Profit, Risk and Incentives under Socialist Economic Planning

By the same author

The Economics and Politics of East–West Trade
The Economics of Socialism
Socialist Economic Development and Reforms

Profit, Risk and Incentives under Socialist Economic Planning

J. WILCZYNSKI

MACMILLAN

First published 1973 by
THE MACMILLAN PRESS LTD
London and Basingstoke
Associated companies in New York Toronto
Dublin Melbourne Johannesburg and Madras

SBN 333 13418 4

Printed in Great Britain by
RICHARD CLAY (THE CHAUCER PRESS) LTD
Bungay, Suffolk

Contents

Preface

THE official adoption of profit as a criterion of enterprise performance and a basis for incentives to labour in the European Socialist countries – Bulgaria, Czechoslovakia, the German DR, Hungary, Poland, Romania, the USSR and Yugoslavia – has caused a good deal of understandable sensation throughout the rest of the world. Many excited observers in the West have taken it as an admission of the failure of Socialist economic planning, whilst the irate ideologues from Tirana to Peking quickly dubbed it a betrayal of Marxism and the world communist movement, all trying to make a good story or political capital out of it.

Apart from the ideological significance, the importance of the Socialist adoption of profit consists in the fact that it has also brought in train other economic reforms. The reforms which are most complementary to profit and incentives to labour include varying degrees of the rationalization of prices, interest rates, taxes and exchange rates, the decentralization of planning and management, the introduction of capital charges on fixed and circulating capital held by enterprises and some reactivation of the market mechanism in general.

The extent of these reforms has differed from one country to another – on the whole they have been advanced furthest in Yugoslavia, followed by Hungary, Czechoslovakia and Bulgaria, and least in the German DR, Poland, the USSR and Romania. Nevertheless, even in the latter countries far-reaching departures from the old Stalinist model of centralized command economy are unmistakable.

It is now widely agreed in the Socialist countries that in the higher stages of economic development directives must be largely replaced by incentives and disincentives, and at the same time enterprises must be allowed considerable independence and encouraged to exercise their initiative. Socialist leaders have also come to realize, although not admitting it openly, that a rigid adherence to Marxian ideas inhibits economic progress.

The driving force behind these reforms has been the determination to advance rapidly to higher levels of efficiency by reducing waste and by accelerating technological progress. The objective is to maintain high rates of economic growth, to step up improvements in living standards and to demonstrate that Socialism is a superior social as well as economic system. Contrary to the assertions made by critics in capitalist countries and in China alike at the time of the reforms, the Socialist adoption of profit and the strengthening of other quasi-capitalist devices have not led to a return to capitalism in any of the eight Socialist countries. Nor has the ultimate Marxian ideal of 'full communism' been abandoned as the ultimate goal. It is not generally realized that the nature and role of profit and other economic levers in a modern Socialist economy are vastly different from those normally identified with capitalism.

Profit, risk and incentives are considered in this book together, because they are obviously closely related under modern Socialism. Although these categories existed under the old system, their role was either non-existent or otherwise small, and certainly there was hardly any correspondence amongst them. The adoption of profit on the one hand, and the extension of the independence of enterprises together with other forms of decentralization, the drive to accelerate technological progress and the strengthening of the role of the market on the other, have all brought the problem of risk to the fore. Incentives to labour are based on enterprise profit, and they are designed to induce the management and workers to maximize profits. Various forms of protection have been developed against risk to promote innovations. At the same time, the authorities now rely primarily on financial incentives and disincentives, rather than on directives, to enhance the working of profit and bonuses and to ensure that they operate in accordance with current policy objectives.

J. Wilczynski

Royal Military College of Australia,
Duntroon, University of New South Wales

1 Historical Background

A. DOGMATIC COMMUNIST VIEWS ON PROFIT

To Marx and his orthodox followers, profit became a symbol of the evil of the capitalist economic system and the ultimate source of egoism, social stratification, class conflict, unemployment, crises, colonialism and wars; but above all responsible for the systematic exploitation and immiseration of the toiling masses. As such it was regarded as bearing the seeds of destruction, bound to lead to the inevitable breakdown of the system of which it became the most distinguishing feature. In his vision of the ideal communist society – to be marked by the social ownership of the means of production, distribution based on the principle 'from each according to his ability, to each according to his needs' and the absence of market relations – Marx saw no place for profit as an economic category.[1]

In Marx's social framework, the profit-seeker is the private capitalist, the villain who in the pursuit of profit opens Pandora's box. He is not interested in satisfying social wants but in squeezing out the maximum gain for himself:

> Use-values must therefore never be looked upon as the real aim of the capitalist; neither must the profit on any single transaction. The restless never-ending process of profit-making alone is what he aims at. This boundless greed after riches, this passionate chase after exchange-value is common to the capitalist and the miser; but while the miser is merely a capitalist gone mad, the capitalist is a rational miser.[2]

[1] K. Marx, *Capital*, London, George Allen & Unwin, 1946, pp. 166–9, 391–426; K. Marx, *Critique of the Gotha Program*, Moscow, FLPH, 1947, p. 27; K. Marx, *Value, Price and Profit*, London, George Allen & Unwin, 1947, pp. 64–74; K. Marx and F. Engels, *The Communist Manifesto*, London, Lawrence & Wishart, 1948, pp. 16–23, 34–5.

[2] *Capital*, pp. 130–1.

Elsewhere Marx describes the doings of the capitalist in the following words:

> . . . the capitalist gets rich, not like the miser in proportion to his personal labour and restricted consumption, but at the same rate as he squeezes out the labour-power of others, and enforces on the labourer abstinence from all life's enjoyment.[1] . . . Capital is dead labour that, vampire-like, only lives by sucking living labour and lives the more the more labour it sucks.[2]

In Marxian economics profit is one of the three components (in addition to interest and rent) of 'surplus value', which is created by the worker in the process of production but appropriated by the capitalist. Marx argued that surplus value is created by the worker during the hours in excess of those necessary to produce the worker's subsistence. In other words, surplus value arises out of the difference between the total value created by labour ('the use-value of labour') and the actual remuneration of labour ('the exchange-value of labour'). Using Marx's terminology, the value of a product is composed of three elements: $c + v + s$ where c means constant capital (depreciation of fixed assets, and raw materials and components used), v is variable capital (the remuneration of labour) and s represents surplus value. The rate of return to capital ($c' + v'$, meaning the total stock of capital) is represented by the formula $(s')/(c' + v')$ and the 'real degree of the exploitation of labour' by $(s')/(v')$ (the relation of 'surplus labour' to 'necessary labour').[3] Marx also maintained that owing to the rapid accumulation of capital under capitalism, the rate of profit had a tendency to fall. However, owing to the rising 'technical' (or 'organic') structure of capital,[4] the rate of exploitation was inevitably increasing.

It must be emphasized that Marx did not regard surplus value as being merely an abnormal phenomenon arising from either hiring labour at less than its actual value or selling products at prices above their real value. The deviations that occur in the labour and

[1] *Capital*, p. 605. [2] Ibid., p. 210.

[3] Ibid., pp. 174–5, 194–201, 400–7; *Value, Price and Profit*, pp. 54–74.

[4] The proportional composition of total capital as indicated by the relation $c':v'$; technological progress leads to a relatively faster growth of constant capital than of wages, so that $(s')/(c' + v')$ tends to rise whilst $(s')/(v')$ tends to fall. *Capital*, pp. 533, 625, 636–42.

product markets and the cheating (which Marx also considered) only affect the size of profit, but not its existence. Marx further insisted that profit (and surplus value in general) was not necessarily a product of the dishonesty of individual capitalists, but a normal and inherent feature of the capitalist economic system.[1]

The views of F. Engels, Rosa Luxemburg and V. I. Lenin on profit were similar to those of Marx. Engels and Rosa Luxemburg stressed the role of profit in the accumulation of capital and the power the latter gives the bourgeoisie over the proletariat. Rosa Luxemburg and Lenin brought out the role of profit in colonial expansion and the greed of international monopolies. They tacitly assumed that the profit motive would cease to exist under communism.[2] In contrast to the four leading ideological founders of communism, K. Kautsky adopted a more realistic attitude to profit and incentives. He foresaw the need for market relations and conceded the possibility of the operation of the profit motive.[3] Lenin despised many of his ideas and described him as a 'swindler' and 'renegade'.[4]

B. ORTHODOX INDICATORS OF ENTERPRISE PERFORMANCE

Marx and other early communist writers gave little thought to the ways of ensuring maximum economic performance. They idealized the future new society, believing that the social ownership of the means of production and the absence of class conflict would be sufficient to induce management and workers to the maximum effort and efficiency. However, when Socialist states were established, reality proved different. After four years of economic chaos following the Bolshevik Revolution, the idealist Marxian principle of distribution 'to each according to his needs', was officially

[1] See especially, *Value, Price and Profit*, pp. 53–4.

[2] F. Engels, *Herr Eugen Dühring's Revolution in Science* (*Anti-Dühring*), Moscow, WCPS, 1934, pp. 230–50; Rosa Luxemburg, *The Accumulation of Capital*, London, Routledge & Kegan Paul, 1951, pp. 419–67; V. I. Lenin, *Selected Works*, London, Lawrence & Wishart, 1944, vol. V, pp. 3–119.

[3] K. Kautsky, *The Social Revolution*, Chicago, C. H. Kerr, 1903, pp. 125, 128–34, 145, 159, 164–6.

[4] V. I. Lenin, op. cit., vol. VII, pp. 105–6, 115.

replaced in the Soviet Union by that of 'to each according to his work'. This measure was meant to be a temporary concession under Lenin's New Economic Policy (1921–8) in transition to 'full communism'.

This move naturally necessitated some criterion for judging the success of enterprises, on which to base incentives to labour and the promotion of managers. It was soon discovered that the period of 'transition' had to be much longer than originally envisaged, and when other Socialist states were established after World War II they similarly had to search for a yardstick of economic performance.[1]

In this search both in the USSR and in the other Socialist countries, not one but a number of indicators of enterprise performance were devised. We shall now briefly examine the different indicators used before the economic reforms, and bring out their weaknesses.

(*a*) *The Volume of Output*

Using this criterion, the success of an enterprise was judged by its output, measured in physical terms (number of units, weight, length, size, capacity, etc.). Incentives to the personnel were

[1] In Marx's and Lenin's writings two stages of communism are distinguished. The 'lower phase', called 'socialism', is still 'stamped with the birthmarks of the old society from whose womb it emerges', and it necessarily embodies several elements of capitalism. The 'higher phase', called 'communism' or 'full communism', is to be marked by a distribution according to needs, a classless society, the absence of money and of market relations, a new man devoid of the acquisitive instinct and the eventual 'withering away' of the state. All the fourteen countries – Albania, Bulgaria, China, Cuba, Czechoslovakia, the German Democratic Republic, Hungary, the Democratic People's Republic of (North) Korea, Mongolia, Poland, Romania, the Soviet Union, the Democratic Republic of (North) Vietnam and Yugoslavia, which are often referred to in the West as 'Communist', are still in the 'lower phase' and describe themselves as 'Socialist'. The USSR, the oldest and ideologically most mature Socialist country, according to the Party Programme announced in 1961 was scheduled to be entering the 'higher phase' by the year 1980. However, owing to the slowdown of economic growth and the incorporation of several elements typical of capitalism into the Soviet economy as a result of the economic reforms, the whole question of the changeover to full communism is now uncertain. If it is to take place, it will be well after 1980 and, of course, even later in other Socialist countries. See V. I. Lenin, *Selected Works*, vol. VII, pp. 16–22, 78–94; *The Road to Communism*, Documents of the 22nd Congress of the Communist Party of the Soviet Union, Moscow, FLPH, 1961, pp. 509–12.

usually linked to the quantitative fulfilment and over-fulfilment of planned targets.[1]

This indicator, which was widely used up to the late 1950s, was least satisfactory of all. First, it was difficult to make comparisons between different types of physical output, and so its applicability was limited. It stimulated enterprises to press for the lowest possible assignment of planned targets (so that they could be easily reached and exceeded) and for the largest possible allocation of raw materials, and to hide their production capacities (the hoarding of labour and materials, and the under-utilization of fixed assets). This led to an extravagant use of inputs irrespective of costs and to the output of goods of poor quality and of doubtful suitability. This basis for incentives produced impressive results on paper in the form of high rates of (quantitative) growth, but they concealed the social utility of the output and the social cost at which it was being attained.

(*b*) *The Value of Output Produced*

In the case of this criterion, the incentive fund was formed as a laid-down proportion of the value of output produced above a particular planned level. Although this yardstick enabled different types of output to be brought to a common denominator, nevertheless it had several serious defects.

It favoured production for its own sake irrespective of users' preferences, which was often reflected in piling up stocks of unsaleable goods, even though shortages prevailed elsewhere. There was a tendency to produce high-priced articles, but not necessarily of high quality, to the neglect of low-priced items. There was also a predisposition for excessive disintegration of production pro-

[1] It may be mentioned as a matter of interest that in Poland between 1957 and 1960 the over-fulfilment of planned targets by a given percentage qualified the enterprise to a corresponding percentage increase in the base salary fund of the managerial and technical staff. It was erroneously thought that an increase in the volume of output was the same thing as an increase in productivity. This practice, of course, added to the inflationary pressure (however well suppressed). Consequently, in 1960 the basis was modified whereby an over-fulfilment of the plan by 1% entitled the personnel to bonuses representing only 0·5–0·6% of their base salary. M. Pohorille (ed.), *Ekonomia polityczna socjalizmu* (The Political Economy of Socialism), Warsaw, PWE, 1968, p. 803.

cesses amongst enterprises because incentives were based not on the value added by each enterprise but on the value of output, with the consequent multiple-counting of materials for the formation of incentive funds. Furthermore, this system tended to irrationalize the process of substitution in production, because the absolute size of the incentive fund could be maximized by using the most expensive inputs.

(*c*) *The Value of Output Realized*

This indicator was an improvement because performance was judged on the output actually delivered and sold, not merely produced, so that it promoted the production of goods for which there was demand. But otherwise, this indicator suffered from defects similar to the preceding one, plus the fact that deliveries tended to become discontinuous, viz. in the last few days of the planned periods (three, six or twelve months) taken for the calculation of incentive funds.

There was also an interesting anomaly. In some countries (such as Poland before 1967) output was valued at industry disposal prices (factory price plus turnover tax; this being a type of sales tax). When the state imposes a high turnover tax, it usually aims at reducing the demand for such an article. But enterprises found it to their advantage to actually step up the production and sale of these items.

(*d*) *The Value of Production*

Further progress was made when this standard of performance was adopted, because the value of materials used was eliminated from the basis and enterprises were rewarded only for value added in the process of production. However, experience soon showed that enterprises became extravagant with labour and tended to substitute it for material inputs, with consequent adverse effects on technological progress. This practice contributed to low labour productivity, an excessive growth of wage funds and inflationary pressure.

(e) *The Volume or Value of Trade Turnover*

These indications were commonly used for determining the performance of trading enterprises. They worked reasonably well if applied to uniform types of goods, but otherwise they produced several adverse effects. When the volume of trade turnover was used, enterprises preferred to wholesale and retail small and simple items, neglecting bulky and complex articles and those for which there was irregular demand. As trading enterprises normally handle a large variety of different goods, there was the problem of comparing the units, weights, lengths, etc., of different items – a rather sensitive question when incentives to the personnel depend on the basis of equivalence chosen.

In the case of the value of trade turnover, enterprises quickly discovered that it was most advantageous to handle expensive items, and so they cared little for ordinary low-priced articles. Retail entities also promoted the distribution of goods carrying high turnover taxes, those goods which the state on economic or social grounds was anxious to curtail (as in the case of tobacco, alcoholic beverages, anti-social luxuries, goods with high import content). In effect, the socially least-desirable items were often well displayed and in plentiful supply whilst there were shortages of common necessities. Whether the volume or the value of trade turnover was applied, trading enterprises showed only remote concern for costs and the quality of service to the public.

(f) *Additional Tasks*

In some cases, enterprise performance was judged and rewarded on the basis of extra tasks executed in addition to the planned targets. These tasks could include new articles, fashionable goods in current demand, improvement in quality and perhaps unscheduled but valuable work or services carried out for other enterprises or consumers at critical times. The authorities' objective was to tap enterprises' hidden production capacities. But in practice results were disappointing. Enterprises continued to hide their reserves and release them gradually, so as to be able to execute 'additional tasks' in each successive year. Moreover, they concentrated on the tasks subject to incentives and neglected their primary planned targets.

(g) *Other Indicators*

There was also a large number of other criteria applied at different times and used for more or less specific purposes. They mostly assumed the form of indices in which, generally speaking, effects (such as output awarded quality marks, output for export, output sold, value of production, value of trade turnover) were related to costs (e.g. circulating costs, employment, fixed assets, prime cost, total capital).

The indices were mostly expressed in value terms, but in some cases they were represented in physical units or in a mixed form. A distinction was also often made between planned and above-plan effects and outlays, and between gross and net values. The number of these indices in use ran into hundreds, and some of them assumed extremely complex forms. Two simple indices may be given for the sake of illustration:

(i) *Index of the turnover of circulating assets:*

$$ItAc = \frac{O}{Ac\,.\,Dn}\,100;$$

O = the value of output at factory prices over the period;
Ac = the average value of the stocks of circulating assets;
Dn = the number of days in the period.

(ii) *Index of the above-plan cost reduction:*

$$IKr = \frac{Ka}{Kp}\,100;$$

Ka = the above-plan reduction in enterprise cost;
Kp = the planned reduction in enterprise cost.

How the indices of enterprise performance were linked to incentives may be illustrated by the index of cost reduction which was in use in Polish industry between 1954 and 1957. For every

1 per cent reduction in the prime cost of the enterprise below the level laid down (planned) by the central planning authority, a sum equal to 5–10 per cent (according to the branch of industry) of the enterprise's basic wage fund was placed in the bonus fund.[1] However, like other indicators, this index produced results far from expectations, even though it was later modified. Thus in the machine-building industry enterprises used to deliberately construct initial models of machinery with useless extra additions, which were gradually reduced and removed in subsequent periods to qualify for bonuses.[2]

It was common that several indicators were in use in an enterprise concurrently. Most of them were employed to determine incentives to the personnel, whilst others were used for analytical purposes and in fact some of the latter are still in use today. Their multiplicity and frequent modifications indicated that none of them was satisfactory. They were in fact partial indicators, and as such measured and stimulated achievements in narrow, specific aspects of economic activity. They produced two types of contradictions, whereby enterprises and individual workers found it to their advantage to act contrary to social interest:

(i) a neglect of production activities not covered by the indicators, and consequently unrewarded by incentives;
(ii) conflicting effects of different indicators, so that attainment in one direction was often offset by detriment in other respects.

C. DISCUSSIONS IN FAVOUR OF THE ADOPTION OF PROFIT

The widespread prevalence of waste and disinterest in efficiency prompted many economists to reconsider the whole question of the economic motivation of enterprises and their personnel. But although some of them became convinced that profit would be a

[1] M. Misiak (ed.), *Bodźce ekonomiczne w przedsiębiorstwach przemysłowych* (Economic Incentives in Industrial Enterprises), Warsaw, PWN, 1963, p. 38.
[2] B. Miszewski, *Postęp ekonomiczny w gospodarce przemysłowej* (Economic Progress in an Industrialized Country), Warsaw, PWE, 1968, p. 71.

superior criterion, for a long time their views could not be easily articulated, and even as late as 1967 a Soviet economist observed that 'no other concept in the political economy of socialism has engendered so much nervousness as profit'.[1] The term itself remained essentially a dirty word. To avoid embarrassment and for fear of being accused of identifying socialism with capitalism, speakers and writers normally employed alternative descriptions, such as: net financial accumulation, net income, net product, net revenue, remainder, residual balance, surplus, surplus product, or used the term 'profit' in inverted commas.

Arguments for the explicit acceptance of the profit criterion were advanced as early as the early 1920s in the USSR, when remarkably free discussions flourished. Some economists thought that profit, like interest, rent and other instruments developed under capitalism could be reconciled with socialism, and they did not want to change the established term. They pointed out that it was essential to distinguish between the two functions of profit – as a means of exploitation and as a measure of enterprise performance. The exploitative connotation of profit associated with pre-socialist social systems should not be a deterrent to the utilization of profit as an instrument for promoting economic efficiency.[2] In fact Lenin himself proposed in 1922 as a tactical retreat that state enterprises be placed on 'the so-called profit basis' and wages be linked to it.[3]

However, under Stalin (who succeeded Lenin in 1924), the freedom of discussion was soon severely curtailed, and for the quarter of a century until his death (in 1954) the question of profit was practically removed from public debate (it may be observed here that between 1928 and 1954 no textbook of economics was written *and* published in the USSR).

In the same year as Stalin died, the first edition of the well-known official textbook of economics was published in the USSR, in which the concept of 'rentability' was examined and favourably evaluated as a criterion of enterprise performance. Rentability was defined as a percentage ratio of net enterprise revenue (profit) to

[1] A. Birman, ('Profit Today'), *Kommunist*, Moscow, 10/1967, p. 99.

[2] e.g., see a book by E. Preobrazhensky (first published in Moscow in 1925), *The New Economics*, Oxford, Clarendon Press, 1965, pp. 196 et seq.

[3] V. I. Lenin, *Collected Works*, Moscow, Progress Publishers, 1966, vol. 33, pp. 184–6.

the prime cost of the realized output.[1] A strong case for the introduction of the rentability index was also put forward by A. Bordag in the German DR two years later.[2] The well-known Polish economist, Oskar Lange, in his book published in 1959, summed up his views on the role of profit under socialism:

> The profit category is retained in the socialist enterprise, but it ceases to be the ultimate goal of its operations – instead it becomes an instrument subordinated to the macrosocial objective postulated in the national economic plan. Profit serves as an incentive for implementing targets and as an indicator of efficiency.[3]

Similar views in favour of profit were expressed by P. Kumin and A. Miloshevskii in Bulgaria, R. Selucky and K. Kouba in Czechoslovakia and R. Nyers and J. Wilcsek in Hungary, not to mention advocates of far-reaching economic reforms, such as F. Behrens (of the German DR), W. Brus (Poland), P. Erdös (Hungary), Ota Šik (Czechoslovakia) and M. V. Vasilev (Yugoslavia).

But the greatest impact was produced, both in the Socialist and capitalist countries, by the arguments advanced by Evsei G. Liberman in the USSR. This is not surprising because it was generally realized that until Big Brother – the ideological leader, effectively backed up by innumerable Soviet divisions stationed all over Eastern Europe – nodded *nihil obstat*, profit would have to remain in semi-disrepute, whatever was said or written elsewhere. Liberman's ideas on profit can be traced back to at least the early postwar years. It is known that in 1948 he explained his ideas at a meeting of economists in Moscow, but he was told by well-wishers to keep quiet about them. After Stalin's death his interest in the subject was further intensified and he published several articles in learned journals, but they went largely unnoticed. It is only the publication of his article in the daily organ of the Communist

[1] Institute of Economics of the Academy of Sciences of the USSR, *Politicheskaya ekonomiya. Uchebnik* (The Textbook of Political Economy), Moscow, GIPL, 1954, p. 475.

[2] A. Bordag, ('On the Rentability Rate'), *Wissenschaftliche Zeitschrift der Technischen Hochschule* (Journal of the Advanced Engineering School), Dresden, no. 4, 1955–6 [quoted from J. Popkiewicz, *Stopa zysku w gospodarce socjalistycznej* (The Profit Rate in the Socialist Economy), PWE, 1968, p. 10].

[3] O. Lange, *Ekonomia polityczna* (Political Economy), Warsaw, PWN, 1959, vol. I, p. 158.

Party, *Pravda*, (with a circulation of 7 million copies) in early September 1962,[1] followed by other writings, that has led to a widespread interest in his proposals.[2]

The publication of Liberman's and of other leading writers' articles on the subject, and more importantly a statement by Khrushchev made in late September 1962 and published in the official gazette of the Presidium of the Supreme Soviet,[3] advanced the discussions on profit from the obscuracy of academic speculation to the public arena. That is why September 1962 is usually regarded as the turning point in the official attitude to profit in the Soviet Union. These developments lent respectability to public discussions on profit and gave the green light to other interested Socialist countries.

Liberman, more clearly and convincingly than anybody else, demonstrated the need for an all-embracing indicator of enterprise performance, and he came to the conclusion that only profit could perform this function. He then pressed his main point – material incentives to the personnel should be placed on a systematic basis and be clearly and directly made dependent on enterprise profit. He stressed that enterprises should receive planned targets only in respect of the total size and broad structure of output, but otherwise should be free to work out their own plans. His arguments appeared simple and reasonable, and could be easily understood even by common Party hacks and ordinary workers. He proposed a scale of deductions from profits for the incentive fund according to the profitability of the enterprise's operations, defined as a percentage ratio of net profit to the value of fixed and circulating assets. There would be no deductions for the fund if profitability was below 5·1 per cent, but if this level was exceeded then

[1] E. G. Liberman, ('Plan, Profit, Bonus'), *Pravda*, Moscow, 9/9/1962, p. 3.

[2] His main contributions appeared in: *Voprosy ekonomiki* (Problems of Economics), Moscow, 6/1955, pp. 34–44; *Kommunist*, 10/1956, pp. 75–92; *Kommunist*, 1/1959, pp. 88–97; *Vop. ekon.*, 8/1962, pp. 102–12; *Pravda*, 17/8/1964, p. 3; *Pravda*, 21/11/1965, pp. 2–3; *Ekonomicheskaya gazeta* (Economic Gazette), Moscow, 51/1965, pp. 6–7; *Literaturnaya gazeta* (Literary Gazette), Moscow, 20/3/1968, p. 10; *Soviet Life*, Soviet Embassy in Washington, July 1965, pp. 36–9; *The Economist*, London, 26/2/1966, pp, 782, 785–6; *International Labour Review*, Geneva, Jan. 1968, pp. 1–14.

[3] N. S. Khrushchev, ('The Development of Economics in the USSR and the Party Leadership in the National Economy'), *Izvestiya*, Moscow, 20/9/1962, pp. 1–2.

deductions would be made on a progressive scale ranging from 2·1 to 5·3 per cent of the value of total assets.[1]

As it turned out, when the profit criterion was officially adopted, it was not in the form advocated by Liberman. Nevertheless, his name will always be associated with profit, and to many observers in the Soviet Union and elsewhere he became a symbol of Socialist economic revisionism. In fact quite undeservedly, because his proposals were most moderate, even timid, and he certainly did not mean to undermine central planning – on the contrary, rather to strengthen it by relieving central planners of unnecessary micro-economic detail. Furthermore, his ideas lacked the originality and sophistication of other thinkers on the subject. An American specialist on the Soviet economy, V. Treml, evaluating the contribution made by Liberman, described him as being noted for 'the modesty of his proposals and his disarming mediocrity'.[2] But even some Soviet scholars took Liberman to task, maintaining that some of his methods were inconsistent and unworkable in practice.[3]

Arguments in favour of profit were also put forward, with some interesting streaks of originality, by a number of other Soviet economists, particularly Z. Atlas,[4] L. Gatovskii,[5] V. S. Nemchinov,[6] B. Sukharevskii,[7] V. Trapeznikov[8] and V. Zinoviev.[9] Some writers, such as A. Bachurin, I. Konnik, G. S. Lisichkin and V. A. Volkonskii, went further by advocating a substantial operation of the market mechanism, in their belief that profit, market and planning could be reconciled and integrated into 'dialectical unity'.[10] Several well-known representatives of the mathematical

[1] *Pravda*, 9/9/1962, p. 3.

[2] V. Treml, 'The Politics of Libermanism', *Soviet Studies*, April 1968, p. 572.

[3] Especially K. Plotnikov and A. Zverev, in *Vop. ekon.*, 11/1962, pp. 93–7, 112–14.

[4] In *Vop. ekon.*, 7/1958, pp. 115–26; 10/1960, pp. 71–82; 8/1961, pp. 112–24.

[5] In *Kommunist*, 18/1962, pp. 60–72.

[6] In *Pravda*, 21/9/1962, p. 3.

[7] In *Vop. ekon.*, 11/1962, pp. 13–27.

[8] In *Pravda*, 17/8/1964, p. 3.

[9] *Pribil i povyshenie effektivnosti sotsialisticheskogo proizvodstva* (Profit and the Improvement in the Effectiveness of Socialist Production), Moscow, Mysl, 1968.

[10] A. Bachurin, ('Problems of the Rentability of Socialist Enterprises'), *Vop. ekon.*, 11/1959, pp. 71–84, and ('Reforms, Planning and the Science of Economics'), *Planovoe khoziaistvo* (Planned Economy), Moscow, 2/1968, pp.

school, notably L. V. Kantorovich, agreed that the criterion of profit and the incentives based on it were consistent with optimal planning.[1]

D. PROFIT BEFORE THE ECONOMIC REFORMS OF THE 1960S

In the pre-1962 editions of the official Soviet textbook of economics, published under the auspices of the Institute of Economics of the Academy of Sciences of the USSR, it was declared:

> In a socialist society, capitalist profit has been eradicated. This being the case, net enterprise revenue is not in fact profit.[2]

This textbook, which was translated into all Eastern European (and many other, including English) languages, was widely accepted in the Socialist bloc as a declaration of creed not to be disputed.

Yet, contrary to what is generally believed in the Socialist, and particularly capitalist, countries, profit has always existed in the Socialist economies in one form or another. This was clearly pointed out by J. Popkiewicz (dean of the School of Economics, University of Wroclaw):

> It is worth noting that profit as an economic category existed in the Socialist economy even when it was formally and officially rejected or when its appearance was negated. It was never possible to give up the comparison of economic effects with the costs incurred to establish the size of the net surplus product created. On the contrary, the calculation of that surplus has always been the objective of economic accounting in Socialist enterprises, irrespective of the valuation on which it was based and of the methods by which it was carried out. The attainment

---

3–16; I. Konnik, ('Plan and Market in a Socialist Economy'), *Vop. ekon.*, 5/1966, pp. 18–30; G. S. Lisichkin, *Plan i rynok* (Plan and Market), Moscow, Ekonomika, 1966; V. A. Volkonskii, *Model optimalnogo vzaimosviaizi ekonomicheskikh pokazateli* (The Model of Optimal Relations amongst Economic Indicators), Moscow, Nauka, 1967.

[1] L. V. Kantorovich, *The Best Use of Economic Resources*, Harvard UP, 1965, pp. 8, 124.

[2] *Politicheskaya ekonomiya. Uchebnik*, 3rd ed., 1959, p. 556.

of this surplus has always been one of the principal targets of the plan, as it determined the capacity for accumulation and thus the rate of economic growth and the standard of living.[1]

It is interesting to note that for a long time the practical application of profit to perform one function or another bore little relation to the discussions and recommendations by theoretical writers, so that up to the early 1960s the two developments were in fact largely independent of each other. Where profit was employed in the state sector its introduction roughly followed this historical pattern in each Socialist country.

After the initial disorder following the takeover by Communist regimes, profit – by whatever name it was known – had to be introduced as an essential element of economic accounting and financial discipline. The role of profit was then gradually extended, although this process was marked with recurrent setbacks. Its earliest link with incentives was established when the latter could be partly financed out of a fixed portion of enterprise profits, instead of out of the wage fund (so that not all profits were handed over to the state). At first, the size of enterprise profits had no influence on the incentive fund, and the latter was used to satisfy certain collective needs of the personnel. Then incentives were made dependent on reaching a planned profit determined by central planners in advance. Later, in addition to a small proportion of planned profits, a larger proportion of above-plan profits was allowed to be used for incentives, including individual cash awards and then bonuses. The use of profits for incentives was possible only after a large number of centrally fixed conditions was met.

Now to quote actual cases of the existence of profit before the early 1960s. As early as the 1920s in the USSR, with the limited revival of private enterprise under the NEP, profit was tacitly tolerated. But even in the socialized sector, profit was often employed to guide the allocation of resources, and the sharing of profit was not unknown – not only in co-operative but even in state enterprises. With the gradual eradication of private enterprise, the development of directive centralized planning after 1927 and

[1] J. Popkiewicz, op. cit., pp. 45–6.

the Stalinist repression, the role of profit was relegated to the obscure background. None the less, profit was never eliminated – rather it was swept under the carpet than vacuum-cleaned out of the system altogether.

In other European Socialist countries profit was widely used over the period 1945–7, being legitimized on the grounds of 'transition from capitalism to socialism'. Repeating the Soviet pattern of the 1920s a reaction against profit soon followed, but it was not completely eradicated, not even in the state sector.

In Yugoslavia in the late 1940s state enterprises already had 'management funds' derived from enterprise profits used for the provision of collective amenities to the personnel, for rewards to innovators and awards to outstanding workers. From 1952 on, profit-sharing was placed on a formal basis, and by the mid-1950s, 5 per cent of personal earnings from work in state enterprises was gained from profit-sharing.[1] In Poland in some state enterprises in the late 1940s 10 per cent of the planned profit and 20 per cent of the above-plan profit could be placed in the bonus fund. In 1950 the inducement to exceed planned profit targets was raised – only 1–4 per cent of the planned profit but as much as 10–30 per cent of the above-plan profit was to be channelled to the bonus fund. (In 1957 the latter percentage was increased to 50 per cent.) In 1957 bonuses, in individual cases, could reach 35 per cent of a person's basic pay.[2] In Hungary, according to the scheme introduced in 1957, profit-sharing was made dependent on the *improvement of the profit rate*, compared with preceding years.[3]

In the USSR in 1962 1–6 per cent of the planned and 30–60 per cent of the above-plan profit could be earmarked for the 'enterprise fund'. Two-fifths of this fund was used for collective incentives (housing, and social amenities and services), two fifths for individual bonuses, special holidays and assistance in need (and one-fifth for the modernization of the enterprise.) In the industries where this scheme operated, incentives derived from enterprise

[1] I. Paj and V. Rakić, 'The Development of the System of Distribution of the Social Product and Net Income', *Yugoslav Survey*, Belgrade, Aug. 1970, pp. 67, 71–2.

[2] M. Misiak (ed.), op. cit., pp. 27, 33, 42–3.

[3] I. Friss (ed.), *Reform of the Economic Mechanism in Hungary*, Budapest, Akadémiai Kiadó, 1969, pp. 69–70.

profits represented from 5·5 to 7·0 per cent of the basic wage funds.[1]

In a sense, profit-sharing has practically always existed in the co-operative sector – in collective farms and co-operative workshops and trading co-operatives. Strictly speaking, the income of co-operative workers consists of sharing their enterprise's income after meeting all their obligations to the state. Profit also played an obvious role in the private sector, which although insignificant has never been completely eradicated in any Socialist country.

There was a renewed practical interest in profit in most of these countries in the early 1960s. In addition to the relatively free discussions on profit and incentives, this was the period of falling rates of economic growth. Over the period 1951–60 the eight Socialist countries as a whole achieved an average annual rate of growth of about 10 per cent, but in the early 1960s the rate dropped to about 4 per cent, or even less (Czechoslovakia experienced a negative rate, viz. −2, in 1963).[2] These developments stimulated experiments with the profit criterion in different forms, which were particularly flourishing over the period 1963–6, and received most publicity in Bulgaria, Poland and the USSR.

It must be emphasized that the instrument of profit before the main economic reforms was applied only to some branches of the economy, mostly in enterprises producing industrial consumer goods, and the proportion of total profits allowed for incentives was on the whole very small. The operation of profit was severely circumscribed by a large number of directive targets, indicators and *ad hoc* administrative instructions, and constant amendments, overriding profit.

E. PROFIT, RISK AND INCENTIVES UNDER THE NEW ECONOMIC SYSTEM

The essential purpose of the economic reforms in the European Socialist countries (Albania excepted) since the early 1960s has been to increase efficiency in the interest of high rates of economic

[1] *Politicheskaya ekonomiya. Uchebnik*, 1962, ed., p. 526.
[2] For further details, see J. Wilczynski, *Socialist Economic Development and Reforms*, London, Macmillan, 1971, esp. pp. 5–8.

growth. Before the reforms, the Socialist growth strategy was based mainly on extensive sources, i.e. on physical increases in the factors of production. This was feasible because there were substantial labour reserves in agriculture and domestic service, an ample supply of capital at the expense of current consumption and even some unused land. However, these reserves were becoming rapidly exhausted by the mid-1960s.

Moreover, owing to the weakness of material incentives and the faulty system on which they were based, there was widespread waste and inefficiency, which were becoming more evident as these countries were entering higher stages of economic development. In spite of the inordinately high levels of investment and continued sacrifices borne by the public, rates of growth were drastically falling and stagnation set in. Theoretical writers and policy makers alike soon came to the conclusion that to sustain rapid economic growth it was imperative to activate intensive sources of growth, i.e. a rapid growth of productivity. In the past, on the whole, only one-third of total growth was derived from productivity increases and two-thirds from extensive sources. This contrasts with the advanced capitalist countries where these proportions are usually reversed.

In this drive towards predominantly intensive growth, the efficiency of enterprises assumes strategic importance. As discussions and practical experience had demonstrated, only profit as the criterion of performance and stronger incentives to labour based on it could ensure efficiency and its steady growth.

Thus profit and incentives have become not only the most distinguishing features of the economic reforms but also the mainstay of intensive growth. The systematic incorporation of the profit lever into the Socialist economic system to perform this function began in the German DR in 1964, in Yugoslavia in 1965 (and partly earlier, in 1952 and 1958), in Poland in 1965, in the USSR in 1966, in Czechoslovakia in 1967,[1] in Hungary in 1968, in Bulgaria in 1968[1] and in Romania (to a very modest extent) also in 1968. As a rule, profit was first applied in industry, but since that time

[1] Bulgaria and Czechoslovakia adopted gross income, i.e. wages *plus* profit, as a criterion of enterprise performance and a basis for incentives. However, since 1970 they have been changing over to the profit criterion as well.

steps have been taken to extend its operation to other branches of the economy.

As an integral part of the economic reforms, enterprises have been granted a greater independence. Central planning is now concentrated on macroeconomic proportions and medium- and long-term developments. To achieve their objectives, the authorities now rely primarily on financial instruments (prices, taxes, interest rates, capital charges, depreciation rates) designed to influence profits and thereby induce enterprises to act in desired directions.

Intensive growth is essentially based on technological progress. This process, particularly if it is accelerated, involves large elements of risk. Under the old centralized and directive system, enterprises were hardly concerned with risk. The imposition of targets and even methods of production in detail from above absolved enterprises from risk-bearing. Even where they had sufficient freedom, enterprises tended to steer away from innovations on their own initiative. But under the new system risk is viewed in a different light altogether. The undertaking of risky operations is conducive to the maximization of enterprise profits, and consequently of incentives to the personnel. With the decentralization of planning and management, risk-bearing has been largely shifted from the state budget to individual enterprises.

As an aftermath of the publicity given in the West to the Socialist acceptance of profit, many outside observers are under the impression that the profit motive now governs the economic process and that the size of profit determines the size of incentives to labour. The actual situation is in fact much more complex and its details are the subject of the remaining chapters of this book. But it is fitting to point out here that the practices followed in the eight countries under consideration are far from uniform, and the role assigned to profit and its relation to incentives differ considerably from one country to another.

2 Profit as a Criterion of Enterprise Performance

A. MERITS OF PROFIT

THE indicators of enterprise performance which were in use before the adoption of profit (Ch. 1B, pp. 4–9) were specialized yardsticks, which often produced conflicting effects, contrary to social interest. The most distinguishing feature of the profit criterion is that it is the most comprehensive of all possible criteria or, as it is described in the Socialist countries, a 'synthetic' indicator. It takes account of both the input and output sides. It can be quantified and expressed as a common denominator for a variety of economic effects. It can be employed not only in its absolute form (the profit mass) but also as a relative indicator (a rate of return). Its applicability is universal, whether in industry, agriculture, trade or 'non-productive' services (finance, insurance, housing administration, entertainment).

One wonders what Marx, Engels and other founding fathers of the communist ideology would think if they saw the eulogies on profit in modern Socialist literature which they would not find even in such Western books as *The Triumph of American Capitalism*. A well-known Soviet academic, N. Fedorenko, stated in the organ of the Central Committee of the Communist Party of the Soviet Union:

> Consequently, it stands to reason that under socialism the maximization of enterprise profits is a step towards the principal objective of our system, viz. the fullest possible satisfaction of the needs of the members of society.[1]

Another Soviet advocate of profit, A. Birman, pointed out in the same journal:

> Profit is not merely an accounting or statistical device. Profits earned indicate that all the economic processes involving all

[1] N. Fedorenko, ('Prices and Optimal Planning'), *Kommunist*, Moscow, 8/1966, p. 87.

those participating in the production of a given article have been satisfactorily carried out and that the needs of society have been satisfied.[1]

A Polish economist, Z. Madej, emphasized that:

> Enterprise profit under socialism represents a sort of macrosocial goal adapted to the microeconomic level. . . . National income can be maximized via the maximization of enterprise profits, and profits can be maximized through the maximization of personal earnings.[2]

A Bulgarian supporter of profit, Z. Stanev, described its importance under socialism in the following words:

> Profitability is a synthetic criterion which is much more effective than the previously used specialized plan indicators, because it reflects changes in costs, in the organization of production and labour and in the quality of the product. It is an overall reflection of the strengths and weaknesses in the activities of an enterprise.[3]

The acceptance of profit has led to some rationalization of the management of enterprises. Under the old system, the usual qualifications for managers consisted in ideological reliability and the ability to carry out detailed directives of a routine nature handed out by higher authorities, and it was the latter who were decision-makers. But under the new system, where enterprises enjoy a good deal of independence, there is a need and scope for professionally competent managers who by their resourcefulness and sound decisions can increase enterprise profits and bonuses to their personnel (including themselves). In all these countries the training of managers has been placed on a new footing, and Western methods are now widely utilized.[4]

The observance of the profit criterion has also stimulated a more business-like approach to costs. To deter enterprises from hiding

[1] A. Birman, ('Profit Today'), *Kommunist*, 10/1967, p. 108.

[2] Z. Madej, *Zysk w gospodarce socjalistycznej* (Profit in a Socialist Economy), Warsaw, PWE, 1963, pp. 69, 84.

[3] Z. Stanev, ('Profit as an Incentive'), *Problemy na truda* (Problems of Labour), Sofia, 6/1970, p. 3.

[4] For details, see Z. Mosna, ('The Training of Managers in the Socialist Countries'), *Hospodářské noviny* (Economic News), Prague, 16/10/1970, pp. 10–11.

idle production capacity (hoarding fixed and circulating capital and labour), capital charges[1] have been introduced and in some countries (Bulgaria, Czechoslovakia, Hungary) payroll tax as well. There is a greater inclination to eliminate or at least reduce subsidies by liquidating loss-incurring enterprises or integrating them with more efficient entities. The level and changes in the profitability of different types of production provide valuable information (where the price structure is reasonably rational) to central planners for the determination of priorities in developmental plans.

One of the features of economic relations amongst Socialist enterprises was a virtual absence of competition, which further aggravated such familiar facts of Socialist economic life as recurring shortages, low quality, poor or no adaptability of production to buyers' preferences, a small range of goods, unattractive and obsolete articles and what came to be known simply as 'sellers' markets' (for further details, see Ch. 8D). It is hoped in the Socialist countries that enterprises' efforts to maximize profits will lead to 'keen competition amongst enterprises, cost reduction, a greater variety of products, better quality, accelerated technical progress and a greater efficiency in general'.[2]

The profit criterion can be used in different forms to determine enterprise performance and material incentives to the personnel. In practice four variants are in use in the Socialist countries under consideration: the profit mass, the rentability rate, the profit rate and gross income (profit plus wages). The reason for using profitability indices (rentability and profit rates) rather than the profit mass or gross income in most Socialist countries is, in general, to give different enterprises the same starting chance, because they may be operating under vastly different conditions (in respect of location, natural resources, equipment, technology, the nature of demand) over which they have little control. This is largely a reflection of the continued distortions in price structures and the inadequacy of the taxation system to absorb differential rent.

In most of these countries more than one of the four profit variants are used. Each variant may be calculated on a gross or net

[1] For details, see Ch. 7A, pp. 159–60.

[2] W. Wilczyński, *Rachunek ekonomiczny a mechanizm rynkowy* (Economic Accounting and the Market Mechanism), Warsaw, PWE, 1965, p. 105.

and on a planned or above-plan basis, and furthermore, various components of costs and revenue may be differently defined and treated. The economic effects of the profit criterion, naturally, vary according to the ways it is calculated and applied. We shall examine these questions in detail in the next four sections of this chapter.

B. THE PROFIT MASS

The simplest form of using profit as a criterion of enterprise performance and a basis for incentives is to take the absolute amount of profit attained by the enterprise in a given period (usually three, six or twelve months). As a rule net profit, rather than gross profit, is taken as a basis for calculating the portion for the incentives fund.[1] A formula (actually used in Poland) for calculating net profit is given below:[2]

$$nP = Os - pK - D + S + B - Cc - rE - iP;$$

Os = output actually sold (at producer prices);
pK = prime cost of the output sold;
D = differential payments to the state budget (according to the advantages possessed by the enterprise);
S = subsidies received from the state;
B = balance of losses and profits on operations outside normal production;
Cc = capital charges on fixed assets in possession;
rE = payments to research establishments for commissioned work;
iP = illicit profit (achieved in ways conflicting with existing regulations or otherwise damaging to social interest).

[1] In Socialist terminology the following concepts relating to profit are employed: global income = total receipts; global income *minus* materials used = gross income; gross income *minus* wages = gross profit (also called 'social profit' or 'net income' or 'net revenue'): gross profit *minus* taxes and other charges payable to the state budget (and in some cases to intermediate organs of economic management) = net profit (also known as 'enterprise profit'); net profit *minus* deductions for other purposes than the incentive fund(s) = incentive fund(s); incentive fund(s) *minus* collective incentives = individual incentives. Also see Table 2, p. 35.

[2] Adapted from *Życie gospodarcze* (Economic Life), Warsaw, 2/8/1970, p. 3.

The approach via the profit mass is followed in Yugoslavia and in Hungary, and in some cases in Bulgaria, Czechoslovakia, the German DR, Poland and the USSR. The way in which net profit is distributed for different purposes is now virtually unrestricted in Yugoslavia, where a workers' council in each enterprise determines the proportions or amounts to be devoted for investment, repayment of credits, incentives, reserves, etc. In Hungary the proportions are broadly regulated. In the remaining six countries the regulations are more detailed and usually a distinction is made between 'planned' and 'above-plan' profits, and in some cases between different degrees of increment in profits (for details, see Ch. 5).

The profit mass can be maximized in three ways within the power of the enterprise: (i) by increasing (or optimizing) output; (ii) by reducing costs; (iii) by changing the structure of output in favour of the most profitable items (another way is by increasing prices, where enterprises are allowed to do it). On which course an enterprise concentrates depends on the profit margin and the nature of costs. If average profit is high, the enterprise endeavours to maximize its output, but if unit profit is low its effort is mostly directed at cost reduction. The enterprise strives to change over to the more profitable articles where profit margins on the different items it can produce differ, and there are no diseconomies of large-scale specialized production.

Consequently, the profit mass is the most suitable standard for adoption in those forms of production where the increase in output and cost reduction are equally important, and where enterprises are not in a position to neglect articles with low profit margins but of high social importance (e.g. common necessities). Experience in the Socialist countries where this standard is not universally used has shown that it is most suitable in the following types of enterprises:

(*a*) Those producing a single commodity or a narrow range of items – e.g. in mines, brickworks, producers of industrial raw materials, oil refineries.
(*b*) Enterprises producing goods to exact specifications and on a large scale so that purchasers control quality – e.g. in electrical engineering, shipbuilding, vehicles and other transport equipment.

(*c*) Enterprises producing goods for which buyers' markets exist because the producer has to adjust the structure of his output to the buyers' preferences – the nearest examples include market gardening, food concentrates, clothing, some consumer durables (radios, TV sets, washing machines, sewing machines).

(*d*) Enterprises producing for both domestic and foreign markets, so that the structure of production can and should be adjusted to the requirements of the most profitable markets and where the maximization of prices is in the social interest.[1]

The main advantage of the profit mass as a criterion is that it is simple for workers to understand and thus it produces a stronger effect on them; moreover, unlike the rentability rate and the profit rate which are abstract concepts, the profit mass is a real magnitude to draw upon for material incentives to the personnel, further development and reserves.

But the profit mass standard also entails several disadvantages, particularly in countries where the profitability of different forms of production varies widely owing to substantial distortions in relative prices. Articles of common use carrying small profit margins may be sacrificed in favour of expensive items. Compared with the profit rate, the profit mass does not indicate or promote the utilization of assets beyond the level of capital charges so that under-utilized capacity may persist. Enterprises may limit their production below the social optimum size by reducing employment; this is likely in older enterprises where the marginal revenue product of labour is declining and especially if enterprises are in a position to increase their prices. As the profit mass can be increased by increasing enterprise assets, this criterion does not sufficiently discourage growth based merely on extensive sources. For these reasons many Socialist countries have turned to indices of profitability, viz. the rentability rate and the profit rate, which we shall examine next.

[1] T. Kierczyński, ('The Place of Profit in the New System of Stimulating and Financing Enterprises'), *Nowe drogi* (New Paths), Warsaw, 5/1970, pp. 53–5.

C. THE RENTABILITY RATE

The term 'rentability' has been used to convey several meanings. In its broadest sense it may simply signify the fact of being 'economically advantageous' from the social point of view (even though attained at a microeconomic loss), or 'profitability', i.e. being gainful to enterprises. Occasionally it was used as an alternative name for the partial profit rate (the percentage ratio of profits to fixed assets), or even for the (complete) profit rate (the percentage ratio of profits to fixed and circulating assets). This usage can be largely explained by the fact that 'rentability' appeared for a long time to be less offensive than 'profit' (and its derivatives), suffering from the tag of the original sin.

However, in its modern precise meaning rentability, or the rentability rate, denotes a percentage ratio of profits to the prime cost, and in this book it is consistently used in this sense:

$$Rr = \frac{P}{pK} 100;$$

P = the profit mass;
pK = the prime cost of the output sold.[1]

This rate has been applied to individual products, or enterprises, branches of the economy or the whole economy. But its greatest practical use is to measure enterprise performance.

This concept was widely discussed as early as the mid-1950s and its application was widely experimented with subsequently. Today it is employed in Poland and in the USSR, but there has been a tendency in recent years to replace it by the profit rate. It can be calculated on a gross or net basis. In the 'gross rentability rate' (gRr), also known as 'social rentability', gross profit is related to prime cost, whilst in the 'net rentability rate' (nRr) it is net profit to prime cost; the latter form is mostly in use.

A distinction is also made between 'planned' and 'above-plan' rentability. Owing to the widely differing opportunities for profit-making in different enterprises, the state sets differentiated 'planned rentability rates', so that all enterprises are impelled to do

[1] Prime cost is, as a rule, composed of materials used (including power and light), wages (including payments for services obtained from outside), depreciation, repairs to plant and interest on bank credits.

their best, irrespective of their differential advantages or disadvantages, to qualify for incentives. If planned rates are exceeded, enterprises qualify for extra incentives, usually on a progressive scale. Thus in Poland in 1967, the planned net rentability rates ranged from 2·68 to 22·53, but the actually achieved rates fell within the range of 2·99–22·77.[1] Sometimes, instead of the ordinary static rentability rate, a 'dynamic' version is used, i.e. profit is related to the prime cost not in the same period but to the prime cost in the preceding (or some other past) period:

$$Rr' = \frac{P_1}{pK_0} 100.$$

As under Socialist conditions prices are usually given and are beyond the control of enterprises, the rentability rate is very strongly influenced by changes in costs. Costs determine the size of the numerator ($nP = Os - pK - T$, i.e. net profit equals receipts from the output sold *minus* prime cost minus taxes, etc.) and of the denominator (prime cost). A reduction in costs is reflected in a larger numerator *and* a smaller denominator, and *vice versa*. This is illustrated in Table 1. Thus a decrease of only 4 per cent in prime cost (from 70,000 to 65,000 roubles) produces an increase in net profit by 50 per cent (from 10,000 to 15,000 roubles) and in the net rentability rate by 62 per cent (from 14·3 to 23·1 per cent). A rise of 7 per cent in prime cost results in a 67 per cent and a 71 per cent fall in net profit and the net rentability rate respectively. From these examples it should be evident that a change in prime cost leads to a greater than proportional change in the profit mass and an even greater one in the rentability rate.

Consequently, the linking of incentives to the rentability rate spurs enterprises above all to the lowering of costs. Its application is most effective in those enterprises in which there is a potential for continued cost reductions and where there are strong cost-induced inflationary tendencies, irrespective of the structure of costs.

At the same time, the rentability rate suffers from several weaknesses. It is useless as an absolute indicator and it cannot be used

[1] *Wiadomości Narodowego Banku Polskiego* (Communications of the National Bank of Poland), Warsaw, 1/1969, p. 18.

reliably for comparing the economic performance of enterprises which have different levels and structures of costs. To serve its purpose, it has to be related to some basic index, such as a planned rentability rate or a rate in some base year. But with this approach

TABLE I THE EFFECT OF CHANGES IN COSTS ON PROFITS AND RENTABILITY RATE

In Thousand Roubles, in Value Columns

Changes in Prime Cost	Value of Output Sold	Prime Cost	Taxes, Capital Charges, etc.	Net Profit	Net Rentability Rate
	Os	*pK*	*T*	*nP*	*nRr*
Original situation	100	70	20	10	14·3%
After a decrease in prime cost	100	65	20	15	23·1%
After an increase in prime cost	100	75	20	5	6·6%

inefficient enterprises may be sheltered whilst in the case of those working under more favourable conditions the incentive effect may be blunted. Small changes in costs cause wide changes in the rentability rate, which may produce considerable fluctuations in incentives and contribute to uncertainty.

By the application of this standard not enough pressure is exerted on enterprises to maximize their output by making full use of their fixed and working capital. Yet the Socialist countries, especially those where the rentability rate is used, are noted for shortages. There is evidence suggesting that enterprises are not inclined enough to utilize their capacity to the full by introducing two- or three-shift work and by speeding up the turnover of circulating assets.[1]

The point is that the social cost of capital is insufficiently reflected in prime cost – only to the extent of depreciation and low interest on bank credits. Capital charges are not normally treated

[1] J. Popkiewicz, *Stopa zysku w gospodarce socjalistycznej* (The Profit Rate in a Socialist Economy), Warsaw, PWE, 1968, p. 81.

as cost but are deductible from gross profits, and moreover many branches of the economy are exempt from them (see Ch. 7D, pp. 170–1).

D. THE PROFIT RATE

The profit rate is a percentage ratio of profit to enterprise assets. By ultra-Marxists it is sometimes described as the 'rentability of production assets' or 'calculational rentability'. This concept received some attention from Yugoslav economists in the early 1950s, and from other Socialist writers in the mid-1950s. But it was thoroughly analysed only during the period 1962–6 and experimented with on a larger scale in the latter 1960s. By 1970 the profit rate was the most important profit standard in the German DR, Poland, Romania and the USSR.

Neither the profit mass nor the rentability rate is clearly indicative of the amount of assets in an enterprise's possession and the degree of their utilization. The profit rate overcomes this disability. Some economists define it as a percentage ratio of profit to fixed assets and as such (including the value of land) it has been proposed for application in state farms.[1] Some writers, steeped in Marxian tradition, would relate profit to what Marx called 'variable' capital, i.e. wages $\left(\frac{s'}{v'}\,100\right)$. This profit variant was experimented with in Yugoslavia in 1952, but it proved unworkable and had to be abandoned after a year.[2]

However, it is now widely agreed that both fixed and circulating assets should be taken into account, so that the formula for the profit rate now commonly accepted is:

$$Pr = \frac{P}{Af + Ac}\,100;$$

P = the profit mass; Af = the value of fixed assets;
Ac = the value of circulating assets (stocks of raw materials, components, semi-finished and finished products).

[1] T. Kierczyński, ('The Profit Rate in the System of Management of State Farms'), *Życie gosp.*, 15/6/1969, p. 8.

[2] L. Sirc, *Economic Devolution in Eastern Europe*, London, Longmans, 1968, p. 41.

In an exceptional case, when the value of assets is equal to prime cost, the profit rate is equal to the rentability rate. According to a study carried out in Poland, differences amongst enterprises in respect of the profit rate are much greater than in respect of the rentability rate.[1]

A given profit rate is more difficult to reach and exceed than a given profit mass or rentability rate. To improve the profit rate it is not enough to increase the absolute amount of profit – the amount has to increase by more (or decrease by less) than the value of assets. This relation applies even more if comparisons are made with the rentability rate (see Table 1, p. 28).

Parallel to the concepts of the rentability rate, the profit rate can be calculated on a gross profit basis, in which case it is known as the 'gross (or "social") profit rate', whilst the 'net profit rate' includes net profit in the numerator. As a rule, the former index is used for comparing the effectiveness of the utilization of assets amongst different branches of industry or the economy, and the latter for evaluating intra-branch effectiveness (amongst different enterprises).

The method of calculating the value of assets varies in different Socialist countries. In some cases the initial value of fixed assets is taken as the basis, in others the depreciated value (usually in mid-year). Newly installed fixed assets may be included either as from the planned or actual date of completion, or when the project is fully operative. Non-production assets, i.e. those used for social or recreational purposes, are not taken into account.

In some cases the state, when setting the minimum profit rate to be achieved, lays down a norm for circulating assets which should not be exceeded in a given type of enterprise. Such an index is called the 'normative profit rate'. If the enterprise exceeds the norm penalties may be applied, so that the actual profit achieved is less favourable.

In employing the profit rate as a basis for incentives to the personnel, the authorities usually set a minimum rate, called a 'planned profit rate', which must be attained before a deduction from enterprise profit can be made for the incentive fund. If this rate is exceeded, additional deductions are made for the fund, usually on

[1] J. Popkiewicz, op. cit., p. 171.

a progressive scale according to the level of the 'above-plan profit rate' achieved. For some time incentives were payable for exceeding the profit rate of the preceding year or some other base period. But experience showed that in such cases enterprises tended to hide their production capacities and utilize them only gradually, so as to quality for incentives in succeeding years. It is now common that the profit rate set by the state is not linked to previous rates.[1]

The use of the profit rate is most suitable in an economy where there is a scarcity of capital in relation to labour. Within a particular economy, its application produces best results in those branches where there is scope for improving the organization of production processes not involving large capital outlays, where economies of scale can be achieved by a greater product specialization and a reduction of overheads, and where the value of assets can be changed in relatively short periods. Experience shows that its application has been most successful in large enterprises and combines.[2] On the other hand, the profit rate should not be used in those branches where the production cycle is long and when sales are not continuous as, for example, in building and construction.

The specific advantages of the profit rate as a criterion of performance can be summarized as follows:

(*a*) It promotes the most effective utilization of the fixed assets in the possession of enterprises.
(*b*) It spurs enterprises to maintain the lowest possible level of stocks of circulating assets.
(*c*) It prods enterprises to the disposal of equipment which is not fully utilized.
(*d*) It provides an encouragement to enterprises to pursue specialization and co-operation with other enterprises as this enables a reduction of overheads.
(*e*) It exerts a restraint on new investment projects, so that only the most profitable ones are selected for implementation.

[1] B. Miszewski, *Postęp ekonomiczny w gospodarce przemysłowej* (Economic Progress in an Industrialized Country), Warsaw, PWE, 1968, p. 120.
[2] T. Kierczyński, *Nowe drogi*, op. cit., pp. 55–6.

(*f*) It makes the profitability of different branches of the economy and of different enterprises comparable, provided assets are rationally priced. As such it provides a guide to central planners in their endeavour to optimize the distribution of resources (especially capital) in their long-range plans.

(*g*) It is the most synthetic of all the criteria of enterprise performance in use. In this sense it is superior to the profit mass and the rentability rate because it includes all the elements reflected in either of the latter two standards, and in addition the effectiveness of the utilization of assets.

The possible disadvantages of the profit rate yardstick are as follows:

(*a*) The introduction of the profit rate favours those enterprises which previously were hiding production reserves, as they are in a better position to improve their profitability than the conscientious enterprises which had no idle capacity before.

(*b*) The maximization of the profit rate is sometimes possible by a reduction of production capacity through the premature scrapping of fixed assets before it is socially desirable.

(*c*) Enterprises are likely to be deterred from embarking on investment projects yielding returns after a long period.

(*d*) Innovations may be adversely affected if they are capital-intensive, i.e. when the increased capital–output ratio is not matched by a corresponding increase in profits. Mechanization and automation may be hampered, as enterprises are likely in some cases to favour manual labour instead. This runs counter to Socialist thinking, according to which labour is essentially the only scarce factor of production and it should be increasingly replaced by capital.

(*e*) The quality of production may suffer. Enterprises may find it profitable to reduce the range (and consequently the size) of stocks of materials and some of these may be less suitable for production, or they may unduly shorten the cycle of treatment of their materials to speed up the turnover of their stocks (e.g. the curing of timber in the furniture industry).

(*f*) Enterprises are likely to shy away from production for unpredictable markets, as spare production capacity and larger stocks of materials and finished products are likely to reduce the profit rate. Yet it may be socially necessary to cater for such production (e.g. in export production).

(*g*) The most suitable minimum period for assessing the profit rate is usually a year. But the payment of incentives to the personnel only once a year reduces their inducement effect. If the rate is calculated on the basis of shorter periods, it is likely to be less reliable; moreover it would show wide variations from one period to another, which would be reflected in considerable fluctuations in incentive payments.

(*h*) Like the rentability rate, it is an abstract criterion and its link with bonuses may appear too obscure to ordinary workers, with a consequent weaker incentive effect. The fact that a given profit rate is more difficult to exceed than either the profit mass or the rentability rate also tends to produce discouragement; to overcome this disability, the authorities may, and often do, scale down (or occasionally raise) the rate during the year, but if this is done it produces uncertainty and demoralization (see Ch. 6D, p. 142).

E. GROSS INCOME

An approach which is different from the preceding three profit standards is represented by the acceptance of profit together with wages, i.e. gross income (the value of production) as a criterion of enterprise performance. This approach has been rationalized by its advocates on the following grounds.

Economic progress is primarily reflected in the rate of growth of national income, i.e. the value of production or 'value added'. Profit (gross) is only one portion of value added, the other being the remuneration of labour, and these two elements combined in application to an enterprise are called 'gross income', equivalent to the (net) value of production. The performance of an enterprise should not be judged merely on the basis of its profits but on its total contribution to national income. Furthermore, 'gross income' is ideologically more palatable because it does not explicitly allude to 'profit'.

Gross income has been adopted as the principal criterion in Czechoslovakia since 1967 and in Bulgaria since 1968. However, it was in use in one form or another in all Socialist countries under the old economic system, but its role was of course severely circumscribed by a large number of directives. It was officially employed in Yugoslavia in the early 1960s, and to a lesser extent before.

As a basis for incentives to the enterprise personnel, gross income can be employed either in its absolute form (the 'gross income mass') or as a rate where the absolute size of gross income is related to some form of social cost, usually fixed and circulating assets held by the enterprise. To make the operation of the gross income standard effective, wage funds have to be decentralized, i.e. freed from central fixation. Instead, wage funds are subject to a (usually progressive) payroll tax.

Gross income as a criterion of enterprise performance and a basis for incentives suffers from three major defects. First, enterprises find it to their advantage to substitute labour for the means of production, which is not conducive to technological progress. There is a tendency to maximize wages, with a lesser concern for the most economical application of labour, so that the growth of labour productivity may be adversely affected. This leads to the second disadvantage, viz. the use of the gross income criterion unduly favours the growth of wages beyond the growth of productivity, with the consequent inflationary effects. The decentralization of wage funds facilitates this process. To cope with this problem both Bulgaria and Czechoslovakia have had to resort to the imposition of ceilings on wage increases in recent years. The third defect consists in perverse relations. The remuneration of labour is lumped together with profits and it depends on profits as well as on itself. Under this set-up it is difficult to gauge opportunity costs before *ex-post* data are available. For these reasons Bulgaria since 1969 and Czechoslovakia since 1970 have been increasingly turning to the profit criterion in the form of the profit rate and the profit mass.

A comparison of the criteria of enterprise performance based on profit together with the methods of their derivation currently used in the eight Socialist countries is presented in Table 2. In conclu-

TABLE 2 COST, REVENUE AND PROFIT RELATIONS IN A HYPOTHETICAL SOCIALIST ENTERPRISE

Details	Symbol	Derivation from Other Magnitudes	Numerical Relations
Prime cost	pK	$Os - gP$	65
Materials, etc., used	Mu	$pK - bW - Df - opK$	30
Base wage fund *	bW	$gY - gP$	25
Taxes, etc., paid to the state	T	$gP - nP$	20
Depreciation of fixed assets	Df	$pK - Mu - bW - opK$	5
Other prime cost	opK	$pK - Mu - bW - Df$	5
Fixed and circulating assets	$Af + Ac$	..	70
Output sold	Os	$pK + gP$	100
Gross income	gY	$bW + gP$	55
Gross profit	gP	$gY - bW$	30
Net profit	nP	$gP - T$	15
Gross income rate	gYr	$\frac{gY}{Af + Ac}$	78·6%
Gross rentability rate	gRr	$\frac{gP}{pK}$	46·2%
Net rentability rate	nRr	$\frac{nP}{pK}$	23·1%
Gross profit rate	gPr	$\frac{gP}{Af + Ac}$	49·2%
Net profit rate	nPr	$\frac{nP}{Af + Ac}$	21·4%

* i.e., exclusive of incentives derived from net profit.

sion, we can restate the profit variant or variants employed in each individual country:

Bulgaria – gross income (also the profit rate and the profit mass);

Czechoslovakia – gross income (also the profit mass and the profit rate);

German DR	– the profit rate (also the profit mass);
Hungary	– the profit mass;
Poland	– the profit rate (also the rentability rate and the profit mass);
Romania	– the profit rate;
USSR	– the profit rate (also the rentability rate and the profit mass);
Yugoslavia	– the profit mass.

F. ABNORMAL AND ANTI-SOCIAL PROFITS

In the Socialist countries a good deal of significance is attached to the processes whereby profits are made, especially those processes which are not indicative of the enterprises' own efforts and those which are considered to be 'anti-social'. For our purposes we can identify seven distinct potential sources of such profits.

(*a*) *Windfall Profits*

Enterprises may make unexpected profit as a result of actions initiated by the state, and not as a consequence of their own efforts. Such actions may include reductions in the cost of certain inputs, in depreciation rates, in social insurance contributions and in import duties on the one hand, and increases in the prices of products on the other. In making changes of this nature, the state may be guided by a variety of social objectives, and the increased profitability of enterprises is only an incidental side-effect.

(*b*) *Profits Derived from Special Advantages Enjoyed by Enterprises*

Some enterprises may be in a privileged position with regard to location, the layout of the plant, the modernity of equipment, the ease of access to raw materials and specialized inputs, soil fertility and climate. Such 'differential advantages' are beyond the control of enterprises.

(c) *Monopolistic Profits*

Contrary to the belief entertained by many Western economists conversant with the Socialist economies,[1] many enterprises in these economies are in a monopolistic position and they are sometimes able to turn it to their own advantage. Socialist countries have always been noted for the prevalence of large entities because they facilitate central planning and management. The processes of integration and concentration were further accelerated in most of these countries in the early 1960s and the trend has reappeared in all of them since the late 1960s. Such monopolistic enterprises may raise prices and resort to other unfair practices, thereby earning super-normal profits.

This has been particularly evident in recent years in Bulgaria, Czechoslovakia, Hungary and Yugoslavia, where certain categories of prices have been freed from state control (for details, see Ch. 4E. pp. 100–4). It appears that abnormal profits are also earned on non-standardized products, even in the remaining Socialist countries, the prices of which are determined by negotiation between the interested parties. Owing to his superior bargaining power, the producer 'dictates the price most advantageous to himself and the purchaser usually accepts it without any argument'.[2]

(d) *Profit Achieved by Neglect*

This can occur when enterprises are lax in protecting socialized property and workers' lives. Thus by failing to maintain and repair equipment and buildings, to provide adequate safety, sanitary and similar facilities, enterprises may 'reduce' their costs at the expense of society.

(e) *Quasi-Illicit Profits*

Enterprises can increase their profits by changing the assortment of their production. They may reduce or phase out articles which

[1] e.g., Joan Robinson, 'Consumer's Sovereignty in a Planned Economy', in *On Political Economy and Econometrics*, Essays in Honour of Oskar Lange, Warsaw, Polish SP, 1965, p. 5 ('. . . the monopoly power of manufacturers [does] not exist in a planned economy').

[2] Z. Wilkosz ('Once Again on Super-normal Profits'), *Finanse* (Finance) Warsaw, 11/1968, p. 42.

are least profitable even though socially indispensable, and instead concentrate on the most profitable items including socially undesirable luxuries. They may also reduce costs by producing goods of lower quality. The prevalence of sellers' markets in the Socialist countries usually enables enterprises to sell whatever they produce. Although by capitalist economy standards such behaviour by enterprises is not considered illegitimate,[1] in the Socialist countries it is officially viewed as anti-social.

(*f*) *Illegal Profits*

The more restricted is the operation of the market mechanism, the more opportunities and temptations there are for making profits by breaking existing laws and regulations. The evidence of these abuses can be found even in published literature. They include selling in black markets above officially fixed prices, the bribing of officials to minimize the enterprise's tasks and to secure extra advantages, the false classification of goods or their content to qualify for higher prices, the over-statement of costs and understatement of receipts in the enterprise's accounts to minimize tax and other liabilities, and the like.[2]

(*g*) *Profits from Private Enterprise*

Private enterprise has always existed in all Socialist countries in one form or another, and the liberalization associated with the economic reforms has in several ways favoured its resurgence,

[1] If goods are in short supply, their prices should rise. Thus by increasing their profitability, supply is increased whilst demand is reduced, so that equilibrium is restored in the market. Similarly, if products of poor quality can be sold profitably, it means there is sufficient demand for them and thus their production is justified.

[2] For evidence, see *Berliner Zeitung* (The Berlin Daily), East Berlin, 30/3/1971, p. 4; *Figyelö* (Economic Observer), Budapest, 21/10/1970, p. 3; *Finanţe şi credit* (Finance and Credit), Bucharest, 8/1970, pp. 23–31; *Rad* (Labour), Belgrade, 10/10–5/11 1970, p. 6; *Shchetovodstvo i kontrol* (Damage and Control), Sofia, 9/1970, pp. 23–4; L. A. Sergeiev, *Reviziya pri rassledovanii prestuplenii* (Auditing in Criminal Investigations), Moscow, Gosiurizdat, 1969, pp. 21 et seq.; *Svět hospodářství* (The World Economy), Prague, 20/5/1971, p. 2; J. Śliwa, *Rola zysku w funkcjonowaniu handlu socjalistycznego w Polsce* (The Role of Profit in the Operation of Socialist Trade in Poland), Warsaw, PWN, 1969, p. 52.

particularly in farming, crafts, catering, short-distance and local transport and personal services.[1] In some of them, as for example in market gardening, catering and building (especially in Poland and Yugoslavia) remarkable fortunes are being made. Thus in Poland in 1969, when average gross (before tax) earnings per person employed in the socialized sector were 29,660 złotys, there were 206 taxpayers owning suburban gardens in the Warsaw district alone whose gross profit exceeded 150,000 złotys each; of these 50 taxpayers netted more than 250,000 złotys each, and 7 taxpayers scored at least 500,000 złotys each.[2]

Windfall and illegal profits existed even before economic reforms,[3] but under the new system – noted for an increased independence of enterprises and fewer controls in general – the

[1] Some examples compiled from statistical yearbooks and journals published in these countries may be quoted here. Of the eight Socialist countries, only in the USSR is all land socialized, but even there individual plots cultivated by private persons for their own benefit (including private sale) have come to play a very important role; in the late 1960s, they contributed 30% of agricultural output (60% of eggs and 40% of livestock, milk and meat). The proportion of farming land privately owned and farmed is 1% in Bulgaria, 5% in the German DR, 6% in Hungary, 9% in Romania, 10% in Czechoslovakia, 84% in Yugoslavia and 85% in Poland. In Poland, the number of persons working in the private non-agricultural sector more than doubled between 1960 and 1970 to 400,000, of whom one-half were entrepreneurs and the other half hired labour; there are 150,000 artisan workshops, 25,000 transport enterprises, 15,000 retail shops, 8,000 kiosks, 5,000 laundries and agencies and 1,000 restaurants, all privately operated. In Yugoslavia, there are now at least 185,000 privately owned enterprises (compared with 130,000 in 1964); one-third of the value of art and craft articles is produced in private workshops; of the total number of dwellings constructed in 1967, more than one-half was privately undertaken and since 1967 the regulations regarding the opening of private retail shops have been considerably liberalized. In the German DR, there are 4,000 private industrial enterprises employing 100,000 persons contributing 12% of total industrial output, and 20% of retail sales is handled by private shops. In Hungary, there are 10,000 private retail shops and the number of artisans working on their own account exceeds 100,000. In Romania, the number of private workshops is over 40,000, and in Bulgaria the number of registered private tradesmen is about 30,000. In Czechoslovakia the number of privately owned enterprises exceeds 2,000 and the number of persons working on their own account is at least 17,000.

[2] *Rocznik statystyczny 1970* (Statistical Yearbook for 1970), Warsaw, Central Statistical Office of Poland, 1970, p. 39; *Życie gosp.*, 17/1/1971, p. 9, and 27/6/1971, p. 8.

[3] e.g., in the Polish pharmaceutical industry windfall and illegal profits represented the following proportions of total profits: 19% in 1957, 20% in 1958 and 15·3% in 1959. In the case of certain enterprises 142% was reached. Z. Madej, op. cit., p. 98.

temptation and scope for making super-normal profits are naturally much greater. But even if windfall and illegal profits are excluded, differences in profitability are still quite wide, as illustrated by the following examples.

In the German DR of the 88 industrial associations investigated in the late 1960s, the gross profit rate amongst different enterprises ranged from −0·5 to 98·0 per cent.[1] In Hungary in 1969 the *average* gross profit rate amongst different *branches* of industry (not enterprises) ranged from 4·1 to 38·4 per cent in the state sector and from 32·5 to 56·0 per cent in the co-operative sector (see Table 3 for details). In Soviet industry in the late 1960s, where the average gross profit rate was 20 per cent or less, about one-fifth of the

TABLE 3 DIFFERENCES IN THE GROSS PROFIT RATE* ACHIEVED IN SELECTED BRANCHES OF INDUSTRY IN HUNGARY IN 1969

Branch	In the State Sector	In the Co-operative Sector
Chemical industry	11·0	53·5
Electricity generation	7·4	—
Food processing	38·4	56·0
Light industry	14·2	40·9
Machine construction	13·7	40·7
Metallurgy	7·7	41·7
Mining	4·1	—
Total industry	10·6	41·3

* Gross profit as a percentage of the value of the assets used.

Source. Közgazdasági szemle (Economic Review), Budapest, 12/1970, p. 1431.

enterprises normally scored 50 to 100 per cent, and some enterprises even more.[2] In Yugoslav industry the average gross profit rate in 1966 ranged from 15·5 (in electric power) to 63·2 per cent (in the rubber industry).[3]

[1] *Gospodarka planowa* (Planned Economy), Warsaw, 10/1969, p. 33.
[2] *Finansy SSSR* (Soviet Finance), Moscow, 9/1970, p. 34.
[3] *Jugoslavenski pregled* (Yugoslav Survey), Belgrade, 5/1969, p. 203.

From the preceding discussion we can generalize that some sources of profits are independent of the enterprises' effort and some are illegal by official Socialist standards. In the case of monopolies and private undertakings, super-normal profits may be made – not necessarily by breaking laws and regulations but by superior efficiency and by performing valuable social functions; none the less their excessive profits cause concern to the socialist state. Taking into account all the sources of abnormal and anti-social profits, this concern is conditioned by the following considerations.

First, the authorities aim at preventing enterprises and individual persons from deriving extra income from sources which are considered socially inethical. Second, attempts are made to exclude such profits when evaluating enterprise performance, as they are not necessarily indicative of the enterprises' own exertion. The third object of concern is that unmerited and illicit profits must be neutralized before they are included in the basis on which incentives to the enterprise personnel are calculated. Guided by these considerations, the authorities administer certain measures designed either to prevent abnormal and anti-social profits from being made or to partly or wholly absorb such profits.

(i) *Differentiated Charges Levied by the State.* The branches of the economy, or even individual enterprises, which suffer from cost disadvantages may benefit from concessional interest rates and capital charges, or even be exempt from them. The state may also manipulate the proportion of depreciation allowances which has to be handed over to the state budget or intermediate organs of economic management (see Ch. 7A for further details).

(ii) *Differentiated Land Taxes and Prices.* These methods are applied mostly to farms to absorb differential rent. On the one hand, farms have to pay taxes which are differentiated according to the quality of land in their possession (see Ch. 4C for further details). On the other, procurement prices payable by the state to farms for a particular type of product vary roughly according to the degree of disadvantage caused by natural conditions. Thus in Poland in

1969 prices for wheat in złotys per 100 kilogrammes paid by the state ranged from 229 to 249 on compulsory deliveries and from 350 to 389 on above-compulsory deliveries (whilst free market prices ranged from 423 to 503).[1]

(iii) *Differentiated Levies on Non-Agricultural Enterprises.* These are fixed charges applied mostly to enterprises in mining, industry, construction and transport. They are so calculated as to neutralize the special advantages enjoyed by enterprises in respect of location, the nature of mineral deposits, the quality of equipment, the layout of plant, etc. On the other hand, other enterprises may benefit from state subsidies differentiated according to the degree of the disadvantage beyond their control.

(iv) *The State Absorption of Windfall Profits.* As a rule, windfall profits have to be handed over to the state immediately and in full. The prevailing official view in the past was that enterprises should neither benefit from such undeserved profits nor, by the same token, suffer in the case of state actions leading to a reduction of enterprise profits. However, under the new system, where financial instruments have assumed an active role, the state may deliberately make such changes designed to influence enterprises' profits and thereby their activities in socially desired directions. In these cases, windfall profits are not anti-social and are not necessarily surrendered to the state budget.

(v) *The State Absorption of Illegal Profits.* These profits have not only to be transferred to the state, but in addition penalties are applied. For example in Poland, according to the revised law of November 1970, a sum equivalent to 150 per cent of illegal profits must be handed over to the state.[2]

(vi) *Progressive Taxation of Profits.* If enterprises still make supernormal profits, in spite of the application of the measures discussed above, they are largely fleeced of such profits by progressive taxation. In Czechoslovakia the proportion

[1] *Rocznik statystyczny 1970*, pp. 348, 350.
[2] *Monitor polski* (Polish Law Gazette), Warsaw, 9/12/1970, p. 579.

of gross profit payable in tax rises from 10 to 55 per cent in the case of consumer co-operatives, from 20 to 70 per cent in the case of trading enterprises and in the case of other enterprises from 30 to 70 per cent.[1] In the German DR, if the annual gross profit per member of a co-operative enterprise is below 500 marks, no profit tax is payable, if the gross profit is from 500 to 750 marks – 5 per cent is absorbed by profit tax, and the proportion of this tax rises to 60 per cent where gross profit per member exceeds 6,900 marks.[2]

(vii) *Progressive Income Taxes.* These taxes are imposed on incomes earned from the private ownership of property and enterprises and in some countries (Bulgaria, Czechoslovakia, Hungary and Yugoslavia) on wage funds. In this way the upper extremes of personal income derived from lucrative pursuits are reduced. Thus in Romania income from letting and sub-letting property (land, buildings, furnished accommodation) is taxed at 6 per cent if such income is below 300 lei a year, but then the percentage rises up to 26·55.[3] In Czechoslovakia, if the average wage in the enterprise increases up to 3 per cent above the preceding year's level, less than 1 per cent of the wage fund is payable in tax; but if it increases by 10 per cent or more the proportion represented by tax rises to over 20 per cent.[4]

(viii) *Differentiated Planned Profitability Rates.* As has been discussed in Sections C and D of this chapter, differentiated minimum rentability or profit rates may be set by the authorities on a planned basis to neutralize special advantages. This approach has several advantages. The rates can be fixed for individual enterprises each year, and even readjusted during the year according to changing production and demand conditions and various state policy requirements.

[1] *Sbirka zakonu* (Law Reports), Prague, 27/11/1970, pp. 473–80.

[2] *Gesetzblatt der DDR* (The Law Gazette of the German DR), East Berlin, part II, no. 97, 16/2/1970, p. 684.

[3] *Buletinul oficial al Republicii Socialiste România* (Official Bulletin of the Romanian Socialist Republic), Bucharest, 30/4/1970, part I, p. 296.

[4] *Sbirka zakonu*, op. cit.

G. LIMITATIONS OF PROFIT UNDER SOCIALISM

Although much has been said and written in the Socialist countries about the advantages of the profit criterion, its importance and usefulness under socialism can be easily exaggerated. Its limitations stem from six basic conditions – the heterogeneity of the indicators of enterprise performance used, the restricted scope for the operation of profit, obstacles to the automatic flow of resources from the less to the more profitable uses, the limited extent and degree of competition, the doubtful correspondence of enterprise performance to economic efficiency and the anti-social manipulation of profits by enterprises and individual persons. The first five of these conditions are peculiar to the Socialist economies, and the sixth – although usually identified with capitalism – has reappeared under the new economic system, or at least has assumed greater proportions than before. We shall now examine these conditions.

The criteria of enterprise performance based on profit assume three primary forms – the profit mass, the rentability rate and the profit rate (and the hybrid form of gross income). Each of these may be used on a gross and net, a planned and above-plan, and a static and dynamic basis. The methods of calculating costs and assets also differ and there is no uniform treatment of revenue items. The profit standards applied differ widely, not only amongst different Socialist countries but even within a country, according to different branches of the economy, industry or even enterprises. A set profit standard may also be changed during the year, even in application to the same enterprise.

Moreover, in several Socialist countries other indicators of enterprise performance not based on profit are still in use, such as the size of output, the normative cost of processing, the foreign exchange effectiveness of investment and others. The different criteria in use may produce contradictory indications. In effect, workers in a particular enterprise may find that according to one criterion they may earn large basic and extra bonuses, but they may not even qualify for basic bonuses according to another (for evidence, see Ch. 6D, pp. 142–3). The very fact of the multiplicity of the standards used indicates that profit, in whatever form employed, has not provided a perfectly satisfactory criterion.

But even where a profit criterion is used, its full application and operation are still hamstrung in several ways, particularly where directive planning and management have survived or reasserted themselves. In all these countries the so-called 'major proportions in the economy' are still centrally determined, often irrespective of profitability. These include the division of national income between consumption and investment, between private and social consumption, between centralized and decentralized investment, and the broad distribution of production amongst the main branches of the economy and regions of the country.

TABLE 4 COMPULSORY PRODUCTION TARGETS IN HUNGARIAN INDUSTRY IN 1968

Type of Products	Number of Products Involved	Number of Enterprises Affected
Chemicals	8	26
Engineering products	3	5
Leather goods	4	4
Paper products	2	4
Products of ferrous metallurgy	2	5
Products of non-ferrous metallurgy	4	19
Sources of energy	5	25
	—	—
Total	28	88*

* This figure represents a total of the figures stated in the column. The actual number of enterprises affected was smaller as some enterprises were bound by targets in respect of more than one product.

Source. Based on I. Friss (ed.), *Reform of the Economic Mechanism in Hungary*, Budapest, Akadémiai Kiadó, 1969, p. 127.

In all of these countries except Yugoslavia, there are still directive targets imposed at least on some enterprises. Even in Hungary, where after Yugoslavia profit plays the greatest role, in 1968 there were compulsory production targets for twenty-eight goods involving about eighty enterprises (see Table 4). Usually there are also other directive tasks or limits binding enterprises, such as basic technological innovations, the amount of foreign exchange to be earned, quotas on the allocation and use of certain scarce materials, limits on capital investments and all these may sometimes be changed at short notice.

Even where differences in profitability are obvious and persistent, resources are not necessarily moved away from the least to the most profitable branches or enterprises. In all the eight Socialist countries loss-incurring enterprises are still tolerated and large subsidies are still paid to them. Even in Yugoslavia 11 per cent of enterprises operate at a loss, and most of them continue in business, carrying over their losses to the next year; they employ 12 per cent of manpower and own 13 per cent of fixed assets in the country; the profitability of an additional 17 per cent of enterprises is less than 2 per cent.[1] In Hungary in 1968–9, 7,600 enterprises were in the red, but of these only 36 were to be liquidated (mostly to be merged with other, profitable, entities).[2] Although some measures have been taken to prune subsidies, these efforts have, on the whole, been half-hearted. In most of these countries 'planned losses' are still a familiar item of Socialist economic plans. But many enterprises in fact incur larger losses than envisaged in the plan. For example, in Romania in the first half of 1970 the industrial enterprises in Bucharest recorded losses 17 per cent greater than their 'planned losses'.[3]

The Socialist economies are still noted for the weakness or absence of competition amongst enterprises and individual workers. Even where enterprises have freedom in conducting their operations, they do not necessarily avail themselves of it with a view to maximizing their profits. The Soviet Minister for Finance, V. Garbuzov, recently complained:

> Many enterprises still stick to the old practices, preferring to receive free allocations from the state instead of relying upon their own resources.[4]

[1] *Privredni pregled* (Business Review), Belgrade, 23/11/1970, p. 10, and 18/5/1971, p. 2.

[2] *Munkaügyi szemle* (Labour Review), Budapest, 5/1970, p. 176.

[3] *Scinteia*, Bucharest, 6/9/1970, pp. 1, 3.

[4] V. Garbuzov, ('Economic Reforms and Financing'), *Kommunist*, 3/1968, p. 51.

The extent of competition is particularly limited where large monopolistic suppliers prevail, and this is still a feature of the Socialist economies.

According to a study carried out in Hungary by the Institute of Economics and the Bureau of Construction in 1968, the weight of the different considerations given by managers in running state enterprises was as follows:[1]

(*a*) Maximization of the size of profit	27%
(*b*) Satisfaction of demand	23%
(*c*) Full utilization of capacity	15%
(*d*) Maximization of output	14%
(*e*) Maximization of *per capita* profit	12%
(*f*) Providing employment opportunities	7%
(*g*) Other considerations	2%
All considerations	100%

It will be noted that although direct profit maximization was the main single consideration, it was in fact outweighed by other objectives of a social nature.

The proportion of gross profits distributed in bonuses is in most cases less than one-tenth, and the proportion of personal earnings from profit-sharing is mostly less than one-fifth, so that the incentive effect on workers is rather weak. But even where profit-sharing, or private profit (in the private sector), does enable high personal incomes, there are definite limits to personal enrichment. The possibilities of acquiring private property or other forms of investment and enjoying prestige and power from such ownership, are clearly limited. A Polish monetary expert, Z. Grabowski, once looking through *The American Encyclopedia* noticed words of recognition in tribute to Lord Keynes as one who also 'knew how to make money'. Reflecting upon this praise, Grabowski remarked: 'Hardly anybody in our society would be proud of such a laurel on his head.'[2]

[1] Z. Román, ('Enterprise Behaviour'), *Közgazdasági szemle* (Economic Review), Budapest, 9/1969, p. 1025.

[2] Z. Grabowski, ('Money Today'), *Życie gosp.*, 4/12/1966, p. 2.

Although the maximization of profits may indicate maximum enterprise performance, it does not necessarily mean maximum efficiency. The reliability of profit as a verifier of efficiency depends largely on the pricing system, and in the Socialist countries this is still far from perfect (for details, see Ch. 4E). The advocates of profit are particularly fascinated with its synthetic character, superior to its specialized substitute predecessors. But as Michał Kalecki pointed out long ago, 'Profit is an all-embracing criterion of enterprise performance. This is its advantage but . . . at the same time its liability.'[1] There are multifarious ways of making profits, and some of them are contrary to social interest. Enterprises tend to be preoccupied with the most profitable articles to the detriment of less profitable items, and yet the latter may be highly desirable on social grounds. It is often not profitable, especially when sellers' markets prevail (as they do in the Socialist countries), to improve the quality and durability of goods. Profits can also be increased (at least in the short run) by neglecting the maintenance of buildings and equipment, by resorting to monopolistic practices, the black market, bribery and the doctoring of accounts.

From the preceding discussion of the shortcomings of profit, it should be evident that it has not been as wholeheartedly and completely embraced by the Socialist countries as the popular literature in the capitalist world has made it appear. Fundamentally, profit has not been accepted as an end but merely a means. E. Liberman, who has been identified by many Western commentators as the symbol of Socialist economic revisionism, was quite emphatic on this point:

> The difference from capitalism is that the goal and the means have changed places. Under capitalism, profit is the goal, and the satisfaction of the needs of the population is the means. Under socialism it is just the other way round. Satisfaction of the needs of the population is the goal, and profit is the means. The difference is not one of term but of substance.[2]

[1] M. Kalecki, ('Workers' Councils and Central Planning'), in *Dyskusja o polskim modelu gospodarczym* (Discussion on the Polish Economic Model), Warsaw, KiW, 1957, p. 36.

[2] E. Liberman, 'Are We Flirting with Capitalism?', *Soviet Life*, Soviet Embassy in Washington, July 1965, p. 39.

As is generally known, not all Socialist countries have adopted the profit criterion, not even with the limitations discussed in this section. The most outspoken opposition to profit has been registered in Albania and China. As a matter of historical fact, there were some economists in China who in the early 1960s openly advocated the adoption of the profit criterion. The most notable of them was Liu Shao-ch'i, who has been described as the 'Chinese Liberman'. But the Communist regime has declared its most determined opposition to these ideas, and the Cultural Revolution dealt a final blow to discussions and experiments in this direction. According to the official stand, profit cannot be accepted as a regulator of enterprise operations, as it is 'egoistic' and 'counter-revolutionary', and in a society true to Marxian ideals politics and revolution should be 'in command' of economic activities. The current official attitude to this question was recently described by a Chinese writer in the following words:

> He [Liu Shao-ch'i] has vainly attempted to corrupt the working masses, the poor and lower-middle peasants and the revolutionary cadres with 'money' and bourgeois counter-revolutionary egoism, so as to make them forget class struggle and proletarian dictatorship . . . We must use Mao Tse-tung's thought as a weapon and continue to criticize and repudiate 'material incentives', 'profit in command' and other reactionary fallacies, and eliminate the influence of Liu Shao-ch'i's counter-revolutionary revisionist line.[1]

[1] Ko Cheng, ('Politics in Command of Economics, Revolution in Command of Production'), *Jen-min jih-pao*, Peking, 24/7/1969 [translation in *Chinese Economic Studies*, New York, Spring 1970, p. 197].

3 Risk and the Socialist Economic System

A. RISK UNDER SOCIALISM AND UNDER CAPITALISM

RISK is a condition where there is a possibility of the occurrence of loss as a result of a deviation from the intended or expected situation. In economics, a distinction is made between 'measurable' and 'unmeasurable' risk. Measurable risk is that which can be estimated fairly accurately as it can be predicted on the basis of past experience and the law of large numbers. As such, this risk is insurable because its probability of occurrence is known, so that the insurance liability and consequently the insurance premiums can be calculated. This type of risk is associated with weather, fire, accidents, illness, theft and the like.

On the other hand, unmeasurable risk cannot be predicted with any degree of accuracy. It usually derives from such circumstances as changes in tastes, discoveries, innovations, shifts in government policies, fluctuations in foreign markets and vagaries in international relations. The inability of an enterprise to anticipate future developments affecting its costs and sales poses a possibility of losses (or profits) which cannot be estimated with any degree of certainty in advance. Economic decisions usually involve a subjective judgement based on limited information, some of which cannot be reduced to quantitative terms, and their outcome is dependent on variables beyond the control of enterprises. This type of risk in most cases cannot be insured against and consequently it is normally of considerable concern to individual enterprises.

In economic theory, following the contributions made by F. H. Knight and G. L. S. Shackle, measurable risk is known simply as 'risk'[1] or 'divisible experiment',[2] whilst unmeasurable risk is termed 'uncertainty'[1] or 'non-divisible experiment'.[2] It is widely

[1] F. H. Knight, *Risk, Uncertainty and Profit*, Boston, Houghton Mifflin, 1921, pp. 19–20, 197–232.

[2] G. L. S. Shackle, *Uncertainty in Economics*, Cambridge UP, 1955, pp. 23–6.

agreed amongst Western economists that profit is a reward for the latter type of risk. In this book, in accordance with the well-established practice in the business world, the term 'risk' is used as a general concept to include both 'measurable' and 'unmeasurable' risk, but the focus of attention is naturally given to the latter type of risk.

If we examine the problem of risk under the two rival social systems of today, it becomes obvious that its extent is in several respects much smaller under socialism than under capitalism. This is made possible by central economic planning and the social ownership of the means of production. Central planning – which is defined as 'a controlled and purposeful management of economic processes consisting in *ex-ante* co-ordination of means to attain desired ends'[1] – facilitates macroeconomic readjustments in the levels of money supply, employment, personal income and current consumption, and the intermeshing and synchronization of production and distribution. Major changes in the economy are not left to the whimsical market mechanism but are shaped on a planned basis. The risk of natural disasters can be reduced by centrally initiated or co-ordinated preventive measures, not impeded by the existence of private property and vested interests, even if they are not immediately profitable (dams, reafforestation, irrigation, etc.) and there is hardly any possibility of deliberate arson to insured private buildings in order to claim insurance.

The microplans of individual enterprises are built into the general economic plan so that much uncertainty can be removed by dovetailing and synchronizing the allocations of inputs and the disposal of output. The risk facing an individual enterprise may be magnified by what is described by some economists as 'secondary' or 'structural' risk.[2] This risk derives from uncertainty as to the actions of competing enterprises in the same or related industry, and it could be very high in the case of cut-throat competition. This source of risk, which is ever-present in a private-enterprise market economy, is largely absent under socialism, where

[1] W. Samecki, *Ryzyko i niepewność w działalności przedsiębiorstwa przemysłowego* (Risk and Uncertainty in the Operation of the Industrial Enterprise), Warsaw, PWE, 1968, p. 240.

[2] e.g., W. Grzybowski, ('Returns to Risk in a Socialist Economy'), *Gospodarka planowa* (Planned Economy), Warsaw, 3/1965, p. 57.

enterprises are socially owned and are supplied with the details of the general economic plan as well as the plans of related enterprises. A Socialist economy is also in a better position to counteract the effects of economic fluctuations originating from foreign countries.

Other sources of risk which are present in a capitalist economy but are non-existent or occasional only under socialism include conflicts arising from the uneven distribution of property and national income, strikes and other forms of antagonism between employers and workers, restrictive practices, price wars, boycotts, takeovers, speculation and trade cycles. The possibility of bankruptcy is very real.

It is therefore not surprising that for a long time the question of risk was almost completely ignored in socialist economic thought. Risk, especially unmeasurable risk, was essentially identified with capitalism – noted for its 'antagonistic property relations', the 'anarchy of production' and the 'class struggle'. This, of course, contrasts with the attitude in Western countries where the problem of risk has received extraordinary attention in both theory and business practice, and where studies of risk go back to the earliest days of capitalism and in fact can be traced back to at least the late Middle Ages.

However, experience has shown that economic activities even under socialism are subjected to risk. A Polish economist, H. Fiszel, noted for his outspoken views on the economic irrationalities existent in the Socialist countries, clearly stated in 1966:

> There is no economic process without risk. Risk must not be ignored in economic calculation because its incidence varies in different branches of production.[1]

Some sources of risk prevail in any type of economy irrespective of the social system in force, whilst others are peculiar to socialism. We can identify six distinct, general causes of risk:

(*a*) *Natural Disasters*. These include droughts, floods, frosts, hail, lightning, earthquakes, fire, geological and physiographic features.[2]

[1] H. Fiszel ('Risk and Reserves in a Planned Economy'), *Ekonomista* (The Economist), Warsaw, no. 5, 1966, p. 979.

[2] The natural element of risk is particularly present in agriculture and in industries depending on agricultural raw materials (food processing, chemical

(*b*) *Consumer Demand.* The demand for consumer goods is subject to changes and once consumers' freedom of choice prevails (as it has since the discontinuation of rationing in the early 1950s), the structure of the output produced may not match that which is actually sold, leading to piling up stocks of some goods and (most likely) shortages of others.

(*c*) *Technological Change.* The introduction of new methods of production and new products, and the implementation of investment projects for these purposes always embody some elements of uncertainty.

(*d*) *The Presence of the Private Sector.* Private enterprise still exists, more in some countries than others, but nowhere is it absent altogether.[1] This sector is more dependent on market forces, and in several ways it competes with the socialized sector for resources and the sale of its goods and services.

(*e*) *Mismanagement and Abuses.* The incompetence of the management, the slackness of the workers, cheating, pilfering, embezzlement, robbery, wilful damage, etc., are facts of economic life, just as omnipresent as in capitalist countries.

(*f*) *Foreign Trade.* No Socialist country is a closed economy and consequently they are exposed to the economic uncertainties associated with the export effort, the availability of imports, prices, credits and payments. These uncertainties are particularly pronounced in trade with capitalist countries.

Moreover, there are certain sources of risk which are more likely

---

and textile industries, exports and, indirectly, imports). To illustrate by reference to Poland: in the 1960s agricultural output fluctuated from year to year by 10% (rye by 17%, and potatoes and sugar beet each by 25%). The point is that agriculture still plays a very important role in the Socialist economies. Taking the eight countries as a whole, it contributes about one-quarter of their national income (by Western accounting and valuation), compared with 4% in the United Kingdom and in the United States. The proportion of export income derived from agricultural products is at least one-quarter (one-third in exports to the developed capitalist countries). Due to adverse weather conditions (and mismanagement), the Socialist countries except Romania over the period 1962–7 had to import large quantities of grain from the capitalist world at a cost of $3,800 million in hard currencies. The figures are based on, *Gosp. plan.*, 8–9/1967, p. 76; United Nations *Monthly Bulletin of Statistics*, 3/1971, p. xxi; International Wheat Council, *International Wheat Statistics 1967*, pp. 40–3.

[1] See Ch. 2F, footnote 1, p. 39.

to be present in the Socialist economies. The most important ones are as follows:

(*a*) *Planning Errors.* Central planning consists in the *ex-ante* setting of patterns of production, distribution and consumption. These plans cover the whole economy consisting of heterogeneous entities, and cover long periods (normally five years, with perspective plans up to twenty years). Planners' decisions may be erroneous at the time of plan construction or rendered obsolete by subsequent developments. The occurrence of bottle-necks, a familiar feature of centrally planned economies, provides evidence of the risk deriving from this source.

(*b*) *Alterations in Central Plans.* These are more frequent than is generally realized and they naturally create uncertainty for individual enterprises over which they have little control.

(*c*) *Inadequate Understanding of the Market.* The degree of risk is magnified by the fact that Socialist planners and enterprise managers are, on the whole, less commercially minded so that the quality of their judgement is unlikely to match that of businessmen in capitalist countries. The appointment of Socialist decision-makers has often been governed more by political considerations than by their business acumen, and at least in the past they were conditioned to control the market, not to follow or anticipate it. The extent and degree of risk have substantially increased as a result of economic reforms owing to decentralization, the profit incentive, innovations and a greater role assigned to the market (see Section C of this chapter, below). There is also evidence suggesting that the existence of central planning side by side with the market mechanism produces new tensions and uncertainties.

(*d*) *Alienation.* Contrary to Marxian expectations, alienation[1]

[1] This concept can be traced back to ancient Greek philosophers, but it was Marx who gave it a social connotation in the modern sense. He discussed it first in his earlier philosophic writings in 1844 (known as the *Paris Manuscripts*) and indirectly in *Capital* (1867). Marx described alienation as estrangement between the capitalist employer and the workers who realize that they have no control over their own labour and the goods they produce, and moreover that the capitalist uses the means of labour (producer goods) produced by labour itself to replace

has also made an appearance under socialism. It became particularly evident under the old economic system – noted for directive, centralized planning and administration and insufficient material motivation. It has manifested itself in indifference and even hostility between the individual and the ubiquitous monolithic state, between workers and management and between enterprises and bureaucracy.[1] It may surprise many readers of Marx to find the following recent description by a Polish economist of the situation in the Socialist countries:

> The socialization of the means of production as a basis for production relations must inevitably breed internal contradictions in a socialist economy. . . . Social ownership based on state and collective appropriation, although historically inevitable, embodies an inherent contradiction between the interests of society on the one hand, and of enterprises and their personnel on the other. This contradiction, in spite of the basic community of interest, arises in enterprises where there is a tendency to secure material gains at the expense of society or other enterprises.[2]

(*e*) *Relations with Capitalist Countries.* In their relations with the capitalist world, Socialist countries are exposed to greater uncertainty than is normally the case amongst capitalist nations, as was most obviously demonstrated by the Cold

---

labour, which leads to continued expansion of the 'industrial reserve army'. See Karl Marx, *Early Writings*, ed. by T. B. Bottomore, London, Watts & Co., 1963, pp. viii–ix, 120–34; K. Marx, *Capital*, Chicago, C. H. Kerr, 1908, vol. I, pp. 89–96, 689–703. Also see a recent study on alienation in the USSR: P. C. Roberts, *Alienation and the Soviet Economy*, Albuquerque, Univ. of New Mexico P., 1971.

[1] An interesting example of this source of risk facing Socialist enterprises is that of arbitrary tax assessment and collection by over-zealous officials, especially if they are members of the Communist Party. Thus in a report presented by the Auditor-General's Office in Poland in 1965, it was concluded that 'the administrative methods used by some officials are not only unnecessary but in fact harmful'. In the three administrative districts examined in 1964–5, taxation offices took legal proceedings against 17,600 peasant farms (mostly privately owned) allegedly for defaulting on tax payments, but it was later demonstrated that in 17,000 cases taxpayers had been unfairly proceeded against as taxes had been fully paid. Z. Abramowicz, *Ryzyko w działalności przedsiębiorstwa handlowego* (Risk in the Operation of the Trading Enterprise), Warsaw, PWE, 1968, p. 23.

[2] Ibid., p. 54.

War. Boycotts, the strategic embargo, arbitrary anti-dumping measures and the withdrawal of credits directly affect Socialist countries' exports and imports, and in addition a deterioration in East–West relations may necessitate the diversion of more resources to defence. In each case economic plans may be disrupted.

The existence of risk under socialism has also been pointed out by several Western economists in the past. Some of them, such as C. Bettelheim, M. H. Dobb and J. A. Schumpeter, concluded that risk prevailed in a socialist economy but it could be reduced or otherwise tackled more effectively in the context of the social ownership of the means of production and central planning.[1] J. Wiseman further deduced that in a liberal collectivist economy not only does uncertainty exist but also the most rational method of meeting it is by the rule of profit maximization.[2] However others, notably L. v. Mises, G. Halm and F. A. v. Hayek, went further by insisting that in some respects the problem of risk was much greater where enterprises were not privately owned, due to the absence of clear responsibility for losses and the reluctance on the part of the management to utilize opportunities for the minimization of losses or the maximization of gains.[3]

In the Socialist approach to the problem of risk there has been a preoccupation with social implications, and not merely with the microeconomic and private aspects. In a capitalist economy enterprise losses are normally borne by private owners; if the loss is caused by the owner himself the state does not concern itself with it, and if other entities suffer a loss the state – if asked to intervene – generally limits itself to the determination of responsibility and

[1] C. Bettelheim, *Studies in the Theory of Planning*, London, Asia Publishing House, 1959, pp. 269–71; M. H. Dobb, *On Economic Theory and Socialism*, London, Routledge & Kegan Paul, 1955, pp. 3–5, 53–4; J. A. Schumpeter, *Capitalism, Socialism and Democracy*, London, George Allen & Unwin, 1947, p. 186.

[2] J. Wiseman, 'Uncertainty, Costs, and Collectivist Economic Planning', *Economica*, May 1953, pp. 118–28.

[3] L. v. Mises, 'Economic Calculation in the Socialist Commonwealth', in *Collectivist Economic Planning*, ed. by F. A. v. Hayek, London, Routledge & Kegan Paul, 1935, pp. 116–22; G. Halm, 'Further Considerations on the Possibility of Adequate Calculation in a Socialist Community', in *Collectivist Economic Planning*, pp. 132–6, 172–5; F. A. v. Hayek, *Individualism and Economic Order*, Univ. of Chicago P., 1948, pp. 152–6, 164–76, 194–203.

compensation between the parties involved. In neither case, especially if compensation is paid, is the loss viewed with great concern as a loss to the economy. Under socialism, enterprise accounting is regarded as a part of public accounting and enterprise losses are seen much more clearly as losses to society, even if such losses are compensated for in some way. Consequently in the Socialist countries there is a much more determined effort to prevent or minimize losses by removing or reducing the sources of risk.

The state in a centrally planned economy is in a better position to command information on the causes of risk and has a more comprehensive administrative machinery for tackling the problem. In all the Socialist countries insurance organizations have well-developed 'preventive measures funds' and it appears that their efforts, on the whole, meet with greater co-operation from local authorities, police, enterprises and farms than is usually the case in capitalist countries. It may also be noted here that in the case of a misappropriation of funds or resources by one Socialist enterprise at the expense of another, the owner, i.e. society, does not lose or gain,[1] but in a private enterprise economy the owner does lose or gain.

B. THE CENTRALIZED, DIRECTIVE MODEL AND RISK

In a highly centralized economy noted for a clearly defined hierarchical structure of authority and responsibility, supply, production and disposal plans are prescribed in detail and imposed on individual enterprises bureaucratically from above. The allocation of materials and equipment, methods of production and targets to be reached are compulsory, or 'directive', enforceable by law. The central planning organ works out the feasibility of the overall economic plan with the aid of input–output tables, synthesized in the matrix of physical inter-branch balances. Enterprises are virtually deprived of the freedom of initiative. The system prevailed in the European Socialist countries before the economic

[1] Unless there is an overall loss or gain of production consequent upon the reallocation of resources.

reforms of the 1960s,[1] and some of its elements still persist, particularly in the German DR, Poland, Romania and the USSR.

Under that system economic calculation was carried out by central planners at the time of the plan construction and all crucial decisions were made at the top level. The central organ also set aside centralized reserves of materials, equipment and finished products to provide for unexpected emergencies. The more complete and careful the planning, the lower is the degree of risk and the smaller the need for reserves. There was little scope for independent decision-making by individual enterprises, and managers in fact acted as passive executors of commands in accordance with 'directive indicators'. Their functions were reduced to routine responsibilities, consisting mostly in the maintenance of the plant, the hiring of labour, the administration of accounts and the provision of information to the planning authorities on production capacities and current plan fulfilment.

Consequently, under this set-up the extent of risk to individual enterprises was very small. Firstly, enterprises were absolved from bearing responsibility for decisions made by higher authorities. Losses were absorbed by the state budget. Secondly, marketing risk hardly existed as the disposal of the enterprises' output was virtually guaranteed. Most output was directly allocated to other recipient enterprises by central planners. Moreover, centralized, directive planning and management coincided in these countries with acute sellers' markets, noted for an excess of demand over the available supply at controlled prices. Even goods not exactly answering buyers' preferences could, as a rule, be easily disposed of owing to the prevalent shortages. Purchasing enterprises were reluctant to complain for fear of jeopardizing their sources of supply in the future, and consumers could do little except exercise 'Hobson's choice'.

Yet the centralized and directive system did not eliminate uncertainty and losses. The basic reasons for this inability stemmed from the planners' imperfect knowledge of not only future developments but even past and present data on which plans were constructed, and the system for the collection and processing of

[1] Up to 1952 in Yugoslavia. Albania still adheres to the centralized, directive system.

information was not sufficiently developed. Furthermore, enterprises tended to supply misleading information to the planning authorities so as to secure the largest possible allocations of resources and to be assigned the lowest possible targets, because this was in their interest in view of the existing system of incentives (see Ch. 1B, pp. 3–9).

The longer the plan period the greater the risk of planners' errors, and the tighter the plan (i.e. the higher the targets laid down in relation to the available resources) the greater the risk of underfulfilment, bottlenecks and plan disruption. It is implicitly assumed that the central planning authority's judgement reflects society's preferences. The validity of this assumption is debatable. It may be argued that society runs the risk of its preferences not being correctly interpreted by central planners, either because of their imperfect knowledge or because of their intentional bias in favour of the interests of the Communist Party and the perpetuation of the social system to which they owe their position and success. And yet so much depends on their judgement. When errors are embodied in the plan, the consequent losses are likely to be high because they occur on a macroeconomic scale, with magnifying effects. The system is noted for inflexibility and it has no automatic error-correcting mechanism – it is too unwieldy and too impersonal to prevent a chain of losses even when they are patently obvious. A Czechoslovak economist, L. Unčovsky, summed up the working of the system thus:

> Centralized management and the concentration of power have led to a neglect of the role which risk plays in a socialist economy. It is possible to hide the consequences of risk by using the great concentration of resources controlled by the state. In the first place it is possible to transfer resources from other sectors to cover the risk. On the other hand, there are central resources earmarked as reserves.[1]

There is ample evidence of planners' errors demonstrated *firstly* by frequent changes in plans, and *secondly* by deviations of actual performances from planned targets. In effect, the element of

[1] L. Unčovsky, 'Some Problems of Risk in a Socialist Economy', in K. Borch and J. Mossin (eds), *Risk and Uncertainty*, Proceedings of a Conference held by the International Economic Association at Smolenice Castle, Czechoslovakia, in 1966, London, Macmillan, 1968, p. 377.

risk faced by individual enterprises under centralized directive planning is considerable. Enterprises are dependent on the central plan for the allocation of raw materials, semi-finished components, machinery and other equipment. Yet experience shows that, to start with, delays occur in sending even the original directives to enterprises. Thus it was reported that in Poland annual plan indicators were, as a rule, handed out after the beginning of the plan period and cases where they were received in the second half of the year were 'not that rare'.[1] But even the current five-year plan in the USSR, for 1971–5, was not approved by the Supreme Soviet till the end of November 1971.

Furthermore, original plans are changed during their currency, and this applies even to annual plans. For example, in Poland in the past some 95 per cent of enterprises had to change their plans during the year, some of them four times or even more.[2] It is known that in the Soviet constituent Republic of Ukraine in 1963, in one economic district (Kiev) plans were changed twelve times and in another (Lvov) sixteen times![3] But the national economic plan is a highly complex document so that, as a Polish economist emphasized, '. . . owing to technical and calculational problems, only some magnitudes are adjusted but not others . . . which leads to maladjustments, confusion and bottle-necks'.[4] Extra-plan additional directive tasks and recommendations issued by the planning authorities during the period of plan implementation were not infrequent.[5] Plans may also be changed secretly without enterprises ever being informed. This element of uncertainty is further enhanced by the fact that changes in plans affect various enterprises to different degrees, and the same enterprise differently at different times so that as a Bulgarian economist, T. Petrov, showed the consequent 'dislocations and losses of profits experienced by some are greater than by others and these vary through time'.[6]

[1] W. Samecki, op. cit., pp. 193–4.
[2] *Finanse* (Finance), Warsaw, 2/1969, p. 35.
[3] S. Góra, *Warunki produkcji a dzialalność bodźców* (Conditions of Production and the Operation of Incentives), Warsaw, PWE, 1967, p. 118.
[4] W. Samecki, op. cit., p. 180.
[5] Ibid., p. 193.
[6] T. Petrov, ('Profit as a Criterion of the Operation of an Industrial Enterprise'), *Planovo stopanstvo i statistika* (Planned Economy and Statistics), Sofia, 1/1966, pp. 45–6.

A study of Soviet experience under the old system suggests that, taking the economy as a whole, the deviations of actual production achievements usually amounted to 10–15 per cent below or above planned targets.[1] It appears that divergencies in other European Socialist countries were of about the same order, and in fact larger in some years. These macroeconomic variations, being averages, of course conceal individual deviations in different industries and enterprises. This is demonstrated in Table 5, showing quarterly plans and results in Polish light industry (consisting of four enterprises producing cotton textiles, clothing and footwear) over the five-year period 1957–61. Quarterly plans have been chosen because, unlike annual, five-year and perspective plans, these are usually final plans, not subject to revisions by the central planners during the course of their implementation.

From Table 5 we can conclude that plans and actual results were matched only in exceptional cases – in 1 per cent of the total number of plans examined. The lowest range of deviations occurred in respect of the volume of output, viz. 10 per cent below and 18 per cent above the plan, and in the value of output, viz. 12 per cent below and 17 per cent above the planned targets. The greatest departures were recorded in respect of profits. In none of the seventy-five cases analysed did the planned profit coincide with the actual profit achieved. The range of the deviations was from 77 per cent below to 244 per cent above the planned levels.

To sum up, from the standpoint of risk, the centralized directive system had some advantages and many defects. In some respects, centrally made decisions reduced the extent of risk facing individual enterprises, and where such decisions caused losses they were absorbed by the state budget. As these countries were in the early stages of economic development and had a small pool of competent managers, the concentration of crucial decisions at the central level minimized total social losses, which might otherwise have been greater.

However, more importantly, the system was singularly unsuited to the undertaking of risky but potentially productive ventures. Firstly, enterprises did not have enough independence to be able to

[1] H. Popławski, *Dopuszczalne ryzyko gospodarcze w przedsiębiorstwie* (Permissible Economic Risk in the Enterprise), Warsaw, PWE, 1970, p. 18.

embark on such ventures, and secondly, even where there was sufficient freedom the management was generally unwilling to take risks. The system of incentives was such that it favoured obedient

TABLE 5 ACTUAL DEVIATIONS FROM QUARTERLY PLANS IN LIGHT INDUSTRY IN POLAND, 1957–1961

Plan Indicator	Total Number of Plans Analysed	Number of Plans Coinciding with Actual Results	Proportion of Cases where Deviations were: Greater than ±1% %	Greater than ±5% %	Total Percentage Range of Deviations below (−) and above (+) Planned Levels %
1. Volume of materials allocated	144	1	93	82	(−63)–(+32)
2. Volume of stocks of materials held	112	0	98	93	(−70)–(+125)
3. Volume of output	77	0	88	18	(−10)–(+18)
4. Value of output	77	0	94	51	(−12)–(+17)
5. Volume of sales	70	0	85	40	(−17)–(+51)
6. Volume of stocks of final goods	79	1	99	92	(−52)–(+150)
7. Structure of the volume of materials allocated	144	1	99*	94*	(−72)–0*
8. Structure of the volume of output	77	1	78*	34*	(−24)–0*
9. Structure of the volume of sales	55	0	96*	73*	(−40)–0*
10. Profit	75	0	93	84	(−77)–(+244)

* These figures show negative deviations only, because an assortment plan cannot be exceeded.

Source. Based on W. Samecki, op. cit., pp. 63–71, 88–93, 102–3, 124–39.

and unquestioning executors of the directives handed down by higher authorities. If a risky decision was successful it was not sufficiently rewarded, but if it proved a failure it could mean a loss of prestige, a lower chance of promotion or perhaps dismissal.

The two decades of the existence of the centralized and directive system after World War II in these countries (less than a decade in Yugoslavia) left a mark on the mentality of Socialist managers. This is particularly so in the more authoritarian countries, where there has been considerable opposition to decentralization and where several ingredients of the old system have been retained. As one shrewd Socialist observer put it:

> Many managers cannot get rid of the old habit . . . in many cases they have lost the ability to distinguish between directives and recommendations. Their economic decisions are still governed by the so-called principle of alibi, viz. decision-makers are preoccupied with securing approvals, permits, documents, etc., just in case they are held legally responsible. Whole armies of clerks are engaged in contriving such alibis.[1]

C. ECONOMIC REFORMS AND RISK

The economic reforms since the early 1960s have placed the question of risk in a new light altogether. After a long period of neglect many studies on risk began to appear in which Western writings and practical experience have been carefully examined with a view to adaptations under the new economic system. In 1966 an East–West conference on risk and uncertainty was held under the auspices of the International Economic Association at Smolenice in Czechoslovakia, where Socialist participants were mostly on the receiving, whilst the Western ones were on the giving, side.[2]

The problem of risk has been given attention not only in Socialist economics but also in other disciplines, namely accounting, mathematics, statistics and law. From the studies carried out in the last decade or so the conclusion has emerged that the elimination of uncertainty under socialism is neither possible nor in fact desirable. Its complete elimination would restrict the freedom of manoeuvrability for the planning authorities, would demoralize enterprises and apply brakes on economic progress.

[1] H. Popławski, op. cit., p. 21.

[2] For details of the papers presented and the discussions, see K. Borch and J. Mossin (eds), *Risk and Uncertainty*, op. cit.

The main elements of the economic reforms are relevant to uncertainty and they include the decentralization of planning and management, a greater price flexibility, the acceptance of profit as a criterion of enterprise performance, the strengthening of material incentives to labour and linking them to profits, the flexible use of financial incentives, some relaxation of the restrictions on private enterprise and a more determined orientation to foreign trade – and the commercialization of economic relations, enhanced competition and a substantial reactivation of the market mechanism in general.

The scope and degree of risk confronting individual enterprises have greatly increased under the new economic system. First, there has been a tendency to exempt the state from the direct risk-bearing associated with its conduct of economic activities by the micro-economic localization of financial responsibilities, i.e. the shifting of risk-bearing to individual entities operating on the basis of commercial accounting. Second, enterprises are no longer assured of a market for whatever they produce. As profits are calculated on the basis of output sold, not merely produced, they have to supply what other enterprises and consumers are prepared to buy.

Third, large proportions of prices have been freed from rigid central control so that they can now fluctuate in response to market conditions. Fluctuating prices affect revenue from sales, even if their volume does not change (for details, see Ch. 4E). Fourth, consumer demand is now more unpredictable. Responding to public pressure for better living and in order to reinforce the effectiveness of material incentives, the authorities are allowing more resources for current consumption. In addition to a larger volume, there is a greater variety of goods and services available, including luxuries with close substitutes. The unpredictability of consumer behaviour is further enhanced by the rising levels of income, and particularly by the growing savings bank deposits which can be spent unexpectedly. Table 6 shows the remarkable growth of these deposits since 1960.

Finally, the new system is more conducive to competition. To maximize their profits, enterprises must meet buyers' preferences. Rising imports, which increasingly include consumer goods, provide alternative sources of supply, and the development of buyers' markets is further enhancing the rivalry amongst enterprises. Under this set-up, the behaviour of other competing enterprises now represents a source of uncertainty, so that 'structural' (or 'derived') risk is no longer the preserve of a capitalist economy but is becoming a factor to reckon with even under socialism.

TABLE 6 THE GROWTH OF SAVINGS BANK DEPOSITS IN THE EUROPEAN SOCIALIST COUNTRIES, 1960–1968

In National Currency at Current Prices per Head of Population

Country	Currency	1960	1965	1968	*Index for 1968 1960 = 100*
Bulgaria	Lev	106	213	342	*323*
Czechoslovakia	Koruna	1,423	2,517	3,415	*240*
German DR	DD Mark	1,018	1,835	2,536	*249*
Hungary	Forint	554	2,009	2,843	*513*
Poland	Złoty	645	1,862	3,087	*478*
USSR	Rouble	51	81	137	*269*
Yugoslavia	Dinar	50	180	481	*962*

Source. Based on *Rocznik statystyczny 1970* (Statistical Yearbook for 1970), Warsaw, Central Statistical Office of Poland, 1970, pp. 583, 670.

The compelling driving force behind the reforms has been the leadership's determination to accelerate the growth of productivity. The reforms have been largely directed at enabling and inducing enterprises to search for more effective methods and patterns of production. To some extent the liberalization of the discriminatory treatment of private enterprise, especially in such spheres as farming, handicrafts, catering and the various consumer services, has created a more favourable climate for private risk taking than in the past. But of greater consequence is the fact that the independence of socialized enterprises has been substantially extended, so that they now have a greater freedom of initiative to embark on innovations.

The strengthening of material incentives to the enterprise personnel and basing them on enterprise profits provide stronger inducements of risk-taking than was the case under the old system.

In addition, a flexible use of other financial incentives is made, all designed to enhance the profitability of the enterprises undertaking projects which although exceedingly risky are of great social importance. These incentives include highly differentiated interest rates, depreciation allowances, tax concessions and special profit mark-ups built into producer prices (see Ch. 4D for details).

The authorities have come to recognize the fact that risk-taking must be adequately rewarded. Unsuccessful ventures lead to a reduction of profits and thus a reduction or loss of incentive payments. Consequently, successful undertakings must provide opportunities for larger bonuses. In general, the size of the incentives to different categories of enterprise personnel is now directly related to their capacity for making decisions involving risk (see Ch. 6D, pp. 143–4). In addition to the provision of positive inducements, several forms of protection have been developed to shield enterprises and their personnel against losses arising out of risky undertakings (for details, see Section E of this chapter).

D. TECHNOLOGICAL RISK

One of the most serious shortcomings of the economic system which prevailed before the reforms was its limited capacity for, and even animosity towards, innovations. Under centralized directive planning and management, plans handed down to enterprises prescribed the allocation of resources in detail and even their methods of production. In effect, enterprises had no freedom in choosing inputs and techniques to pursue the most effective patterns of the substitution of inputs. The system of incentives favoured the fulfilment and over-fulfilment of quantitative targets, so that cost reduction, improvements in quality and the introduction of new products were all of remote concern.

This approach to production was a reflection of what has come to be known as the 'extensive growth strategy'. To maximize the rates of economic growth, the authorities concentrated on physical increases in output gained mostly by expanding employment, the size of capital and occupied land, rather than by increasing productivity. A Soviet economist frankly conceded as late as the mid-1960s that under Socialist conditions 'technological progress produces adverse effects on the basic indicators of enterprise performance. Innovations disrupt the existing structure of production and lead to an immediate drop in profitability.'[1] The share of national income devoted to research and development was much smaller than in the developed capitalist countries – only about half the proportion spent in Western countries.[2]

Consequently, the Socialist countries continued to lag behind Western nations in technology, particularly in its industrial applications. An American economist, M. Boretsky, who carried out a comparative study on Soviet and US technological progress, showed that in 1962 the USSR was some twenty-five years behind the USA in the application and dissemination of technological know-how in industry. Boretsky also concluded that the Soviet lag in civilian technology was greater in 1962 than in 1940. The lag of Poland in 1960 was estimated in a Polish source to have been forty-three years behind Britain, or nine years behind France.[3]

The economic reforms of the 1960s were primarily prompted by the determination of these countries to arrest the decline in the rates of growth which prevailed in the early 1960s, by mobilizing intensive sources of growth, i.e. by rapid increases in efficiency. This necessitates an acceleration of technological progress, namely the rationalization of the methods of production, improvements in the quality of resources and output and the introduction of new products more effectively satisfying the needs of producers and consumers.

Another propulsive force behind the technological drive is the

[1] G. D. Anisimov, *Materialnoe stimulirovaniye vnedreniya novoi tekhniki* (Material Stimulation of New Technology), Moscow, Ekonomika, 1966, p. 61.

[2] The percentages of national income (as defined by the Western method) in the early 1960s were 5·1, 4·0, 2·0 and 2·0 in the USA, Great Britain, the FR of Germany and France (in that order), compared with 2·1, 2·0, 1·5, 1·5 and 1·0 in the USSR, Czechoslovakia, the German DR, Hungary and Poland respectively. Based on: *Czechoslovak Economic Papers*, Prague, no. 8, 1967, p. 48; *Figyelö* (Economic Observer), Budapest, 4/6/1969, p. 3; *Życie gospodarcze* (Economic Life), Warsaw, 15/11/1970, p. 3.

[3] M. Boretsky, 'Comparative Progress in Technology, Productivity and Economic Efficiency: USSR versus USA', in US Congress, Joint Economic Committee, *New Directions in the Soviet Economy*, Washington, GPO, 1966, part II-A, pp. 149–50, 156–9; *Życie gosp.*, 10/8/1969, p. 3.

Socialist leaders' ambition to bridge the 'technological gap' separating them from the most advanced capitalist countries, and indeed to surpass them in order to demonstrate the superiority of socialism not only as a social but also as an economic system, not to mention as a military power. Between 1960 and 1970 expenditure on research and development in the Socialist countries more than doubled, and it is being further increased – in the early 1970s it represented about 3 per cent of national income. The current five-year plans (1971–5) also include scientific–technical plans for the acceleration of technological progress.

Technological change represents a major source of uncertainty, but of course this type of risk can be most productive. The traditional aversion of Socialist enterprises to technological innovational risk has been viewed with increasing concern by many economists and by the authorities for many years now. As early as 1955 a Soviet writer, A. J. Omelchenko, stressed the productive ('creative') implications of risk-taking. He also criticized Soviet managers for their timidity and advocated appointments to managerial positions on the basis of the capability of making decisions involving risk; he also proposed that persons in a position of authority refusing to take risks should be dismissed.[1] The most determined effort to forge ahead with innovations is apparent in the German DR, which has had to rely on intensive sources of growth more than any other Socialist country.[2]

The extent of technological risk has been greatly increased under the new economic system due to two developments with far-reaching consequences. First, several measures have been taken by the authorities to accelerate research and innovations. Under the old system technological improvements were introduced into the economy predominantly through the construction of centrally determined new projects. The present drive is, in addition, to induce enterprises to innovate on their own initiative by modernizing

[1] A. J. Omelchenko, *Tvorcheskii risk i iego gossudarstvenno-pravovaya okhrana* (Creative Risk and Its Economic and Legal Protection), Moscow, Izd. Moskovskogo Universiteta, 1955, p. 8.

[2] In contrast to other Socialist countries, the German DR even before the economic reforms had had no reservoir of underutilized labour to draw upon. In fact between 1950 and 1966, owing to the continued illicit stream of refugees to West Germany and low birth rates, her population declined from 18·4 million to 17·0 million.

their plants, rationalizing their production processes and producing new or improved articles.

Particular attention is being given to research, experimentation and the dissemination of solutions. The risk involved in this drive is obvious, particularly under central planning. Research projects may fail to provide solutions which are satisfactory from technical as well as economic standpoints. The cost of research or of innovation may exceed planned levels, or the planned timings may not be realized, with consequent disruptions. There is also a considerable degree of risk associated with the development of joint research schemes and joint business undertakings, which involves all or some member countries of the Council for Mutual Economic Assistance (CMEA) and which have been mushrooming since the early 1960s.

Second, the Socialist countries under consideration are entering higher stages of economic development, where it is typical for economies to increasingly rely on pure technological progress for the growth of national income. Thus in what are now economically mature capitalist countries, such as France, Germany, the UK and the USA, the proportion of total growth derived from this source was one-quarter or less (and three-quarters from the extension of resources) whilst today it is one-half or more. In the European Socialist countries before the economic reforms, one-third, or in most cases less, of growth was contributed by technological progress, but it is expected that the proportion will be about one-half in the next decade or two.[1]

As an economy becomes more developed, production processes become elongated and broken up into separate phases, each often handled by a different department in the enterprise or by other enterprises, so that co-ordination is increasingly more difficult. The number of alternatives confronting planners as well as enterprise managers multiplies rapidly. The increasing scale of production, mechanization and automation make breakdowns more and more costly.

On the other hand, technological progress itself facilitates a reduction of risk in several respects. Progress being made in the

[1] For details, see J. Wilczynski, *Socialist Economic Development and Reforms*, London, Macmillan, 1971, pp. 25–46, 233–59, 323–7.

application of advanced mathematical methods and high-memory computers in planning and in technical and market research enable multi-variant analysis for optimal solutions, promising the greatest probability of gain and the smallest chance of loss.

Computers reduce the possibility of human error, particularly where routine, monotonous handling of data and calculations is involved. Computers are increasingly being utilized for ensuring maximum economies in the use of inputs, for quality control, the optimal regulation of stocks, the discovery of idle capacity and the co-ordination of investment plans.[1] The pool of competent managers and specialists is increasing, and positions of responsibility are now less commonly entrusted to persons who are merely good communists. Great importance is now attached to the dissemination of technological data and the results of research and experiments, and not only on a national but also on a CMEA scale.

E. PROTECTION AGAINST RISK

For a long time Socialist economists saw little point in protection against risk, considering that in the context of the social ownership of the means of production the accumulation of reserves on the one hand and the payment of compensation on the other merely constituted transfers from one socialized entity to another. However, this attitude has been largely (but not completely) abandoned under the new economic system. It is now widely accepted that, as risk exists under socialism, persons, social property and enterprises must be properly safeguarded against possible losses. Otherwise the production capacity of assets may be impaired and enterprises and their personnel will steer away from risky undertakings.

The Socialist countries have developed three major sources of risk cover – the state budget, insurance funds and enterprise reserve funds. In the last decade there has been a tendency to shift risk-bearing away from the state budget to the operational level. This move conforms to the general trend towards decentralization, and it has been rationalized by the desirability of shifting the burden of risk to where it occurs, and at the same time prodding

[1] A. Kierczyński, ('Computerized Investment and Economic Accounting'), *Życie gosp.*, 8/11/1970, pp. 1, 3.

the entities affected to take preventive measures as far as that is possible. But the actual set-up in each Socialist country is different and it lacks a systematic and consistent approach. One Socialist writer described the set-up as a 'mosaic of *ad hoc* practices'.[1]

This is surprising in view of the prevalance of the social ownership of the means of production, central planning and the opposition to individualism and group interests. This reflects the fact that protection against risk is still in the process of evolution. We shall now examine the following aspects of protection against measurable and unmeasurable risk in the Socialist countries: social security and social insurance, the insurance of socialized property, the legal exemption of managers from permissible business risk, insurance against the uncertainty facing enterprises, reserve funds, and other forms of risk shifting or spreading.

(*a*) *Social Security and Social Insurance*

In Socialist terminology *social security* is concerned with the provision of benefits to persons disabled from birth (blindness, deafness, infirmity) or by war, and the scheme is financed out of the state budget but administered by specialized institutions. *Social insurance* covers persons who are employed in the socialized sector, it is financed by contributions paid by the employing entities (not by the insured, as a rule),[2] the system is at least partly administered by trade unions and it provides cover against accidents at work, illness, maternity and old age. There is normally no provision made for unemployment, because the right to work is guaranteed and there is no involuntary unemployment of any significant duration.[3]

[1] S. Dmochowski, *Ubezpieczenie mienia państwowego w gospodarce planowej* (The Insurance of State Property in a Planned Economy), Warsaw, PWE, 1966, p. 58.

[2] In capitalist countries social insurance, if it is provided, is usually contributory – up to two-thirds of the total, the balance being provided by the employer, the state and in some cases by other sources. However, in the Socialist countries in some cases the insured person may also contribute small amounts. For example in Poland, under the scheme operating since January 1968, persons employed may pay 3% of their salary towards retirement pensions.

[3] Except in Yugoslavia, where unemployment has ranged in the last decade from 5 to 10%, averaging 200,000 persons, of whom one-tenth has been receiving unemployment benefit in recent years. *Statistički godišnjak Jugoslavije 1970* (Statistical Yearbook of Yugoslavia for 1970), Belgrade, Federal Institute of Statistics, 1970, p. 116.

As one would expect, both these forms of social protection are very well developed in Socialist countries, and they had existed as such even before the economic reforms.

This type of risk is measurable and it is borne partly by the state directly and partly by enterprises. As far as the latter are concerned, in the case of social insurance, risk is transformed into cost.[1] It may be observed that some Socialist thinkers believe that, strictly speaking, under socialism 'social security and social insurance and consequently the social service funds disappear once the state takes over total responsibility for the welfare of its citizens and allocates the necessary funds out of the state budget'.[2] Their arguments are that social insurance contributions made by employing entities represent a form of the consolidated budgetary revenue, there are no earmarked social insurance funds and social benefits come from the state budget.

(*b*) *Insurance of Socialized Property*

Some Socialist economists are opposed to the insurance of socialized property, believing that common and predictable risk should be borne by the whole community, i.e. met out of the state budget. They stress that the administration of insurance involves substantial cost, whilst the payment of insurance contributions and of compensation merely represent transfers within the same framework of social ownership. In fact a few writers maintain that even where the insurance of socialized property exists now, it is a transitional device which will gradually lose its justification and will be completely eliminated under full communism.

[1] Social insurance contributions on the average represent the following proportions of the enterprise wage fund: in the USSR, 7%; Czechoslovakia, 10%; Bulgaria and Romania, 12% each; Poland (a uniform rate), 15·5%; the German DR and Hungary, 17% each. With the exception of Poland, the actual proportions are usually differentiated according to the branch of the economy – for example, in the USSR they range from 4·5 to 9·0%. Social insurance contributions on the average constituted 5% of the enterprise prime cost in Poland in 1965. Z. Abramowicz, op. cit., p. 77; S. A. Allakhverdyan (ed.), *Soviet Financial System*, Moscow, Progress Publ., 1966, p. 258; *Gosp. plan.*, 4/1970, p. 57, and 11/1971, p. 684; *Planovo stopanstvo i statistika*, 4/1969, p. 53.

[2] Lila Mackiewicz-Golnik, *Funkcje ubezpieczenia społecznego* (Functions of Social Insurance), Warsaw, PWE, 1969, p. 29.

But others, concerned more with the requirements of the new economic system than dogmatic rectitude, point out that the incidence of risk is not uniform amongst different types of enterprises. It is a sound economic accounting principle, irrespective of the social system, to maintain centralized insurance funds out of decentralized sources and to link the size of insurance contributions to the degree of risk, and such contributions should be treated as a cost to enterprises. Compensation should be received only by those enterprises which contribute to insurance funds. It is further stressed that under socialism the purpose of insurance is not the maximization of profits for the owner but the protection of social property, and consequently insurance contributions can be lower than in capitalist countries.

Soon after the communist takeover, insurance was socialized in all Socialist countries, and today in each of them there is at least one state insurance office concerned with the insurance of socialized fixed and circulating assets (including crops and livestock). Insurance is partly compulsory where overall social interest is clearly involved (need for the continuity of vital production processes, and for protecting the health and life of people), and insurance contributions are treated as cost. Insurance is as a rule voluntary where possible losses are merely of microeconomic consequences (damage to vehicles, breakage of windows, bursting of pipes, theft) and contributions usually have to be met out of enterprise profits.

In a planned economy, to provide compensation for losses there must be not only a financial provision but also a planned provision of resources for the restoration of damage to the production capacity of the enterprise concerned. The system is best developed in Yugoslavia. Insurance is compulsory for state entities against natural risks. Insurance contributions in the case of state non-economic organizations are paid out of the state budget. State enterprises pay insurance contributions themselves and they are accepted as cost, but if insurance is against non-listed risks, contributions have to be paid out of profits. Insurance agencies are run on an efficient commercial basis, they compete amongst themselves and since January 1968 they have been free to operate on a national basis. Prospective policy-holders have a choice of agencies and the latter have the right to determine policy conditions independently.

The least developed set-up now exists in the USSR where state property, with the exception of state-owned dwellings, merchant vessels and goods in foreign trade, is uninsured.[1] Losses to state property are covered directly from the state budget in the normal course of financing investment and repairs. Property held by co-operative enterprises (including collective farms) and public bodies is insured on a voluntary basis. A similar system prevails in Bulgaria, Hungary and Romania. In all Socialist countries goods in the process of being exported or imported are subject to compulsory insurance.

(c) *The Legal Exemption of Managers from Permissible Business Risk*

In the first twenty-five years of communist rule in the European Socialist countries managers could be held legally responsible for the losses incurred by enterprises, whether caused by fraud, incompetence or ordinary business risk. However, as early as 1929–32 in the USSR guidelines were issued to courts whereby cases of economic losses arising in the ordinary course of risky operations were not necessarily to be indictable. But these guidelines were too vague and did not go far enough. The practical effect of the Socialist legislation before the early 1960s was that the managers' freedom and inclination to take risky decisions were severely limited.

However, the need for innovations under the new economic system has placed the question of the responsibility for risky decisions in a different light. There was a lively discussion in Socialist literature and several conferences were held on this question in the early 1960s, in which not only economists but also technocrats and lawyers participated.[2] To remove the barrier to

[1] General insurance of state property has been discontinued since Jan. 1956.

[2] For thorough inter-disciplinary discussions of these questions, see M. S. Grinberg, *Problema proizvodstvennogo riska v ugolovnom prave* (The Problem of Productive Risk in Criminal Law), Moscow, Gosiurizdat, 1963; B. Nietyksza,

reasonable risk-taking by enterprises, since the early 1960s legislations have been explicitly amended in the European Socialist countries, or the courts have been interpreting the law more leniently than before. To illustrate, Article 217 of the Polish Criminal Code amended in 1969 reads:

> No person commits an offence if his acts are directed at increasing gain to the socialized economy, whether in respect of research work or technical or economic experiments, and if he acts within the limits of risk which is permissible in the context of existing knowledge, in particular if the probability of gain considerably exceeds the probability of possible loss.[1]

(*d*) *Insurance against Uncertainty Facing Enterprises*

Some Socialist countries have introduced, or been experimenting with, insurance designed to protect enterprise profits, especially against innovational risk. In the German DR since January 1970 the State Insurance Office has been testing a voluntary insurance scheme against the risks encountered in scientific and technical research and development. The cover applies to foreseeable damage which can arise during the application of new methods of production, the testing of new products or processes and the initial stage of the manufacture of new products.[2]

In Hungary the State Insurance Office now (since 1968) accepts insurance against the loss of production time and damage to machinery. In Poland an insurance scheme is being tested whereby comprehensive insurance is offered to enterprises to cover a variety of risks which may affect the interests of the enterprise concerned. In Yugoslavia insurance against business risk is widely practised along Western lines wherever the degree of unpredictability is not too great.[3]

Eksperyment–ryzyko–odpowiedzialność karna (Experiment–Risk–Legal Responsibility), Warsaw, KiW, 1967; D. Seidel, *Risiko in Produktion als gesellschaftliches und strafrechtliches Problem* (Risk in Production as a Social and Legal Problem), East Berlin, Staatsverlag der DDR, 1968.

[1] Quoted from H. Popławski, op. cit., p. 60.

[2] I. Topfstaed, ('Protection against Technical Risks'), *Die Wirtschaft* (The Economy), East Berlin, 19/11/1970, p. 16.

[3] J. Kalfus, ('Insurance Entities in the Socialist Countries'), *Svět hospodářství* (The World Economy), Prague, 10/12/1970, p. 3.

(*e*) *Risk Reserve Funds*

The possibilities for enterprises taking insurance against the risk associated with production are fairly limited, because this type of risk is largely unmeasurable. Yet this is the most 'productive' form of risk and at the same time it is liable to lead to fluctuations in profits, and thus in incentive payments. To meet this contingency, risk reserve funds have been evolved in the eight Socialist countries under consideration. They are either held by enterprises or are attached to branch associations, economic ministries, or local or regional authorities to protect a group of enterprises. The reserve funds are normally maintained out of enterprise profits and are used to absorb fluctuations caused by irregular supplies of materials, changes in the methods of production, the introduction of new products, and other forms of uncertainty.

To illustrate, we may take the case of Hungary. An enterprise has now to place 12·5 per cent (10·0 per cent before 1971) of its Sharing Fund and of its Development Fund into the Reserve Fund until the latter reaches 8 per cent of the enterprise's payroll and 1·5 per cent of the value of its assets. The Reserve Fund is used for covering losses, for the repayment of credits if the Development Fund is exhausted, and for supplementing the Sharing Fund should the latter fall below the level of the preceding year. The Reserve Fund must be brought back to the required level within five years from the funds which drew on it. In some branches of industry, where uncertainty is exceptionally high, enterprises may be permitted to form Special Reserve Funds, the maintenance of which is accepted as enterprise cost.[1]

Other funds which absorb risk include 'technological innovations funds' and 'trade risk funds' which can either exist in enterprises or be attached to branch associations. In addition, there can be centralized reserve funds, usually held by the ministries. For example, in Poland there are the Reserve Fund for State Farms, the Animal Diseases Compensation Fund, the Mining Compensation Fund and the Central Office of State Materials Reserves. Moreover, local authorities are allowed to set aside reserves for

[1] *Magyar közlöny* (Hungarian Gazette), Budapest, 27/10/1970, pp. 910–16.

emergency purposes, not exceeding 1·5 per cent of their total expenditure.[1]

(f) Other Forms of Protection

A method of reducing risk to farms as well as the state is the widely practised contract procurement system, under which the state guarantees to purchase agreed agricultural products at laid down prices. There is a tendency for these contracts now to cover periods longer than one year. For example, in the USSR according to the new 'forward contract procurement system', effective since 1970, the state guarantees the prices and quantities of grains, meats, fruits, potatoes, vegetables, grapes and other products to be purchased five years ahead (with the possibility of annual renegotiation). But farms have to pay fines amounting to 5 per cent of the value of the produce not supplied according to the contract terms.

In some Socialist countries, notably in the German DR and Yugoslavia, banks are allowed to charge mark-ups above basic interest rates on loans according to the degree of risk borne by the bank. A common method of protecting enterprises against innovational risk consists in novelty mark-ups which are allowed in producer prices over and above production costs and 'normal' profit margins (see Ch. 4D for details). Research and experimental entities are now usually protected against the risk of failure in the case of work commissioned by enterprises, as payment has to follow even if results are of no commercial value.

F. CONFINES OF PERMISSIBLE RISK

As can be concluded from the discussion in this chapter so far, the scope for making risky decisions by enterprises has been considerably enlarged under the new economic system. Several limitations on the enterprises' freedom of initiative (directive allocations, targets and methods of production and managers' legal liability) have been relaxed or removed, inducements to engage in risky but productive undertakings have been strengthened (profits and incentives to the management and workers) and some forms of

[1] S. Dmochowski, op. cit., pp. 46–7, 75–7.

protection against possible losses (insurance, reserve funds) have been developed.

This situation creates or enhances what may be described as 'social risk'. There is the possibility of recklessness on the part of the emancipated enterprises, of indulgence in ventures beyond a reasonable chance of success, or otherwise in anti-social operations however successful they may be from the microeconomic standpoint. Even though enterprises are now largely independent financially, they still represent social entities, and their losses diminish social property and national income, and consequently adversely affect the potential for economic growth – facts which are taken very seriously by the Socialist state.

The balancing of expected profits with possible losses is the essence of any economic decision in the context of uncertainty. Consequently, as one would expect, the legal attitude in the Socialist countries is that the size and probability of gain should exceed the possibility of loss. To be within the limits of permissible risk, M. S. Grinberg, a Soviet authority on the legal aspects of risk-taking, formulated the following four conditions:

(i) The undertaken risk must clearly correspond to the goal.
(ii) The goal cannot be achieved in any other, riskless, way.
(iii) Risk must not be manipulated so as to deliberately cause losses.
(iv) Risk may involve material losses only; it must not endanger human health and life.[1]

A Polish jurist, A. Mącior, stipulated five conditions:

(i) The goal of the risky undertaking must be socially gainful.
(ii) The risky undertaking must be the indispensable means of achieving the goal.
(iii) The probability of failure is small.
(iv) The risky undertaking must be carried out with all possible precautions and by legitimate means.
(v) Consent is obtained from persons whose health or life may be endangered by the undertaking.[2]

[1] M. S. Grinberg, op. cit., p. 95.
[2] Quoted from H. Popławski, op. cit., p. 70.

We have noted in the preceding section of this chapter that legislations have been amended in the Socialist countries to exempt managers from liability for losses arising out of decisions within the scope of permissible risk. But at the same time the responsibilities of managers and the limits to risk-taking have been clarified and spelled out. Thus Article 217, § 1, of the Polish Criminal Code clearly states that legal action is to be taken against 'persons employed in the socialized sector who fail to discharge their duty or exceed their powers and thus, even though unintentionally, cause damage to the assets or allow their misuse, or bring about some other loss to the social economy'.[1] To illustrate, the number of indictable cases of mismanagement and the losses associated with them in Poland in the late 1960s were as follows:

	The Number of Indictable Cases of Mismanagement		*Losses Caused*
	Total	*Per 100,000 of Population*	*In million zlotys*
1967	3,741	11·7	104·8
1968	3,167	9·8	91·7
1969	3,440	10·5	n.a.

n.a. = not available

Source. Ekonomika i organizacja pracy (The Economics and Organization of Labour), Warsaw, 10/1970, p. 451.

The industrial distribution of these offences in 1969 in percentages was: 49 per cent in light industry, 13 per cent in mining and power generation, 12 per cent in heavy industry, 12 per cent in food processing, 11 per cent in forestry and the timber industry and 3 per cent in the chemical industry.[2] It must be pointed out that these cases did not include deliberate sabotage, theft, embezzlement, fire or industrial accidents normally covered by workers' compensation.

The problem of the incidence of material responsibility on the management and workers for risk-taking beyond permissible limits has been widely debated in the Socialist countries, but so far no general agreement has been reached amongst theoretical writers, and there is no uniformity in actual practice. Some theoreticians

[1] Quoted from ibid., p. 41. [2] Ibid., p. 42.

believe that personal liability for losses caused by actions which are not deliberately fraudulent is essentially immoral in a socialist society. But others argue that as losses under socialism affect the whole society, not merely individual owners, persons should be deterred from acting in anti-social ways – even though unintentionally – and they should be penalized by deductions from their earnings. Some participants in the controversy have advocated that the person responsible, or the whole personnel of the enterprise concerned, should be deprived of not only incentives but also of up to 25 per cent of base pay.[1]

[1] Z. Madej, *Zysk w gospodarce socjalistycznej* (Profit in a Socialist Economy), Warsaw, PWE, 1963, pp. 292–4.

4 Prices and Profits

A. THE QUESTION OF EFFICIENCY PRICES

AN indispensable condition for enterprise profit to be indicative of efficiency is that prices must be rational, in the sense of reflecting cost–preference relations. This has hardly been the case in the Socialist countries, and certainly it was not so before the economic reforms. In each country price determination was highly centralized – it was vested in the hands of the Council of Ministers and the State Price Planning Commission.

The most distinguishing feature of the Socialist price system was the two-tier price structure. One tier embraced producer prices, i.e. those payable to producing enterprises.[1] They were normally fixed at the average prime cost level of the branch of industry, plus a planned profit mark-up. These prices remained fixed for long periods (usually 5–15 years), even though cost and demand conditions changed, as they did owing to the rapid transformation of these economies. The other tier represented retail prices, i.e. prices of consumer goods and services sold directly to the public in retail establishments. These prices were changed more frequently but their purpose was to adjust existing or desirable demand to planned or available supply. The two categories of prices were separated by relatively high and widely differentiated turnover taxes and subsidies which could be changed at short notice.[2] By varying these taxes, the authorities could neutralize changes in costs or consumers' preferences.

Some prices were highly differentiated so that for an identical type of article different producers, or even the same producer (see

[1] These prices are also known as 'wholesale prices', but this description is misleading and should be avoided. Wholesale prices include a wholesale trade margin and in some (exceptional) cases also turnover taxes, and neither of these mark-ups is received by producers.

[2] e.g., in Hungary in 1967 (before the price reform of 1968), only 10% of consumer goods was sold at prices reflecting costs; 30% was retailed at prices above and 60% was below production costs (i.e. was subsidized). B. Csikós-Nagy, *Pricing in Hungary*, London, Institute of Economic Affairs, 1968, p. 11.

Section C below), received different prices from the state. Similarly, different prices were charged to purchasers according to the use of the article and the classification of the buyer. Price determination procedures differed in detail in each Socialist country and the level and structure of prices were insulated from those in other Socialist countries and from world market (capitalist) prices.

On ideological grounds, it was generally believed, in accordance with the labour theory of value, that prices should be based on the 'socially necessary labour' embodied in the product. Rent, interest (beyond that on bank loans, usually not exceeding 3 per cent p.a.) and capital charges were denied as contributing to costs or value. In reality, the authorities hardly ever conformed to the Marxian ideal, and fixed prices to suit their practical policy objectives. These objectives were governed by three overriding considerations – the desired distribution of national income amongst different social groups, the postulated level of accumulation (i.e. saving) and the safeguarding of the plan fulfilment (by eliminating disruptions which might be caused by changes in costs and preferences).

These pricing policies, together with the centralized, directive system of planning and management had important implications as far as profit and efficiency were concerned. Prices were not, and could not, be used to ensure the most effective utilization of resources. Neither at the macro nor the micro levels did prices perform the allocative function. Central planners determined the allocation of resources first of all in accordance with the broad objectives laid down by the Communist Party and in patterns dictated by physical balances (input–output relations). At the enterprise level, the management was bound by so many directives that its patterns of the substitution of resources as well as of products were narrowly limited.

When indicators of enterprise performance other than profit were employed, the defects of the distorted price structures were less obvious. But with the profit criterion and the greater independence of enterprises, scarcity or efficiency, prices are of strategic importance because otherwise, as a Polish economist put it, 'irrational prices can de-rationalize profit'.[1]

[1] J. Popkiewicz, *Stopa zysku w gospodarce socjalistycznej* (The Profit Rate in a Socialist Economy), Warsaw, PWE, 1968, p. 119.

According to an East German economist, H. Mann, for a price system to be rational in respect of efficiency four conditions must be satisfied:

(i) A systematic improvement of the structure of prices by an application of the principle of 'production price', i.e. the inclusion of non-labour costs and a profit mark-up based on full cost (not merely on wage cost).

(ii) A rational determination of the *levels* of prices and of profitability in the economy.

(iii) The evolution of a mechanism for the determination of optimal perspective prices on which perspective (long-range, 15–20 year) plans should be based.

(iv) The co-ordination of prices with other economic levers, i.e. financial instruments and material incentives to labour.[1]

Rational prices in this sense can be evolved either by computation or by the forces of supply and demand operating in free markets. Both of these lines of approach have been followed to varying extents in different Socialist countries in recent years. A good deal of theoretical work on optimal prices has been done since the late 1950s. These prices are derived from the 'optimal plan', i.e. the plan which from a given quantity of resources enables the maximum possible output (or a given output is obtained from the lowest possible outlay of resources). By an iterative process, different resources can be assigned coefficients according to their contribution to the optimal plan. In these calculations all social costs, including the use of non-labour resources (land and capital) are accounted for. The original inventor of this theory, L. V. Kantorovich of the USSR, calls these coefficients 'objectively determined valuations', which in effect are scarcity factor prices. Kantorovich adds that the condition of optimality is that 'production must be justified by being profitable'.[2]

The derivation of optimal prices and their practical application have so far proved to be visions over the rainbow, owing to the immense number of calculations involved. But the advocates of the

[1] H. Mann, ('Economic Effectiveness and Price'). *Wirtschaftswissenschaft* (Economic Studies), East Berlin, 1/1969, p. 49.

[2] L. V. Kantorovich, *The Best Use of Economic Resources*, Harvard UP, 1965, esp. pp. 5–33, 121–51.

planometric centralized model believe that this solution to Socialist pricing is feasible once the Socialist countries are equipped with sufficient networks of high-memory computers. In the meantime, less ambitious computational prices have been used by central planners. In working out central plans 'programming prices' have been applied to guide the broad allocation of resources. These prices embody corrections for social cost–benefit, they apply only to selected resources, they are close to 'scarcity prices' and are used only as 'shadow prices', i.e. they are not used in actual transactions as they would be in conflict with the desired distribution of national income. Most progress has been made along these lines in the German DR, Hungary, Poland and the USSR.

More importantly, since the official adoption of the profit criterion all the eight Socialist countries have carried out far-reaching reforms of transaction prices, mostly producer prices:

Bulgaria	– 1968–69, 1971
Czechoslovakia	– 1967–68
German DR	– 1964–66, 1970–2
Hungary	– 1966–68
Poland	– 1967, 1971
Romania	– 1970–71
USSR	– 1967, 1972–73
Yugoslavia	– 1965

Periodical price revisions had also taken place before, but they had consisted merely in bureaucratic price adjustments to catch up with changed conditions. However, in the recent price reforms these countries have not only endeavoured to recast their price structures but also to introduce new principles of price formation in order to more closely reflect all social costs. The features of the new price systems conducive to efficiency include an increase in the levels of producer prices, designed to reduce the number of deficit-incurring enterprises, some progress made in improving the correspondence between retail and producer prices (see Section B of this chapter), a changing attitude to the pricing of primary products (Section C), the decentralization of price determination where market forces are also allowed to play an important role (Section E) and a closer relation between domestic and foreign prices (Ch. 9A). In this chapter we shall also examine the differentiation of profit mark-ups in prices and then bring out the shortcomings of Socialist prices in providing a rational basis for the profit criterion and efficiency.

B. PRODUCER AND RETAIL PRICES

The price reforms carried out since the mid-1960s have primarily concerned producer prices because they are the prices received by producing enterprises and thus directly affect enterprises' profits. By these reforms the prices of some products have been increased and of others reduced, but on the whole their levels have been substantially raised. Thus their level was increased by 18 per cent in the German DR over the period 1964–6,[1] by 8 per cent in Hungary in 1968 (whilst retail prices were reduced by 1 per cent)[2] and also by 8 per cent in Poland in 1971.[3] These increases have been conditioned by three objectives: to reduce the need for subsidization, to enhance the capacity of enterprises for self-financing and to enlarge the role of profit as a source of budgetary revenue (in comparison with turnover taxes).

In contrast to previous practice, capital charges on fixed and circulating assets[4] have been embodied (at least by implication) in higher prices. In general these charges range from 3 to 6 per cent of the value of assets employed (for details, see Ch. 7A, pp. 159–60). Capital charges can be regarded as a minimum macrosocial profit mark-up. In addition, attempts have been made in some cases to include ground rent in producer prices. The factor cost structure (excluding ground rent) in the branches of the Hungarian economy contributing to national income (material production) according to the new price system is shown in Table 7. In Poland gross profit

[1] *Ekonomicheskaya gazeta* (Economic Gazette), Moscow, no. 5, Jan. 1971, p. 20.

[2] *Társadalmi szemle* (Social Review), Budapest, 6/1969, p. 6.

[3] *Nowe drogi* (New Paths), Warsaw, 12/1970, p. 44.

[4] With the exception of Romania, where capital charges have not been introduced on a systematic basis. In Poland, only fixed assets were taken into account in working out the new prices effective since Jan. 1971. Only in Czechoslovakia and Hungary are capital charges treated as part of the enterprise's outlay, elsewhere they are deducted from gross profits.

TABLE 7 PERCENTAGE COST STRUCTURE IN THE BRANCHES OF MATERIAL PRODUCTION IN HUNGARY IN 1968*

Type of Cost	Industry	Con-struc-tion	Agri-culture	Trans-port	Trade	TOTAL
Material costs	76	67	52	39	35	*66*
Wages	13	27	43	26	42	*22*
Depreciation	4	2	4	20	4	*5*
Capital charges and interest	6	4	0	14	18	*6*
Land tax	1	—	1	1	1	*1*
TOTAL	100	100	100	100	100	*100*

* Exclusive of ground rent.

Source. Based on I. Friss (ed.), *Reform of the Economic Mechanism in Hungary*, Budapest, Akadémiai Kiadó, 1969, p. 144.

mark-ups for industrial branch associations, incorporated in the new producer prices effective since January 1971, were calculated according to the following formula:[1]

$$Pb = \frac{\frac{5}{100}\,nAf + \frac{3}{100}\,gAf + \frac{3}{100}\,pK}{pK};$$

Pb = the profit rate for the branch of industry;
nAf = the net value of fixed assets in the branch of industry;
gAf = the gross value of fixed assets in the branch of industry;
pK = the prime cost of commodity production in the branch of industry.

The average gross profit rates (before taxes and other deductions) in industry assumed in planning the new producer prices were (expressed as a percentage of the fixed and circulating assets employed): 13 per cent in Bulgaria, 15 per cent in the German DR and also 15 per cent in the USSR; in Czechoslovakia the rate was 6 per cent *plus* 22 per cent of the wage fund (the latter percentage including 10 per cent for social insurance, which in Czechoslovakia is not treated as a cost but is deductible from gross profit); in

[1] *Bank i kredyt* (Bank and Credit), Warsaw, 12/1970, pp. 469–74.

Hungary, where capital charges are regarded as a cost, the rate was 6 per cent *plus* 25 per cent of the wage fund (including 17 per cent for social insurance).[1]

With the exception of Hungary and Yugoslavia, the price reforms did not include radical alterations of retail prices.[2] Nevertheless, these prices have been subjected to several revisions since the mid-1960s. These revisions have been prompted by four (usually conflicting) considerations:

(i) in accordance with the traditional practice, to ensure reasonable equilibrium in the consumer goods market by adjusting market demand to the planned or available supply;
(ii) to regulate the cost of living;
(iii) to reinforce the effectiveness of material incentives to labour by lowering the prices of certain luxuries and semi-luxuries;
(iv) to make retail and producer prices more closely interdependent.

From the standpoint of the efficiency of the distribution of resources, and especially the role of profit in this process, the latter two considerations are of particular relevance. The role played by luxuries and semi-luxuries in the material motivation of labour is examined in Ch. 6E, pp. 148–53. Here we shall consider the relation between retail and producer prices.

Equilibrium in the consumer goods market, maintained by manipulating retail prices (and consequently the size of turnover taxes, or subsidies) so as to adjust demand to the centrally determined supply, does not ensure the most efficient allocation and utilization of resources. This was pointed out by Mrs Joan Robinson as early as 1960 in an article written for a Polish journal:

> If market forces are to influence the structure of production, it is imperative that producer prices are shaped in proportion to retail prices formed in the market. Only then can enterprise managers, striving to maximize total revenue and minimize total cost, become agents for equating supply with demand within the existing production possibilities. At the same time, the relative

[1] *Ekonomista* (The Economist), Warsaw, no. 6, 1969, pp. 1390–4.

[2] Retail prices apply to consumer goods and services sold directly to consumers. Components of a retail price include the producer price *plus* a wholesale margin, *plus* a turnover tax (or *minus* a subsidy), *plus* a retail margin.

> profitability of the different branches of production (as indicated by the turnover tax proceeds) will provide guidance to the planning authorities as to which industries should be given priorities for development.[1]

To enable cost–preference relations to be reflected in prices, it is necessary that there must be a close correspondence between producer and retail prices. On the one hand, changes in costs should influence retail prices and consequently demand, and on the other changes in buyers' preferences should be transmitted through retail to producer prices, so that producers confronted with altered profit margins respond in appropriate directions.

The reconciliation of the two price levels is one of the most complex problems under Socialist economic conditions. The two-tier price systems still prevail in all the European Socialist countries and they will probably never be eliminated. But most of the countries have embarked upon some rationalization designed to reduce the level and particularly the differentiation of turnover taxes separating these two types of prices. Most progress has been made so far in Hungary and Yugoslavia. In Hungary, in the price system existing before 1968, producer and retail prices were insulated by a gap equivalent on the average to 14 per cent (38 per cent before 1957) of retail prices; at the same time there were over 2,500 different turnover tax rates, *plus* several tens of thousands of specific tax levies applicable to individual types of goods. By the reform of 1968, the gap between the two price levels was narrowed down to 4 per cent, the size of turnover taxes was about halved and the number of different tax rates was reduced to about 1,000 (and the latter figure is planned to be pruned in the future to 300–400).[2]

C. DIFFERENTIAL RENT

As is well known, production costs differ widely under different natural conditions, especially in agriculture, forestry and mining. This is so irrespective of the social system, i.e. whether land is privately owned or socialized. The differences in natural conditions are particularly wide in the USSR; thus the range of unit production

[1] Joan Robinson, ('Philosophy of Prices'), *Ekonomista*, no. 3, 1960, p. 543.

[2] I. Friss (ed.), *Reform of the Economic Mechanism in Hungary*, Budapest, Akadémiai Kiadó, 1969, pp. 135, 156–8.

costs between enterprises operating under the most favourable (treated in all cases below as 1·0) and the least favourable conditions in the mid-1960s was – in lumbering: 1·0–2·1; in cement production: 1·0–7·9; in grain farming: 1·0–10·0; in coal-mining: 1·0–16·1; in electric power: 1·0–37·0 and in natural gas: 1·0–96·1.[1]

In a capitalist economy, the market prices of land products are normally determined by the cost of production on marginal (least favourable) land, so that the owners of intra-marginal land can charge differential rent according to the productivity of land. Differential rent is treated as cost and it is a factor which equalizes the profit rate earned from different grades of land in the economy. This rent can also be regarded as an element of price, i.e. if the price of the product is uniform, differential rent is highest in the case of articles produced on the most productive land and it is nil (or lowest) on marginal land. Thus in the USSR, where the cost of producing one ton of grain ranges from 15 to 150 roubles, differential rent in the case of grain produced on the best land amounts to 135 roubles per ton.[2]

The question of differential rent was first thoroughly examined from the social and economic standpoints by Marx (profiting from the writings by A. Smith, T. R. Malthus and D. Ricardo). Marx distinguished two types of this rent – *differential rent I* deriving from natural differences in the quality of land (physiography, soil fertility, climatic conditions, distance from markets), and *differential rent II* arising from the application of man-made improvements producing better results on some land than on other.[3] He regarded differential rent as a constituent of 'surplus value' (in addition to interest and profit), and as such a form of exploitation of agricultural workers and society by landowners.

The attitude to differential rent in the Socialist countries has, of course, been conditioned by Marx's writings. Traditionally there has been official opposition to it on three grounds:

(i) as a possible source of unwarranted personal income;
(ii) as a possible component of cost; as land is not a product of

[1] *Voprosy ekonomiki* (Problems of Economics), Moscow, 3/1968, p. 46; *Kommunist*, Moscow, 4/1968, p. 65.
[2] *Kommunist*, 4/1968, p. 65.
[3] K. Marx, *Capital*, Moscow, FLPH, 1959, vol. III, pp. 740–6.

labour, it has no value and consequently its use – however productive a piece of land may be – cannot represent cost;

(iii) more recently, as a result of the adoption of the profit criterion, differential rent is viewed as a factor distorting enterprise profit, i.e. enterprises (including farms) may make abnormal profit merely due to natural advantages, and thus their personnel may undeservedly earn excessive bonuses.

In a practical confrontation with these problems, the authorities have resorted to several measures designed to minimize the occurrence of differential rent and to channel it to the state budget. First, the retail prices of primary (as of other) products have, in general, been set at levels close to production costs under average (or better-than-average) conditions, rather than on marginal land or in marginal enterprises. In effect, differential rent occuring in enterprises operating under above-average conditions is reduced, whilst production elsewhere is subsidized. This policy is further justified by the Socialist state as a method of maintaining the low cost of living for the masses.

In all the Socialist countries substantial sums are paid out of the state budget to subsidize such primary products as foodstuffs and domestic fuels. In Hungary in 1968 subsidies, on the average, represented the following percentages of retail prices – meats: 19, bread and flour: 21, milk and dairy products: 48; the average subsidy on basic foodstuffs was 25 per cent. Subsidies on fuels and transport represented 45–50 per cent of their retail value.[1] In Poland 36 per cent of state farms in 1967–8 (57 per cent in 1963–4) operated under loss, and subsidies paid to them represented 16 per cent (27 per cent in 1963–4) of their output.[2] In the USSR in 1967, 8,000 collective farms (of the total number of 37,000) were in the red, or earned no profit.[3]

The second device consists in the administration of differentiated procurement prices payable by the state to agricultural producers. By paying prices roughly according to the regional

[1] *Figyelö* (Economic Observer), Budapest, 11/11/1970, p. 11; *Pénzügyi szemle* (Financial Review), Budapest, 2/1970, pp. 101–2.

[2] *Życie gospodarcze* (Economic Life), Warsaw, 20/4/1969, p. 8, and 15/6/1969, p. 9.

[3] *Zakupki selskokhoziaistvennykh produktov* (Procurements of Agricultural Products), Moscow, 3/1970, p. 18.

conditions of farming, the state absorbs a large portion of differential rent. As enterprises in primary production usually operate under increasing costs, in most Socialist countries the state further differentiates in prices according to the size of output. Priority output for compulsory deliveries to the state is paid lower prices than extra output for above-compulsory deliveries. Output over and above the deliveries to the state may be sold in free markets, where prices are again higher. In other words, the state endeavours to absorb differential rent and even within individual farms.

TABLE 8 THE DIFFERENTIATION OF THE PRICES OF FARM PRODUCTS IN POLAND IN 1969

In Zlotys per 100 Kilogrammes

PRODUCT	Regional Range of Procurement Prices Paid by the State: On compulsory Deliveries	Regional Range of Procurement Prices Paid by the State: On above-compulsory Deliveries	Regional Range of Prices Prevailing in Free Markets (Officially Quoted)
Barley	155–244	283–341	348–423
Calves for veal*	1,037–1,180	1,559–1,882	n.a.
Cattle for beef*	372–438	1,020–1,581	n.a.
Oats	152–164	272–294	321–438
Pigs for bacon*	1,203–1,273	2,395–2,448	n.a.
Pigs for pork*	947–1,002	1,739–2,090	3,765–4,933 ‡
Potatoes	56†	120†	111–158
Rye	183–189	290–305	318–388
Wheat	229–249	350–389	423–503

* Live weight.
† National average; data on regional differences not available.
‡ Pork.
n.a. – not available.

Source. Based on *Rocznik statystyczny 1970* (Statistical Yearbook for 1970), Warsaw, Central Statistical Office of Poland, 1970, pp. 347–50.

The difference between the free market price and the price paid by the state on compulsory and above-compulsory deliveries roughly indicates the unit size of differential rent absorbed by the state in this way. This is illustrated in Table 8 by reference to

Poland. In fact, price differentiation for some products was even greater, but for the sake of simplification it is concealed in the table. For example, in the case of pigs for pork the prices paid by the state in złotys per kilogramme of live weight ranged as follows: on compulsory deliveries – from 3·72 to 4·38, on non-contractual above-compulsory deliveries – from 10·20 to 13·84, and on contractual above-compulsory deliveries – from 14·17 to 15·81 (whilst free-market prices ranged from 37·65 to 49·33).[1] In the USSR, the Russian Republic is divided into five farming zones; the procurement prices paid by the state to collective farms over the period 1965–7 for 100 kilogrammes of beets were 2·70, 2·80, 2·90, 3·20 and 4·00 roubles according to the zone.[2]

There may also be price discrimination between socialized (state and collective) and private producers. For example, in the USSR in 1968 the average price per kilogramme of live weight of pigs paid by the state to socialized farms was 1·40 roubles but only 1·24 roubles to individual plot holders.[3] In the same year in Yugoslavia socialized farms received 95 dinars and private farms 91 dinars per 100 kilogrammes of wheat, and 86 and 75 dinars for barley respectively.[4] Another, less cumbersome method of absorbing differential rent is by the application of differentiated land taxes. In Czechoslovakia, according to the scale introduced in 1967, land tax ranges from 0 to 930 korunas per hectare, depending on the quality of land.[5] In Hungary agricultural land is divided into eleven classes (six classes before 1971) and land tax on the best class of land is 7·5 times higher than on 'marginal' land; in addition to the agricultural land tax, there is also differential rent charged on non-agricultural land ranging from 0·80 tto 16·50 forints per square metre.[6]

There are also other measures administered to absorb not only

[1] However, compulsory deliveries have been abolished since 1971, and instead a greater use is now made of price incentives, as has been the practice in most other Socialist countries for many years.

[2] *Dengi i kredit* (Money and Credit), Moscow, 9/1969, p. 14.

[3] *Izvestiya Akademii Nauk SSSR – Seriya ekonomicheskaya* (Communications of the Academy of Sciences of the USSR – Economics Series), Moscow, 6/1970, p. 33.

[4] *Finansije* (Finance), Belgrade, 7–8/1969, pp. 383–4.

[5] *Życie gosp.*, 21/4/1968, p. 7.

[6] *Ekonomista*, no. 6, 1969, p. 1400; *Pénzügyi szemle*, 9/1970, p. 718.

differential rent but also portions of quasi-rent (rent accruing to superior capital and labour whose supply is not fixed in the long run). Mining, industrial, construction and transport enterprises have to make 'differential payments' to the state if they enjoy above-average advantages in such respects as the location and quality of mineral deposits, climate, proximity to markets, the quality of equipment, etc. Similar effects are produced by the progressive income taxes applicable to collective farms and other co-operative enterprises, and the more progressive rates applied to private farms, craftsmen working on their own account and independent professions (doctors, lawyers, actors, painters, sculptors, writers). Up to 90 per cent of such income is payable in tax.

The state absorption of differential rent served a useful purpose in the past – it provided a large source of accumulation to finance ambitious industrialization programmes. But although it was probably inevitable in the past, it has produced several adverse effects on primary production. The artificially depressed price level of primary products favoured their wasteful use on the one hand, and discouraged their output and the expansion of production capacities on the other. The continuous 'planned' losses incurred by enterprises in less favourable positions produced demoralizing effects on the management and workers. The practice of intercepting differential rent via widely differentiated procurement prices has proved cumbersome and wasteful in implementation.

The pricing approach to primary products contrasts with the price policies applied to industrial consumer goods, which have been traditionally subject to heavy turnover taxes. This disparity of prices has also prevailed in trade amongst the member countries of the Council for Mutual Economic Assistance, where the prices of raw materials (especially of fuels, timber, metal ores, mineral fertilizers) have been disproportionately low in relation to manufactures, so that many primary products have become 'hard' items in the region (see Ch. 9B).

The adverse repercussions of these practices became obvious to many Socialist economists long ago, and more recently to the authorities as well. Some economists, such as I. Kozodoiev and A. Pashkov of the USSR, argued more than two decades ago – in defiance of the official policy line – that the value of agricultural products is determined by the conditions of production on marginal land.[1] The supporters of optimal planning implicitly accept differential rent as cost in their valuation of natural resources, to ensure that different grades of land are allocated to their most effective uses.[2] But some economists go further, advocating explicit recognition of differential rent as cost in practical economic management.

It is generally accepted amongst theoretical writers that the prices of primary products should be raised in relation to manufactures, and a substantial portion of differential rent should remain in primary industries. But there is no agreement on the extent of this retention. The majority of writers, such as H. Chołaj of Poland and P. A. Klemyshev of the USSR, believe that all or a large portion of differential rent I should be intercepted by the state (and ploughed back as centralized investment in primary industries), but that most or all of differential rent II should be retained by farms as an incentive to the intensification of agriculture.[3]

Several practical steps have been taken since the economic reforms, amounting to a departure from previous policies. In the German DR the average increase in the industrial price level by the reform of 1964–6 was 18 per cent, but the prices of metals were raised by 95 per cent and of fuels by 92 per cent.[4] Further price increases are planned for fuels in 1972: brown coal by 20 per cent and oil by 50 per cent.[5] In the Hungarian price reform of 1966–8 industrial products were increased by 8 per cent, but agricultural products by as much as 20 per cent, and further sharp increases

[1] I. Kozodoiev and A. Pashkov, *Zemelnaya renta v sotsialisticheskom selskom khoziaistve* (Ground Rent in Socialist Agriculture), Moscow, Gosplanizdat, 1959, p. 23.

[2] e.g., see L. V. Kantorovich, op. cit., pp. 99–100.

[3] H. Chołaj, *Cena ziemi w rachunku ekonomicznym* (The Price of Land in Economic Calculation), Warsaw, PWE, 1966, p. 19; P. A. Klemyshev, *Fondoemkost selskokhoziaistvennoi produktsii i rezervy ei znizheniya* (Capital Intensity and the Possibilities of its Reduction in Agricultural Production), Moscow, Ekonomika, 1966, esp. p. 114.

[4] *Ekonomicheskaya gazeta*, no. 5, Jan. 1971, p. 20.

[5] *Sozialistische Demokratie* (Socialist Democracy), East Berlin, 11/9/1970, p. 4.

followed in 1970.[1] In the Polish reform of 1971 the average level of producer prices was raised by 8 per cent, but the prices of the products of heavy industry (relying heavily on mining raw materials) were raised by 13 per cent and of timber products by 24 per cent, and furthermore there have been gradual and substantial increases in the procurement prices of farm products in recent years; at the same time, the prices of chemical manufactures were reduced by 11 per cent.[2]

The Soviet reform of non-agricultural prices of 1967 resulted in an increase of about 25 per cent in the average level; however, the prices of oil were raised by 230 per cent, iron ore by 127 per cent, coal by 78 per cent, metals by 43 per cent and timber products by 30 per cent, whilst chemical products were raised by only 5 per cent. Moreover, the procurement prices of farm products were increased by 50 per cent in 1965 and they are to be increased by another 50 per cent during the current 1971–5 plan period.[3] In Yugoslavia over the two decades following the price reform in 1952, by 1970 the wholesale prices of agricultural products rose by 419 per cent, whilst those of manufactures increased by only 56 per cent.[4]

Further evidence of the more liberal and commonsense approach to differential rent is provided by some steps taken to eliminate the differentiation of procurement prices, the discontinuation of the exploitative compulsory deliveries and a reduction of the overall tax burden on agriculture. Uniform prices are, of course, more conducive to financial discipline and rational economic accounting, and differentiated land taxes are a sounder method of the interception of differential rent by the state where it is desirable.

D. THE DIFFERENTIATION OF PROFIT MARK-UPS

The operation of profit provides the Socialist state with a unique opportunity of selective promotion and the discouragement of particular types of production by differentiated profit mark-ups

[1] *Acta oeconomica* (Economic Papers), Budapest, vol. 4, no. 1, 1969, p. 13; *Gospodarka planowa* (Planned Economy), Warsaw, 4/1970, p. 9.

[2] *Nowe drogi*, 12/1970, pp. 43–4.

[3] *Planovoe khoziaistvo* (Planned Economy), Moscow, 7/1967, pp. 15–16; *Vop. ekon.*, 10/1970, p. 61.

[4] *Statistički godišnjak Jugoslavije 1970* (Statistical Yearbook of Yugoslavia for 1970), Belgrade, Federal Institute of Statistics, 1970, p. 116.

embodied in producer prices. The application of these mark-ups is consistent with the independence of enterprises and is proving more effective than directives imposed from above. The flexible use of prices, by directly varying or influencing profit margins for different products is known in the Socialist countries as 'target (or "goal") pricing'. It must be realized that target pricing is now more effective than it could have been under the old system, because enterprises are in a better position to respond to changes in prices.

The widespread use of this differentiation amounts to a recognition by the state of the continuous changes in cost and demand conditions, and in particular of the unequal incidence of risk in different forms of production. Profit mark-ups must differ to provide *ex-post* as well as *ex-ante* compensation to enterprises. According to some economists, the utilization of profit in a Socialist planned economy in fact reduces to flexible price setting.[1] The differentiation of the profitability of different products embodied in producer prices is practised in the Socialist countries in three forms: branch-of-industry differentials, quality mark-ups and novelty mark-ups.

The profitability differentials for different branches of industry and the economy have been constructed into the new price systems of producer goods. In the Hungarian price structure adopted in 1968 the average gross profit rates for different branches of industry were planned to be as follows (gross profit as a percentage of the value of fixed and circulating assets; capital charges in Hungary are treated as cost):[2]

Light industry	9·8
Chemical industry	9·5
Machine construction	9·2
Building materials	7·3
Average for all industry	6·5
Food processing	5·6
Metallurgy	3·4
Power generation	2·6
Mining	1·6

[1] e.g., T. Kierczyński, ('The Place of Profit in the New System of Incentives and the Financing of Enterprises'), *Nowe drogi*, 5/1970, p. 62.

[2] I. Friss (ed.), op. cit., p. 146.

According to the Guidelines for the new price structure for 1970 in the German DR, the average gross profit rate is planned to be 15 per cent, but for most individual industries the rate ranges from 12 to 18 per cent, and for some branches it is as high as 25 per cent.[1] In the USSR – where, as in the German DR, capital charges are not treated as cost but are deducted from gross profit – the gross profit rate achieved in different branches of industry in 1968 was:[2]

Light industry	39·6
Petrochemical industry	30·3
Oil extraction and refining	25·5
Food processing	22·4
Machine construction	21·2
Average for all industry	*20·1*
Ferrous metallurgy	19·2
Chemical industry	16·2
Building materials	14·2
Power generation	10·6
Coal-mining	8·2

Czechoslovakia represents an exception as in her price model, in principle, no differentiation in the profit rate is made according to the branches of industry. Instead a uniform mark-up amounting to 6 per cent of the value of production assets plus 22 per cent of the wage fund is embodied in her producer prices. However, in reality considerable differences in the actual profit rate have occurred.[3]

One of the effects of the emphasis on the quantitative fulfilment of targets under the old system was the prevalence of a poor quality of production. This question is now treated very seriously and most Socialist countries[4] administer special prices which incorporate profit mark-ups for high quality and penalty mark-downs for poor quality. These prices apply only to certain types of products, mostly consumer goods. Such goods are usually classified into three categories: top quality, good average quality and sub-standard quality (Categories I, II and III).

[1] *Gosp. plan.*, 10/1969, p. 34.

[2] *Narodnoe khoziaistvo SSSR v 1969 g.* (National Economy of the USSR in 1969), Moscow, Statistika, 1970, p. 744.

[3] *Zahranični obchod* (Foreign Trade), Prague, 8/1969, p. 3.

[4] Czechoslovakia, Hungary and Yugoslavia rely primarily on competition and market discipline (with varying degrees of success).

In Bulgaria goods awarded the top quality classification receive a 10 per cent mark-up above the basic price (which includes a 'normal profit' mark-up), whilst to sub-standard products a mark-down of up to 20 per cent of the basic price is applied. In the German DR the mark-ups on good quality range from 2 to 5 per cent of the basic price; a mark-down of up to 10 per cent was administered on poor quality before 1971, but this classification has since been dropped. In Poland products rated in the top and good quality categories receive a profit mark-up of up to 50 per cent higher than the 'normal profit' mark-up in the basic price. In Czechoslovakia the prices for goods in the top-quality category can be set by enterprises themselves according to the market demand, whilst on sub-standard products enterprises have to pay a penalty, equal to 5 per cent of the producer price, to the state budget.[1]

The differentiation of profit margins is also widely used now to promote technological progress on a planned basis. Selected types of goods, which must be standardized and produced on a large scale, are usually classified into three special categories, Classes A, B and C, according to the degree of novelty. Products in the two upper classes are entitled to what may be called 'innovation' mark-ups above the basic price, whilst those in the lowest classification (obsolete goods) are subject to penalty mark-downs or only a 'normal profit' mark-up.

This practice is most elaborate in Poland. The profit mark-ups allowed on Class A and B products amount to 15 and 7 per cent respectively, and they usually apply for the initial two (with a maximum of five) years. In the first year 20 per cent, and in subsequent years 50 per cent, of these 'super-normal' profit earnings are handed over to the state budget, the rest being retained by the enterprise and the relevant industrial association. In the case of obsolete products, either there is no special mark-up or there is a penalty mark-down of about 10 per cent of the basic price; the over-fulfilment of targets of these goods does not entitle the personnel to bonuses, and enterprises may be directly instructed to discontinue the production of such items. This scheme has apparently proved quite successful. The value of 'novelty' in-

[1] *Vop. ekon.*, 8/1969, p. 60; *Gosp. plan.*, 3/1970, p. 12; *Železnicní doprava a technika* (Railway Transport and Technology), Prague, 6/1970, p. 180.

dustrial consumer goods rose from 750 million in 1963 (when the scheme was introduced) to 11,110 million złotys by 1970, or from 1·0 to 8·4 per cent of total sales.[1] A similar system is administered in the German DR and the USSR, where technological mark-ups are about 20 per cent, but the novelty period is normally less than fifteen months.[2] In most Socialist countries there are also special mark-ups for spare parts, especially those not in mass production, and for prototypes of new products.

From the point of view of financing risky forms of production, enterprises prefer special mark-ups on costs to allocations from their profits, because the former provide a regular flow of finance whilst the latter are naturally subject to fluctuations and consequently a greater uncertainty.[3]

E. DECENTRALIZATION AND FLEXIBILITY

In the past the Socialist countries were noted for their predilection for fixed (usually described in official parlance as 'stable') prices. Price determination in each country was centralized in the State Price Planning Commission, but the most important prices were reserved for the Council of Ministers. However, the decentralization of planning and management and the acceptance of the profit criterion have naturally necessitated considerable price flexibility. Only then can changing cost–preference relations be reflected in prices, and at the same time enterprises can respond to changing profit opportunities.

The changing views on price flexibility in the Socialist countries were clearly described by a Polish economist:

> There is a well-rooted conviction that the stability of prices is evidence of the superiority of the socialist economic system. This sort of view is merely a product of *conventional wisdom.* Changes in economic conditions should be reflected in prices. It is ridiculous to maintain that as prices are fixed in a socialist

[1] *Finanse* (Finance), Warsaw, 7/1970, p. 42; *Gosp. plan.*, 3/1970, p. 12.

[2] *Ekonomista*, no. 6, 1969, p. 1403; *Ekonomicheskaya gazeta*, no. 31, July 1969, p. 11.

[3] M. Marlewicz, ('Problems of Financing Technological Progress in the Context of Its Peculiarities, Risk and Contradictions'), *Finanse*, 12/1966, p. 37.

> economy no changes in economic processes take place. The artificially maintained stability of prices does not prove that economic conditions remain unchanged. . . . A flexible price is like a lens through which all changes in economic conditions are reflected.[1]

This new attitude is present even in the German DR, where up to the late 1960s pricing constituted about the most rigid element of planning, and where the flexible approach to prices is now known as the 'dynamic price policy'. In that country as well as in Romania (another country noted for rigid planning) a good deal of importance is attached to a gradual reduction of prices, where the growth of productivity warrants it and where profits would otherwise be excessive.

The evolution of more flexible price systems has proceeded along two different paths – the decentralization of price fixing and the extension of the role of the market, and both of these aproaches have been followed in all the eight Socialist countries. But the former approach has been concentrated upon in the economies which have departed least from centralized planning and management (the German DR, Poland, Romania and the USSR), whilst the more market-oriented countries (Bulgaria, Czechoslovakia, Hungary and Yugoslavia) have chosen to rely more on the market mechanism.

There is now a large number of bodies concerned with price determination. In addition to the central authorities, there are regional price offices, and some categories of prices can be determined by industrial branch associations, by the councils of co-operative enterprises, by trading entities and even by the parties to particular types of transactions by negotiation. In the latter two cases, prices are virtually formed by the conditions of supply and demand. Decentralized price setting is carried on in accordance with broad regulations laid down by the state.

The extent of the dispersion of price determination by administrative methods under the new system is illustrated in Table 9 by reference to Poland. In the German DR the State Price Planning

[1] W. Samecki, *Ryzyko i niepewność w działalności przedsiębiorstwa przemysłowego* (Risk and Uncertainty in the Operation of the Industrial Enterprise), Warsaw, PWE, 1967, pp. 200–1.

TABLE 9 PRICE-FIXING ORGANS IN POLAND

Price-Fixing Organ	Types of Products
1. Council of Ministers	(*a*) Basic supplies for production and investment.
	(*b*) Basic agricultural procurements (grains, livestock, milk, potatoes).
2. Relevant ministries	(*a*) Some supplies for production and investment
	(*b*) Machinery and equipment.
	(*c*) Chemical products.
	(*d*) Books.
3. State Price Planning Commission	(*a*) Retail prices of key industrial products.
	(*b*) Some goods produced by local industries.
4. Regional Price Commissions	(*a*) Retail prices of goods produced by local industries.
	(*b*) Ceiling prices for fruit and vegetables.
5. Central Co-operative Unions	(*a*) Goods produced by co-operative enterprises.
6. Trading enterprises	(*a*) Goods purchased from private craftsmen.
	(*b*) Vegetables and fruit.
7. Parties to the transaction	(*a*) Goods for export.
	(*b*) Prototypes and non-standardized goods.
	(*c*) Intermediate products covered by industrial co-operation.

Source. M. Pohorille (ed.), *Ekonomia polityczna socjalizmu* (The Political Economy of Socialism), Warsaw, PWE, 1968, pp. 815–16.

Commission is responsible for the administration of price determination, but in working out prices it has to seek the approval of the following organs: the Council of Ministers (for 6 per cent of all industrial prices), ministries (29 per cent) and industrial branch associations and individual concerns (65 per cent).[1] In the USSR

[1] *Gosp. plan.*, 10/1969, p. 36.

about one half of all prices is now determined on a decentralized basis. On the other hand, in Romania, by the decree of 1970 restructuring the institutional set-up for price fixing, there now appears to be a greater centralization to 'avoid overlapping and divergencies'; however, there is a wider representation of different bodies in the State Price Planning Commission.[1]

The growing inclination in several Socialist countries to allow the market to shape defined categories of prices has been prompted by two considerations. First, it has been found necessary to relieve the administrative organs of the unnecessary routine work associated with setting prices for articles of small consequence, each of which may run to dozens of different types according to size, durability, aesthetic design, etc. The number of different prices handled by the State Price Planning Commissions before the reforms ranged from about one million in Bulgaria to over five million in the USSR.

The second consideration has consisted in the authorities' desire to infuse a greater measure of rationality and discipline, particularly in the formation of those prices where consumer preferences are important and at the same time unpredictable. 'The strengthening of price discipline by the market,' B. Csikós-Nagy (the well-known architect of the Hungarian price reform) recently stated, 'is essential if production is to respond to demand'.[2] In fact, as Mrs Joan Robinson pointed out:

> . . . the arguments for the formation of prices in accordance with market demand are stronger in the case of a socialist than a capitalist economy, because under capitalism the distribution of purchasing power amongst households largely depends on the unequal distribution of wealth . . . so that it is reasonable to expect that under socialism effective demand should determine prices.[3]

An interesting development in the sphere of price formation under the new system are the so-called 'complex' (also known as 'flexible' or 'mixed') price systems. Under these systems only

[1] *Bullletinul official al Republicii Socialiste România* (Official Bulletin of the Romanian Socialist Republic), Bucharest, 18/3/1970, pp. 134–6.

[2] B. Csikós-Nagy, ('Elements and Tasks of the Price Policy'), *Pénzügyi szemle*, 2/1970, p. 97.

[3] Joan Robinson, op. cit., p. 541.

some prices are fixed, whilst some can rise up to laid-down ceilings, some are free to move within specified ranges and others are freely determined in the market without restrictions. In general, controlled prices (the first three categories) cover key materials and the common necessities entering the cost of living, whilst free-market prices apply to the less important materials and luxury and semi-luxury consumer goods. Table 10 provides an example of the proportion of prices falling within each category for different types of products in Hungary.

Similar price systems exist in Bulgaria, Czechoslovakia and Yugoslavia. In Czechoslovakia in 1967 14 per cent of producer prices was fixed, 81 per cent could move up to specified ceilings or within specified ranges and 5 per cent was freely determined in the market.[1] In Yugoslavia agricultural prices are mostly determined in free markets and about one-half of industrial prices is similarly formed. In the German DR there are four categories of prices – 'stable', 'ceiling', 'calculated' (where sellers can quote their own prices in accordance with state regulations) and 'contractual' (negotiated by the parties concerned). In all the eight Socialist countries free-market prices exist for farm products grown or raised privately and sold directly to consumers.

F. DEFICIENCIES OF SOCIALIST PRICES

In the preceding sections of this chapter we have examined the relation of Socialist prices to profit, and in particular the reforms designed to rationalize price formation with a view to increasing the performance of their economies. However, although a good deal of progress has been made, Socialist prices are still far from being conducive to maximum efficiency. Price distortions were too great in the past to be removed in a short space of time, and so far the reforms have not gone far enough. Prices are still partly used for achieving social objectives which are in conflict with efficiency, and moreover the reforms carried out have created new problems.

On the whole, Socialist prices still suffer from four major shortcomings in the context of profit as a criterion of enterprise efficiency

[1] *Ekonomicheskaya gazeta*, no. 5, Jan. 1971, p. 20.

TABLE 10 THE COMPLEX PRICE SYSTEM IN HUNGARY

The Proportion of the Value of Output or Retail Trade Turnover in Each Category of Prices in 1968

Types of Products	Fixed Prices %	Ceiling Prices %	Free-Range Prices %	Free-Market Prices %
1. *Producer Prices of Raw Materials and Intermediate Products*	*30*	*40*	*2*	*28*
Building materials (excl. wood)	—	40	—	60
Fuel and power	75	10	—	15
Hides, skins, leather	—	60	—	40
Metals	—	85	5	10
Raw materials for heavy industry (excl. fuel and power)	10	25	—	65
Textile fibres	—	75	—	25
Wood and paper materials	10	30	—	60
2. *Producer Prices of Manufactured Goods*	*3*	*16*	*3*	*78*
Building structures	—	—	—	100
Chemical products	10	35	5	55
Engineering products	0	30	5	65
Foods, processed	5	5	5	85
Furniture and paper	—	—	—	100
Textiles and clothing	—	10	—	90
3. *Procurement Prices of Agricultural Products*	*60*	*10*	*20*	*10*
Animal products	73	—	21 *	6
Plant products	44	—	41 †	15
4. *Retail Prices of Goods for Private Consumption and Use*	*20*	*30*	*27*	*23*
Clothing	—	21	54	25
Construction materials	20	70	—	10
Foodstuffs	31	29	27	13
Fuel	100	—	—	—
Miscellaneous industrial goods	7	50	22	21

* Loosely regulated.

† About one-half of the products in this category is tightly, and about one-half loosely, regulated.

Source. Based on I. Friss (ed.), op. cit., pp. 148–51.

and a basis for incentives to labour, namely continued divergencies from social cost, the disregard of consumer demand, price differentiation, the distortions produced by the complex price systems and the limitations of state-initiated price changes.

(a) *Divergencies from Social Cost*

There are still large proportions of prices which deviate from factor cost to reflect the opportunity cost of the utilization of land, capital and labour. In effect, substantial subsidies on the one hand and heavy turnover taxes on the other are continued. There is no systematic inclusion of ground rent in planned prices and there are some branches of the economy (especially agriculture and service industries) which are exempt from capital charges; moreover, only in Czechoslovakia and Hungary are capital charges treated as cost.

TABLE 11 DEVIATIONS OF CONSUMER PRICES FROM SOCIAL COSTS IN HUNGARY IN 1968

Products or Services	Ideal Price	Actual Price
Non-essentials (spirits, tobacco, etc.)	100	120–150
Miscellaneous industrial products	100	135
Light industrial products	100	132
Building materials	100	126
Engineering products	100	118
Foodstuffs	100	70–90
Electricity	100	82
Transport and communications	100	74
Coal	100	55
Housing (rent)	100	30

Source. Based on I. Friss (ed.), op. cit., p. 140.

The divergence of actual prices from the efficiency ideal exists even in Hungary, where price reforms have been more radical than in other Socialist countries except Yugoslavia. In a study of the prices reformed in 1968 it was demonstrated that the prices of consumer goods deviated by as much as 70 per cent below and 50 per cent above 'ideal' prices, i.e. prices reflecting all social costs. The details are shown in Table 11. On the whole, realized producer prices (i.e. including taxes) in industry were 6 per cent below, and in agriculture 17 per cent above, 'ideal' prices (without taxes, the respective percentages were 47 and 43 per cent below 'ideal' prices).[1] These divergencies appear to have increased further in 1971 owing to a substantial increase in state subsidies (by 1,300m forints, or by 5 per cent).[2]

(*b*) *The Disregard of Consumer Demand*

The opposition to utility as a determinant of value is still strong because it is considered to be 'subjectivist' and conflicting with the labour theory of value, and consequently anti-Marxian. Some consumers' preferences are regarded as anti-social (e.g. for large, powerful cars) and some irrational (for current rather than future consumption). As Socialist economic planning is incompatible with consumer's sovereignty, consumers' preferences cannot be fully expressed in the market, or if they are they are ignored by the authorities or tampered with through 'consumption steering'.

The two-tier price systems, which are retained in all these countries with the qualified exception of Czechoslovakia and Yugoslavia, can still be used to insulate the effect of consumers' preferences on production. The advocates of optimal planning and the mathematical determination of prices are opposed to the formation of prices by the market; if computational price determination is perfected and extended, planners' preferences may further displace consumers' preferences.

(*c*) *Price Differentiation*

This practice is still widespread. Different planned prices are administered for different types of buyers and sellers for essentially the same product. Prices in private dealings (as for example in food), whether in officially recognized free markets or in black markets, are usually well above officially administered prices. There are also highly differentiated freight charges, interest rates and capital charges.

[1] I. Friss (ed.), op. cit., p. 138. [2] *Figyelö*, 6/1/1971, p. 3.

(*d*) *Distortions Produced by the Complex Price Systems*

Although price reforms have been aimed at gradually removing price distortions by introducing complex price systems, in reality the problem has in some ways been aggravated. When all prices were fixed, there was reasonable stability and undesirable tendencies could be controlled. But under the complex price system, whilst fixed prices have remained stable other prices have tended to rise alarmingly, and furthermore some of them faster than others, so in effect creating new distortions. These processes add to uncertainty, and its incidence is uneven on different enterprises and consumers.

These problems have become most evident in Czechoslovakia, Hungary and Yugoslavia. In Czechoslovakia, where the complex price system was introduced in 1967, by 1970 producer prices in other than the controlled categories rose by about one-third, and even inefficient enterprises made high profits. In this process, enterprises in a monopolistic position played a prominent part, even to the extent of limiting their output. These developments created considerable inflationary pressures so that the government had to declare an interim 'price moratorium' in 1969, and since then price controls have been extended.[1]

In Hungary uncontrolled prices have also increased so that the average profit rate in 1968 and 1969 rose to 9·4 per cent, compared with the planned rate of 6·5 per cent. There was also a wide range of profit rates recorded in different enterprises owing to the distortions produced by fixed and free prices.[2] In Yugoslavia, where the new price system was introduced in 1965, over the period 1965–70 industrial producer prices rose by 25 per cent, agricultural procurement prices by 35 per cent, retail prices by 57 per cent and the cost of living by 60 per cent.[3]

[1] *Hospodářské noviny* (Economic News), Prague, 2/10/1970, pp. 3–4, and 30/12/1970, pp. 8–9.

[2] G. Molnár, ('The Price Reform in Practical Experience'), *Közgazdasági szemle* (Economic Review), Budapest, 12/1970, pp. 1429–36.

[3] Based on: *Statistički godišnjak Jugoslavije 1970*, p. 116; *Borba* (Struggle), Belgrade, 31/12/1970, p. 7.

(*e*) *Limitations of State-Initiated Price Changes*

Although to varying extents in different Socialist countries, the state still retains the power to change fixed prices and other price controls. By a single act of changing prices on its own initiative, it can reshuffle the whole pattern of profitability, even though the methods of production in enterprises may have remained essentially unchanged. The state in its price policy is still guided by a variety of social goals, of which efficiency is only one. There is hardly any evidence of a systematic and objective study of the social cost–benefit of departures from efficiency prices.

But even where the price changes initiated by the state do reflect new cost—preference relations, there is no assurance that producers (or even consumers) will respond accordingly. Price elasticity of supply as well as demand is still much lower in the Socialist than the capitalist countries. According to a recent study, Hungarian managers fail to react to price changes as high as 10 per cent, and it may take several decades before they develop a price sensitivity typical of their counterparts in Western countries.[1]

We can thus conclude that owing to continued price distortions, Socialist enterprise profit is not necessarily indicative of efficiency, certainly less so than in a capitalist market economy. These distortions are prejudicial to the optimum distribution of resources and the maximization of social welfare in accordance with the principle of equi-marginality. Resources should be allocated in such patterns as to equate their marginal productivity in different applications. The multiplicity of prices for the same type of resource and product introduces elements of incongruity and makes the comparative evaluation of costs and effects in different enterprises well-nigh impossible.

Socialist writers are prone to blame enterprises for greed and anti-social distortion of the structure of production. It is argued that enterprises, taking advantage of their newly won independence, strive to maximize their profits by concentrating on the most lucrative articles and neglecting the production and distribution of

[1] S. Kopatsy, ('The 1968 Producer Prices and Profits'), *Közgazdasági szemle*, 6/1970, p. 733.

items of low profitability, however socially indispensable the latter may be.[1] In the context of the new economic system, this is a perverse argument. The fault primarily rests with the distorted price structure, viz. the profitability of the latter-type of products is too low in relation to the former. The state should either readjust the planned profit mark-ups or create conditions for effective competition so that profit margins are rendered accordant by the market forces.

[1] e.g., D. Allakhverdyan, ('Economic Reforms in the European Socialist Countries'), *Vop. ekon.*, 9/1969, p. 110; T. Kierczyński, op. cit., pp. 50–1.

5 The Growth and Distribution of Profits

A. THE GROWTH OF PROFITS

THERE has been a remarkable growth of profits in all the eight Socialist countries, particularly since the economic reforms. This trend can be explained on the following six grounds. First, as material incentives to labour have been based on enterprise profit, both management and workers have been anxious to increase the level of profits or profitability to qualify for larger bonuses. In fact in some Socialist countries (the German DR, Poland, Romania and the USSR) incentive payments have been made dependent not so much on the level of enterprise profits or profitability but on their *increases* in comparison with the preceding or some other base year (see Ch. 2B, C, D). The greater independence of enterprises has naturally made it possible to conduct enterprise operations in such ways as are also most beneficial (however indirectly) to the enterprise personnel.

Second, the scope for increasing profits has been substantial owing to the presence of excess capacity in most enterprises. Whilst under the old system it was to enterprises' advantage to resort to precautionary 'hidden reserves', the profit basis for incentives has prodded enterprises to tap such reserves. Third, in the last decade Socialist countries have carried out some radical reforms of planned producer prices (wholesale prices received by producing enterprises), designed to reduce the need for subsidization. The increase in the general level of these prices has raised the overall profitability of production (see Ch. 4B, pp. 85–7). Fourth, in addition to the increases in planned prices there have been marked increases in the free-market prices charged by enterprises. This has been the case particularly in Czechoslovakia, Hungary and Yugoslavia, where under the 'complex' price systems price controls on specified categories of goods and services have been relaxed or lifted altogether (Ch. 4E, pp. 100–4).

Fifth, in contrast to previous practice, the margins allowed to wholesale and (especially) retail trading enterprises have been increased. A higher level of profitability is now considered to be essential to enable trade to provide better facilities and service to consumers (Ch. 8A, pp. 175–6). Sixth, there has been some revival of free enterprise, motivated by private profit, especially in crafts, repair-work and maintenance, sub-contracting, market gardening, catering, local transport and personal services. This revival has been facilitated by a relaxation of restrictions on private ventures, particularly where socialized entities have proved incapable of supplying goods and services of the assortment and quality required by consumers (see Ch. 2, footnote 1, p. 39).

The growth of profits can be best illustrated by reference to the USSR, the country which is willy-nilly watched by other 'fraternal' Socialist countries to see which way the winds are blowing. The growth of gross profits (i.e. before budgetary deductions) in different years over the period 1950–72 is shown in Table 12. Profit is only one of several sources of financial accumulation in a socialist economy. The latter concept also includes turnover taxes, income taxes, differential payments, fines and other payments for the state (it must not be identified merely with budgetary revenue). Once deductions are made for incentives, financial accumulation becomes the macroeconomic source for financing investment, an increase in stocks and reserves and the collective needs of society. In real terms it corresponds to the 'net product for society'. The figures for financial accumulation are given in Column 2 of Table 12.

In the same table, annual rates of increase in financial accumulation, gross profits and national incomes are also shown (Columns 5–7), together with the proportions represented by gross profits in financial accumulation (Column 3). Two significant conclusions emerge from the table. On the whole, gross profit has been rising faster than either financial accumulation or national income. Over the period 1950–72 financial accumulation rose about five times, national income nearly six times but gross profit about twenty times. Gross profits represented less than one-fifth of financial accumulation in 1950, but by 1971 the proportion had risen to three-fifths. Over the relatively short period 1960–70 considerable

TABLE 12 THE GROWTH OF GROSS PROFITS IN THE USSR, 1950–1972

Year	Financial Accumulation*	Gross Profits*	$\frac{3}{2} \times 100$	Annual Rate of Growth of:		
				Financial Accumulation*	Gross Profits*	National Income†
	Million roubles		%			
(1)	(2)	(3)	(4)	(5)	(6)	(7)
1950	27,100	5,221	*19*	—	—	—
1960	65,200	25,184	*39*	—	—	—
1961	n.a.	26,789	—	—	6·4	6·8
1962	n.a.	30,599	—	—	14·2	5·7
1963	n.a.	30,676	—	—	0·3	4·0
1964	n.a.	34,885	—	—	13·7	9·3
1965	83,300	36,960	*44*	—	5·7	6·9
1966	89,400	44,096	*49*	7·3	19·3	8·1
1967	104,900	55,873	*53*	17·3	26·7	8·6
1968	112,800	67,496	*60*	7·5	20·8	8·3
1969	121,700	72,693	*60*	7·9	7·7	4·8
1970	139,300	86,989	*63*	14·5	19·7	9·0

* Excluding collective farms.
† According to the Socialist concept (Net Material Product).

Sources. Based on *Narodnoe khoziaistvo SSSR* (The National Economy of the USSR), Moscow, Statistika (different years).

fluctuations in the rates of growth of profits were recorded – ranging from 0·3 to 26·7.

The growth of gross profits in different branches of the Soviet economy over the two decades 1950–70 is represented in Table 13. It will be noted that two branches, state farms and construction, which incurred large losses in 1950, have shown a noteworthy growth of profits. Since the economic reforms officially adopted in 1965, state farms, construction and industry have recorded the fastest whilst municipal undertakings, consumer co-operatives and transport and communications the slowest rise; in some branches gross profits actually declined. Industry, the most important branch of the economy, contributes two thirds of total profits (disregarding collective farms). The profit rate in industry, i.e. gross

TABLE 13 THE GROWTH OF GROSS PROFITS IN DIFFERENT BRANCHES OF THE SOVIET ECONOMY, 1950–1970*
In Milllion Roubles

Branch of the Economy	1950	1960	1965	1970	*Index for 1970 1965 = 100*
Industry	3,211	14,017	22,548	55,956	248
State farms	–238	104	100	6,117	6,117
Transport and communications	1,124	4,489	6,830	11,523	169
Construction	–481	1,099	1,605	4,736	294
Supply and disposal of producer goods	96	847	892	1,696	190
Trade (consumer goods)	389	1,579	1,398	2,859	205
Municipal undertakings	199	591	748	984	132
Consumer co-operatives	188	817	898	1,321	147
Other branches*	733	1,641	1,941	1,797	–7
TOTAL	5,221	25,184	36,960	86,989	235

* Excluding collective farms.
Source. Based on *Narodnoe khoziaistvo SSSR v 1970 g.*, p. 703.

profit as a percentage of the value of fixed and circulating assets, has, on the whole, been rising remarkably, as shown by the figures below:

1960 – 13·6	1966 – 13·3
1961 – 13·4	1967 – 17·1
1962 – 14·8	1968 – 20·1
1963 – 14·0	1969 – 20·5
1964 – 14·0	1970 – 21·5
1965 – 13·0	

Source. Narodnoe khoziaistvo SSSR v 1969 g., p. 744, and *v 1970 g.*, p. 706.

The increase in the profit rate since 1967 is partly due to the increase in industrial producer prices effective since July 1967.

Similar tendencies are also evident in the other Socialist countries. In Bulgaria the gross profit earned by enterprises per 100 leva of fixed assets employed rose from 12·96 leva in 1965 to 14·62 leva in 1968.[1] In Hungary in 1968 and 1969, where the 1968 price reform provided for the average profit rate of 6·5 per cent (of the value of fixed and circulating assets), the actual average rates reached were over 9 per cent, and co-operative workshops scored 40 per cent.[2] In Poland the official attitude to profit is less enthusiastic than elsewhere in Eastern Europe. Yet in the 1960s the gross profits earned by socialized enterprises more than doubled – from 46,980 million in 1960 to 108,010 million złotys by 1970. The share of gross profit in financial accumulation rose from two-fifths to nearly one-half over the same period.[3] In Romania in 1970 profitability in industry is reported to have been 80 per cent higher than in 1966, and losses from unprofitable enterprises to have been cut by 40 per cent.[4]

In his greatest work, *Capital*, Marx predicted that in capitalist economies, owing to technological developments, the profit rate must inevitably be falling.[5] A century of experience since the publication of *Capital* has produced no conclusive evidence in support of Marx's speculations. It is doubtful if Marx ever had a clear picture of the role of profit, and what the tendency for the profit rate might be, in a socialist economy. By analogy, technological progress should also lead to the profit rate falling in non-capitalist economies. Experience in the European Socialist countries so far clearly contradicts such speculations.

B. THE DIVISION OF GROSS PROFITS BETWEEN THE STATE AND ENTERPRISES

The importance of profit, in addition to its role as a criterion of enterprise performance, largely depends on how the profits earned

[1] *Planovo stopanstvo* (Planned Economy), Sofia, 4/1970, p. 67.

[2] *Közgazdasági szemle* (Economic Review), Budapest, 12/1970, pp. 1432–3; *Munkaügyi szemle* (Labour Review), Budapest, 5/1970, p. 175; *Pénzügyi szemle* (Financial Review), Budapest, 2/1970, p. 90

[3] *Rocznik statystyczny 1970* (Statistical Yearbook for 1970), Warsaw, Central Statistical Office of Poland, 1970, p. 551.

[4] *Scinteia*, Bucharest, 2/7/1970, p. 1.

[5] K. Marx, *Capital*, Chicago, C. H. Kerr, 1909, vol. 3, pp. 72, 247 et seq.

by enterprises are distributed. The Socialist state has the power to regulate the bases on which profits are divided and the purposes for which they are subsequently used. This further widens and strengthens the part played by profit in a socialist economy. Gross profits are partly transferred to the state budget and partly left at the disposal of enterprises (including their associations). In this section of the chapter we shall consider the bases on which budgetary deductions are made, examine the extent of these deductions and bring out recent trends in this sphere.

Strictly speaking profits, in the first instance accruing to socialized enterprises, are considered, on ideological grounds, as belonging to society. A portion of these (gross) profits is then 'deducted' for the state and it constitutes one of the sources of budgetary revenue. Thus these deductions are regarded as 'transfers' rather than 'taxes'.

In the most general sense, budgetary deductions from the enterprises' gross profits are conditioned by the accumulation needs of society (as viewed by the authorities) and by other sources of financial accumulation (turnover taxes, income taxes, payroll tax, etc.). But more specifically, by absorbing the profits accruing to enterprises not due to their own legitimate efforts and by levying charges on the assets held, the state endeavours to stimulate enterprises to a greater effort and efficiency. The deductions usually assume the form of capital charges on fixed and circulating assets, differential payments and the interception of abnormal profits.

Capital charges normally range from 3 per cent (in Bulgaria) to 6 per cent (in the German DR and the USSR) annually of the value of fixed and circulating assets in the enterprise's possession (for further details, see Ch. 7A, pp. 159–60). Differential payments are collected from enterprises enjoying special advantages in respect of natural conditions or those created by society. Abnormal profits include illegitimate and windfall profits made intentionally or unintentionally. Residual profits, i.e. the balance remaining in the enterprise after profits have been distributed amongst the different 'funds' according to the regulations laid down by the state, have also (in most Socialist countries) to be transferred to the state in full.

In some countries (as in Czechoslovakia), payroll tax represents another budgetary claim on enterprises' gross profits. In some cases (as in Bulgaria and the USSR), interest on loans and (as in Bulgaria) depreciation on investment with high and quick returns are also paid out of profits rather than treated as components of enterprise costs. The profits of enterprises owned collectively and privately (mostly found in agriculture, crafts and personal services) are taxed on a different basis, viz. in the form of progressive income taxes.

There are two distinct views in the Socialist countries on the stability of norms to regulate budgetary deductions. The traditional approach has been for the norms to be used 'flexibly', i.e. to be changed from year to year, or even more frequently according to changing conditions and the state's short-term policy objectives. This approach is still largely followed in Poland, Romania and the USSR. However, in recent years there has been an increasing inclination, particularly in Bulgaria, Czechoslovakia, the German DR and Yugoslavia, to rely on stable deduction scales fixed for longer periods – from two to (now mostly) five years. Enterprises prefer this basis because it reduces uncertainty, facilitates the planning of investment and is conducive to stability and the growth of efficiency.

Although there has been a remarkable growth of the profits earned by enterprises in all the Socialist countries, the proportion (but not the absolute amount) absorbed by the state budget has tended to decline under the new economic system. The most dramatic decline is evident in Yugoslavia, where the proportion before the reforms of the early 1950s was about three-quarters but today it is usually less than one-third. In Romania the percentage has dropped from 90 to 65, in Bulgaria and Poland from 80 to 70 and in Czechoslovakia and the USSR from 75 to 60.[1] This general trend can be explained by the fact that the authorities have been more inclined to leave larger financial resources at the disposal of enterprises in order to strengthen their capacity for 'self-financing'. By the same token, the role of budgetary allocations in financing enterprises' investment has been diminishing (for details, see Ch. 7C).

[1] *Planovoe khoziaistvo* (Planned Economy), Moscow, 3/1970, pp. 70–4; *Scinteia*, 2/7/1970, p. 1.

The distribution of the gross profits of those industrial enterprises in the USSR which have changed over to the new system of planning, management and incentives since 1965 is represented in Table 14. It will be observed that over the relatively short period

TABLE 14 PERCENTAGE DISTRIBUTION OF THE GROSS PROFITS OF INDUSTRIAL ENTERPRISES OPERATING UNDER THE NEW SYSTEM IN THE USSR, 1966–1970

Forms of Distribution	1966	1967	1968	1969	1970
Budgetary Deductions	*73*	*68*	*67*	*62*	*62*
Deductions for the period preceding the changeover to the new system	59	37	19	7	4
Capital charges	4	8	13	17	17
Differential levies	—	5	5	5	5
Irregular and residual profits	10	19	30	33	36
At the Disposal of Enterprises	*27*	*32*	*33*	*38*	*38*
for basic investment projects	4	7	10	15	14
for material incentive funds	9	13	12	14	14
for other purposes	14	12	11	9	10

Sources. Narodnoe khoziaistvo SSSR (different years).

of five years the proportion of the gross profits of these enterprises absorbed by the state budget fell from over 70 to about 60 per cent. Capital charges and irregular and residual profits now represent the main forms of budgetary deductions – about one-half of these enterprises' total profits.

C. PROFITS AS A SOURCE OF BUDGET REVENUE

The growth of profits has been paralleled by their increasing role as a source of revenue for the state. This increase has been taking place not only in absolute terms but also relatively, compared with other sources of budgetary revenue – turnover taxes, personal income tax, social insurance contributions and other, minor, sources.

Before the economic reforms, turnover taxes represented the

main source of revenue – in fact at one stage one-half of the total. However, in recent years deductions from enterprise profits have become the mainstay of budgetary revenue, now contributing about one-third of the total, compared with about a half of this proportion in the 1950s. This is so even in the countries where profit and economic reforms in general have been adopted with least enthusiasm. This is illustrated in Table 15 by reference to Romania and the USSR.

The role of profit as a source of budget revenue must be studied against the background of two developments. On the one hand, as we have demonstrated in Section A of this chapter, total profits in the economy have been growing most remarkably, especially since the early 1960s. On this score one would expect increasing deductions from gross profits for the state in absolute, and perhaps in relative, terms. On the other hand, to enhance the enterprises' capacity for self-financing, the state has been leaving larger proportions of profits at the disposal of enterprises. In effect, while deductions from enterprise gross profits have been contributing increasing proportions of the total budget revenue, at the same time larger proportions of gross profits are being left to enterprises. In other words, gross profits have been rising at faster rates than budgetary deductions (cf. Tables 12 and 15, pp. 112 and 119).

The fact that profit has replaced turnover taxes as the main source of budget revenue has significant implications from the point of view of risk bearing. Under Socialist economic conditions the proceeds from turnover taxes are fairly stable or at least easily predictable. These taxes are levied, as a rule, on consumer goods. The level of consumers' income is subject to careful planning, and fluctuations in personal income, where they exist, are small as there are no deviations from full employment (except in Yugoslavia). Non-labour incomes, which in capitalist countries are the most unstable elements of personal income, are practically non-existent. Consequently, consumer spending as a whole can be predicted with reasonable accuracy and the yield of turnover taxes does not involve much uncertainty.

But the profits earned by enterprises are liable to fluctuate erratically. Changes in natural conditions, in the methods of production, in central plans, not to mention errors by planners, are bound to affect either costs or receipts. Furthermore, as has been discussed in Ch. 3c, economic reforms have increased the extent and degree of the risk facing enterprises, owing to more flexible prices, enhanced competition, a greater orientation to foreign trade and the

TABLE 15 DEDUCTIONS FROM THE GROSS PROFITS OF STATE ENTERPRISES AS A SOURCE OF BUDGET REVENUE IN ROMANIA AND THE USSR 1950–1970

Year	Romania		USSR	
	In Million Lei	As a % of the Budget Revenue	In Million Roubles	As a % of the Budget Revenue
1950	2,860	14.9	4,400	9.5
1955	6,700	15.1	10,300	18.2
1960	13,530	23.3	18,600	24.2
1965	20,680	21.3	30,900	30.2
1966	22,490	20.7	35,700	33.6
1967	30,360	23.5	41,800	35.7
1968	38,190	27.5	48,000	36.7
1969	44,870	30.5	48,000	34.3
1970	28,830	21.6	54,200	34.6

* Preliminary figure.

Sources. Annuarul statistic al Republicii Socialiste România (Statistical Yearbook of the Romanian Socialist Republic); *Narodnoe khoziaistvo SSSR.*

fact that they have to be more self-reliant. In some countries (as in Czechosovakia, Hungary and Yugoslavia), enterprises have at least some freedom in allocating their profits to different 'funds'; as each of these funds is taxed at different levels and scales, the transfers to the state budget entail uncertainty depending on the enterprises' own policies.

The degree of risk to the state budget could be minimized if deductions from profits were laid down in terms of fixed absolute figures for each enterprise and if such deductions had precedence over the enterprises' own requirements. This procedure would be most difficult to administer, it would involve a duplication of settlements in the case of enterprises incurring losses (whether on a planned or an unplanned basis) and, of course, the brunt of uncertainty would have to be wholly – or almost wholly – borne by enterprises. If, on the other hand, enterprises had the first claim on their profits for their own needs (including incentives to their personnel), the state budget would receive residual profits and consequently risk would be fully borne by the state.

Neither of these extreme methods has been adopted in any Socialist country. In practice the budgetary deductions are based on complex procedures, naturally differing in detail from country to country, and even from one branch of the economy to another within each country. To generalize, the state budgetary sharing in profits is based on a percentage system, i.e. the state lays down the proportions of gross profits to be transferred to the budget. These proportions may be defined as fixed percentages of planned profits, of above-plan profits, of total actual profits or of the increase in total actual profits.

In Czechoslovakia as from 1970 65 per cent, and in the case of some enterprises up to 85 per cent, of gross profits is transferred to the state budget.[1] In Hungary the portion of gross profits placed in the enterprise's Development Fund is taxed at a uniform rate of 60 per cent and that in the Sharing Fund on a progressive scale ranging from 40 to 70 per cent.[2] In Romania at least 10 per cent of planned profits (irrespective of the profitability of the enterprise), and about 50 per cent of above-plan profits, is absorbed by the state budget.[3] The average proportion of gross profits channelled to the state budget in the USSR in 1969 was 60 per cent in industry and 48 per cent in construction.[4]

From the procedures followed in the Socialist countries we can conclude that the risk of fluctuations in the profits earned by enterprises is partly shared by the state budget and partly by the enterprises themselves. As a consequence of the economic reforms, budgetary revenue is subject to greater uncertainty because not

[1] *Plan. khoz.*, 3/1970, pp. 72–3.
[2] *Pénzügyi szemle*, 9/1970, p. 713.
[3] *Voprosy ekonomiki* (Problems of Economics), Moscow, 9/1969, p. 110.
[4] *Ekonomika stroitelstva* (The Economics of Construction), Moscow, 6/1971, p. 25.

only have profits become the main source of revenue but also profits themselves are now liable to greater fluctuations. However, these sources of instability have been partly countervailed by the fact that the state budget no longer automatically absorbs all residual profits and losses. Owing to substantial decentralization and self-financing, risk has been largely shifted to individual enterprises, and the predominantly proportional division of gross profits between the state budget and enterprises in effect means a sharing of the risk of fluctuations in profits.

To make precise comparisons between Socialist and capitalist countries on profit as a source of budgetary revenue is a difficult task. In the former countries a much larger proportion of national income passes through the budget – about 50 per cent, compared with about a half this proportion in the latter countries (using the Western basis for national income accounting). The concept of profit also differs. It appears, on the whole, to be broader in the Socialist countries, because rents and interest, where they are earned by enterprises, are included in gross profits (and it is gross profits that are taxable). Nevertheless, the following general observations may be of interest.

In the Socialist economies profits earned by enterprises are now the main source of budgetary revenue, whilst in the Western countries personal income tax is, as a rule, the chief source. This is only natural, considering the existence as private property of the means of production, the larger proportions of enterprise profits being distributed to taxpayers and the highly progressive scale of taxation. In the Socialist countries, personal income tax represents only a minor proportion of budgetary revenue,[1] and for obvious economic, social and ideological reasons the taxation of enterprises is preferred. The profit tax (or, as it is also known, 'corporation' or 'company' tax) still represents fairly large proportions of the budget revenue in the developed capitalist countries, but it is of lesser importance in underdeveloped regions.

Fluctuations in the budgetary receipts from profits are, on the

[1] Except in Yugoslavia, where it provides about one-fifth of the budget revenue. In other European Socialist countries the proportion is one-tenth or less. The declared objective is to abolish this tax altogether as soon as economic conditions permit.

whole, smaller in the Socialist countries. As economic activities are planned on a central and long-term basis, there are virtually no booms and recessions, and large proportions of prices of the means of production and of products are controlled, all of which promotes the stability of costs and receipts in enterprises. Moreover, those fluctuations which do occur can be more easily faced because the Socialist state has a more effective machinery for absorbing budget deficits and surpluses, so that public spending does not have to suffer from the vagaries in enterprise profits.

D. THE INTERNAL ALLOCATION OF ENTERPRISE PROFITS

Before the economic reforms the amount of profits that could be retained by enterprises was small – in most Socialist countries this proportion was one-third, and in some as little as one-tenth. Most of the financial needs of enterprises were met directly from the state budget in the form of non-repayable grants.

But that practice has been greatly modified under the new system. The proportion of gross profits now left at the disposal of enterprises is about one-third in Bulgaria, Poland and Romania, nearly one-half in Czechoslovakia, the German DR, Hungary and the USSR and two-thirds in Yugoslavia. These proportions represent considerable increases in absolute terms, owing to the remarkable growth in the size of total profits since the economic reforms. Where the intermediate level of economic management is well developed, as in Bulgaria, the German DR, Poland and Romania, a portion of enterprise profits is usually held by such entities for meeting the collective needs of the associated enterprises. The emphasis has shifted to what is known as 'self-financing', i.e. the practice of enterprises financing most of their developmental needs out of their own resources.

The financial resources of enterprises are mostly derived from profits (and partly from retained depreciation allowances, the sale of unwanted assets and in some cases from state subsidies). The resources are channelled into earmarked enterprise 'funds'. The freedom of the distribution of enterprise profits[1] is virtually unlimited in Yugoslavia, whilst in the remaining Socialist countries it is in some ways regulated by the state. In industrial enterprises, there are usually three basic funds to be used for the further development of production, incentives, reserves, etc.

For example, in Hungary these funds are known as the Development Fund, the Sharing Fund and the Reserve Fund. The gross profit of an enterprise is first divided between the Development Fund (commonly called the 'R Fund') and the Sharing Fund ('F Fund'). Normally four-fifths is placed in the former and one-fifth in the latter fund, and then budgetary deductions are made from each of these two funds according to different formulae. The Reserve Fund is formed by deducting 12·5 per cent of the (net) 'R Fund' and 12·5 per cent of the 'F Fund'.[2] The distribution of profits for different purposes in a typical Hungarian enterprise is shown diagrammatically on p. 124. In the Soviet industrial enterprises operating under the new system, the three basic funds are the Production Development Fund,[3] the Material Incentive Fund, and the Socio-Cultural and Housing Construction Fund. The planned proportions of net profits in industry as a whole to be distributed amongst these funds in 1968 were roughly five-tenths, four-tenths and one-tenth respectively.[4] The basic funds into which net profits are distributed in the German DR are the Capital Investment Fund, the Working Capital Fund and the Bonus Fund.

In addition to the basic funds, there may be other funds to cater for the specific needs of enterprises in different branches of the economy. Examples of such funds are the Director's Fund (at the disposal of the enterprise manager for special awards and for odd purposes), the Technological Progress Fund, the Stabilization Fund, the Price Reduction Fund, the Crop Failure Fund, the Special Emergency Fund and the Welfare Fund.

[1] The designation 'enterprise profit' or 'net profit' is commonly used in the Socialist countries to describe that portion of gross profit which is left at the disposal of the enterprise after budgetary deductions.

[2] *Magyar közlöny* (Hungarian Gazette), 27/10/1970, pp. 910–16.

[3] This Fund is formed not only from a portion of profit but also from retained depreciation allowances and from the proceeds of the sales of surplus equipment.

[4] *Kommunist*, Moscow, 3/1968, p. 51.

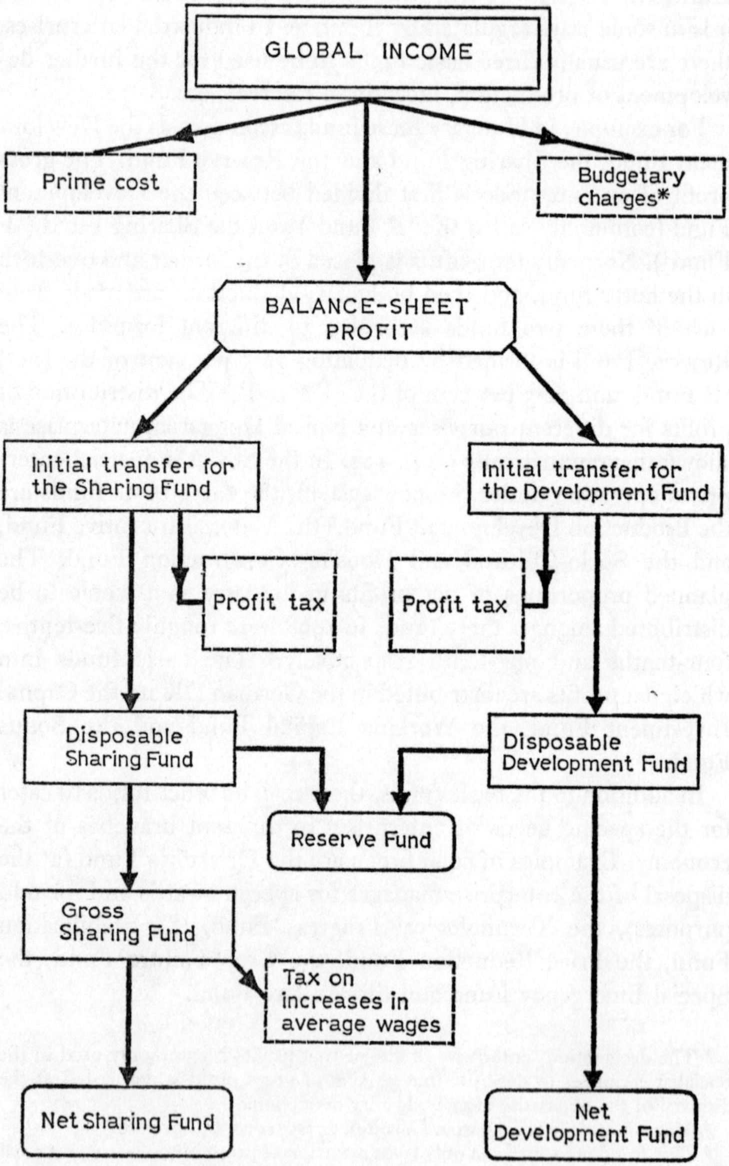
GLOBAL INCOME
Prime cost
Budgetary charges*
BALANCE-SHEET PROFIT
Initial transfer for the Sharing Fund
Initial transfer for the Development Fund
Profit tax
Profit tax
Disposable Sharing Fund
Disposable Development Fund
Reserve Fund
Gross Sharing Fund
Tax on increases in average wages
Net Sharing Fund
Net Development Fund

It is worth pointing out that the formation of these funds has been greatly facilitated by the growth of gross profits, and particularly by the increased proportions of these profits being placed at the disposal of enterprises. This development, more than any other, has effectively strengthened the enterprises' independence, self-respect and responsibility, and their capacity and inclination for profit-making. As far as the enterprise personnel is concerned, the most dynamic effect is produced by that portion of profit which is channelled into individual and collective incentives funds. Because of the importance of this problem under the new economic system, we shall devote a separate chapter to this question.

6 Material Incentives to Labour

A. THE CASE FOR MATERIAL INCENTIVES UNDER SOCIALISM

ONE of the ideals postulated in Marxian ideology was the principle of the distribution of personal income – 'from each according to his ability, to each according to his needs'.[1] Marx believed that in a communist society the workers would rid themselves of greed and acquisitive ambitions, and instead they would be responding only to 'superior' motives so that there would be a complete identification of personal and social interest. In his view the gulf between white-collar and blue-collar workers and between managerial and operative functions would disappear, and so would money – the breeder of egoism and contradictions.

But the Socialist reality turned out to be at variance with communist idealism, as was first demonstrated by the attitude of the masses in the first four years of communist power in the Soviet Union. Lenin himself recognized this hard but undeniable fact, and as a tactical concession the principle of distribution was modified to 'from each according to his ability, to each according to his work'. This basis of income distribution was at first meant to be temporary – transitional on the road to 'full communism', a move which has been described as 'a step backwards to make two steps forward'. Incentives were placed on a firm footing, payable according to the quantity and quality of work. Furthermore, basic pay became differentiated, reflecting the social value attached to different types of skills, industries, regions, etc. This approach was found to be more effective than the direction of labour. Other European Socialist countries also repeated the Soviet experience and practice.

Communist leaders have always attached a good deal of importance to 'moral' incentives, i.e. non-material forms of stimulating

[1] K. Marx, *Critique of the Gotha Program*, Moscow, FLPH, 1947, p. 27.

workers to a greater and better effort. This type of motivation is calculated to appeal to the workers' ideological convictions, the spirit of competition, pride, creativity, professional satisfaction, responsibility, the craving for public recognition and patriotism. Instead of material rewards individual, or groups of, workers may be invited to make public appearances, offered membership of the Communist Party, awarded certificates, pennants or medals, or their names may be inscribed on the lists of honour, etc. However, experience had shown that non-material incentives might produce extra effort for limited periods of time and then most workers, especially the less skilled ones, become immune to appeals not backed up by tangible benefits.

In examining past experience, a Polish economist deduced the following law of the motivation of labour under socialism:

> In the periods of intense revolutionary transformation, ideological fervour provides a strong inducement to the masses to step up their exertion. But later, when further consolidation and acceleration of economic development become of prime importance, it is material incentives that assume key significance.[1]

Similarly, negative non-material incentives in the form of organized self-criticism sessions, public reprimands, threats of withholding privileges, forced labour camps, have never proved to be a sound basis for calling forth the best effort on the part of labour. On occasions, some writers and administrators advocated a mild level of unemployment as a method of ensuring a stricter labour discipline. However, no Socialist country has ever resorted to such a drastic measure deliberately. The advisability of such a possibility was again examined at the Conference on the Use of Resources held in Budapest in 1968 under the auspices of the Council for Mutual Economic Assistance (CMEA), but most national delegates strongly rejected such a solution.

Before the economic reforms, in the late 1950s and in the early 1960s there was a tendency for the differentiation of earnings to be reduced, mainly by raising the level of wages in the lowest paid occupations and in the traditionally depressed branches of the economy, especially in agriculture, trade and services. However,

[1] B. Fick, ('The Differentiation of Earnings'), *Nowe drogi* (New Paths), Warsaw, 11/1969, p. 32.

under the new economic system the question of material incentives has been raised to an unprecedented level of importance. A Soviet economist described the situation in the following words:

> Socialism's vast superiority lies in liberating the productive forces from the bonds of private ownership and man from exploitation, thus providing new stimuli for the growth of social production. But if these objective advantages of socialism are to be used to maximum effect, we must constantly perfect the forms and methods of material incentives.[1]

The Deputy Minister of Finance in Romania, I. Tulpan, pointed out:

> In the redistribution of national income equity cannot be identified with the equality of incomes, but rather with remuneration according to the quantity and quality of work and its importance to society.[2]

A Czechoslovak writer attributed the following six magic powers to material incentives under the new system:

(i) the expansion of production;
(ii) the flexible adaptation of production to social needs;
(iii) an improvement in the quality of products;
(iv) a growth of the productivity of labour, achieved by economies in the use of labour and materials, the maximum effectiveness of investment and trade discipline;
(v) the rapid introduction of innovations;
(vi) the optimum combination of the factors of production and of products leading to the lowest possible social cost and the highest possible social benefit.[3]

A Polish economist concluded that:

> The changeover from extensive to intensive growth places material incentives to labour in a new light altogether. To achieve a steady growth of productivity, it is essential that moral appeals be replaced by material incentives.[4]

[1] B. Sukharevsky, 'The Problem of Incentives in CMEA Countries', *Peace, Freedom and Socialism*, Prague, 8/1970, p. 28.

[2] I. Tulpan, ('Material Incentives as a Lever of Economic Growth'), *Finanţe şi credit* (Finance and Credit), Bucharest, 11/1970, p. 11.

[3] J. Libus, ('Material Incentives under the New System of Management'), *Plánované hospodářství* (Planned Economy), Prague, 3/1965, pp. 39–40.

[4] L. Pasieczny, ('The System of Material Incentives and Intensive Economic Growth'), *Życie gospodarcze* (Economic Life), Warsaw, 26/1/1969, p. 7.

Before the economic reforms, a large proportion of incentives was paid merely for the quantitative over-fulfilment of norms (planned minimum targets to be achieved by individual workers, or a group of workers), usually irrespective of the quality and efficiency of production. Under this set-up, workers on piece-work rates often earned incentives equal to their base wage and sometimes much more than skilled workers on time-rates. Piece-work was widespread in the 1950s, when two-thirds of the work-force was remunerated on this basis. However, today the proportion is about one-third, roughly the same as in capitalist countries.

Of special significance under the new system is, of course, the fact that incentives have been systematically linked to profits and profits accepted as a criterion of economic performance. Experience has shown that the maximization of performance means little to most workers unless their personal interest is clearly involved. The payment of incentives based on this criterion provides convincing proof and acts as a constant reminder to the personnel of what is good to it, and indirectly to society. Recent experience has also shown that sharing in enterprise profit, in addition to the obvious material benefit to the personnel, provides a strong moral uplift to individual workers, as it enhances their pride of achievement and co-ownership.[1]

Consequently, a considerable differentiation of personal income has become a well-accepted fact of Socialist economic life. In some Socialist countries such as the USSR – ironically the country with a head start of a quarter of a century in transitioning to the higher phase of communism – the (gross) incomes of successful top managers, engineers, architects, scientists, actors and writers are up to a hundred times, and even more, the incomes of unskilled workers.[2] These disparities in the earnings from work have in fact become greater than in many capitalist countries.

There was a heated discussion amongst theoretical writers in recent years on whether the incentives received from enterprise

[1] J. Śliwa, *Rola zysku w funkcjonowaniu handlu socjalistycznego w Polsce* (The Role of Profit in the Operation of Socialist Trade), Warsaw, PWN, 1969, p. 121.

[2] For details, see J. Wilczynski, 'Differentiation of Income under Modern Socialism', *Jahrbuch der Wirtschaft Osteuropas/Yearbook of Eastern European Economics*, Munich, 1972.

profits in a socialist economy represent remuneration for entrepreneurship, ownership or labour. Although there is no complete accord on this question, the majority of thinkers appear to agree that profit-sharing under socialism constitutes a portion of the earnings from one's own labour. In a socialist society, labour is the only factor of production that can receive remuneration. Only those who actually work in the enterprise in question are entitled to such incentives, and sharing is in proportion to the quantity and quality of one's work.[1]

B. THE FORMATION OF INCENTIVE FUNDS

The Socialist countries under consideration have experimented with a variety of ways in which to establish and maintain incentive funds. For a long time, particularly before the adoption of the profit criterion, the finance for incentive funds was usually derived from enterprise wage funds or from earmarked budgetary allocations. In several cases, these sources have been employed under the new system as well, even though the size or the method of distribution of the entitlements have been linked in some way to profit.[2]

However, today it is common that incentive funds are formed directly from enterprise profits. The precise bases and methods governing the formation of such funds differ widely from country to country and even within each country, depending on the branch of the economy or the category of workers. In some countries two (or more) bases may be used in application to enterprises in the same branch. Arguments have been advanced to introduce some uniformity in the formation of these funds in the CMEA member countries, as one of the measures designed to facilitate the comparability of costs for determining intra-CMEA specialization. Since 1969 regular annual conferences have been held on 'Wages

[1] e.g., see A. Melich, ('The Operation of Synthetic Incentives'), *Finanse* (Finance), Warsaw, 10/1966, pp. 3–4.

[2] e.g., in the USSR, as reported in 1971, only 40% of the Individual Incentives Funds in the construction industry was derived directly from enterprise profits and the balance of 60% came from other sources. *Ekonomika stroitelstva* (The Economics of Construction), Moscow, 6/1971, p. 25.

and the Labour Force' under the tutelage of CMEA, but so far little uniformity has been achieved in practice.

The following five bases (or sources) for the formation of incentive funds have been in use:

(i) a portion of the total actual profit;
(ii) a portion of the above-plan profit, i.e. that achieved above the level laid down by higher authorities;
(iii) portions of planned and above-plan profits (the percentage of the latter usually being higher than that of the former);
(iv) portions of planned and above-plan increases in profits;
(v) a fixed quota representing a portion of the profit in the initial (base) period *plus* a portion of the increase in the profit above the base period.

The actual amount of profit channelled to the incentive fund is still linked in most cases to the size of the enterprise base wage fund to prevent too great disparities in incentive payments to workers in different enterprises.

On the whole, there is a tendency to link incentive funds to total actual profits. This basis is simplest to administer and is most easily understood by ordinary workers. But basing incentives on the above-plan profit has a stronger incentive effect, particularly on the management in mobilizing reserves and utilizing capacities which otherwise might remain hidden. However, in this case, incentive funds are exposed to greater fluctuations, and the extent of risk to the personnel is greater. Virtually all the Socialist countries have now abandoned the annual growth of profit alone as a basis. Bases (iii), (iv) and (v) represent a compromise whereby the advantages of each approach are hoped to be achieved, but with varying degrees of success in reality.

In some Socialist countries each enterprise maintains one, all-purpose incentive fund but in others there may be more than one fund, earmarked for manual workers, the managerial and administrative staff, socio-cultural facilities, housing needs and other special purposes. In some cases such funds may be attached not to individual enterprises but to an association of enterprises representing an intermediate level of economic management. Taking the region as a whole, about one-tenth of gross profits, or about one-third of net profits (after deductions for the state budget), is placed in incentive funds. Now, to illustrate how incentive funds are formed in some countries.

In Hungarian industrial enterprises the incentive fund, called the Sharing (or F) Fund, is derived from the actual balance-sheet profit. Disregarding exceptions, the portion of the actual balance-sheet profit allowed for the Sharing Fund is determined by the following formula:[1]

$$itSF = \frac{aW \times 3}{aW \times 3 + Af + Ac} bsP;$$

$itSF$ = the initial transfer from the balance-sheet profit for the Sharing Fund;

aW = actual wages paid during the period;

Af = the average value of fixed assets held during the year (on the initial value basis);

Ac = the average value of circulating assets held during the year;

bsP = the balance-sheet profit.

A basic minimum of this placement is tax-free and the rest is subject to a progressive tax ('deduction') ranging from 40 to 70 per cent and transferred to the state budget. From the amount so left up to 12·5 per cent is transferred to the enterprise's Reserve Fund, and a tax is payable to the state budget on wage increases; the remaining balance then becomes the (net) Sharing Fund.[2] In 1968 the proportion of the balance-sheet profits finally received into the Sharing Funds (and available for incentive payments)

[1] The balance-sheet profit is the difference between total receipts and total outlays. Total outlays include the prime cost, capital charges, differential payments and the so-called 'social cost of production', the last item amounting to 25% of the wage fund (8% as the payroll tax and 17% for social insurance). Over the period 1968–70 the wage-fund multiplication factor was usually 2; but beginnining in 1971, to increase the portion of the balance-sheet profit for the Sharing Fund, the factor of 3 has been in use in the majority of the branches of the economy; however, in some branches a higher or a lower factor may be applied.

[2] *Munkaügyi szemle* (Labour Review), Budapest, 5/1970, p. 175; *Pénzügyi szemle* (Financial Review), Budapest, 9/1970, p. 713.

in different branches of the economy worked out as follows (in percentages):

Agriculture	21
Transport	15
Construction	12
Industry	9
Trade	8
Services	4

Source. Figyelö (Economic Observer), Budapest, 29/10/1969, p. 3.

Since 1971, Sharing Funds in Hungary have been in fact greater than the above percentages suggest. Firstly, the wage-fund multiplication factor for industrial enterprises has been raised from 2 to 3. Secondly, according to the Decree on Enterprise Income and the Wage System (also effective since the beginning of 1971), the Sharing Fund may be supplemented with cash awards made by various authorities for special achievements, net proceeds from the institutions maintained by the Fund (such as child-minding centres), interest earned on housing loans financed by the Fund and with income from the sums invested by the Fund for approved purposes.[1]

In Polish enterprises, typically two main incentive funds are administered. The Enterprise Incentive Fund, applicable to manual workrs, is formed by deductions from a portion of the net profit to the tune of 3·5–5·5 per cent (according to the branch of the economy) of the enterprise's planned wage bill for manual workers, provided the planned profit or rentability rate is reached. If it is not reached, the deductions are progressively reduced, and if the degree of non-fulfilment exceeds 20 per cent the enterprise loses the right to the formation of this Fund. If, on the other hand, the planned profit or rentability rate is exceeded, deductions for the Fund are made on a progressive basis amounting to up to 8·5 per cent of the wage bill. The Economic Achievements Incentive Fund, designed for white-collar workers, is more related to enterprise performance. The allocation from net profit represents from 10 to 35 per cent of the planned salary bill, according to the degree of fulfilment of the planned profit (or rentability) rate and of the

[1] *Magyar közlöny* (Hungarian Gazette), Budapest, 27/10/1970, pp. 910–16.

assortment. If the plan is under-fulfilled, the allocation to this Fund is reduced, and if the degree of under-fulfilment is 5 per cent or more no incentives are payable.[1] In the state farms, State Farm Incentive Funds are maintained. As from 1971 the size of the allocation to these funds depends wholly on results, and the former limit of 80 per cent of the wage fund has been dropped; but there is a condition that 90 per cent of the Fund is used for individual incentives and 10 per cent for socio-cultural and housing purposes.[2] In the late 1960s the proportion of gross profits placed in these three funds was 10 per cent.[3]

The system prevailing in the USSR is again different. There are essentially two incentive funds maintained in the enterprises operating under the new system – one for cash awards to individual (blue- and white-collar) workers and one of a collective nature to finance social and cultural services and housing (also open to all workers of the enterprise in question). The Individual Incentives Fund is formed from a portion of the net profit on the basis of two regulators: a percentage increase in the size of the output sold *or* the net profit reached, and the percentage achievement of the planned profit rate. The scales are differentiated according to the branches of the economy, industry or other groups of enterprises. For example, as reported in 1969, the norms applied in a Moscow factory producing metal-working machinery were: for each 1 per cent of the increase in the volume of output sold above the preceding year an amount equivalent to 0·9 per cent of the Wage Fund was channelled for individual incentives, *plus* for each 1 per cent of the planned profit rate achieved 0·2 per cent of the Wage Fund was similarly transferred.[4] In addition, a portion of profit equal to 3–4 per cent of the Wage Fund is allocated to the Socio-Cultural and Housing Construction Fund, and up to 30 per cent of the

[1] Based on: *Nowe drogi*, 5/1970, pp. 48–62; *Finanse*, 6/1970, pp. 11–24. For the period 1971–5 this system was to have been replaced by one based on the achieved increases in the profit rate above the base year level of 1970. However, owing to the widespread opposition to the proposed scheme, it was dropped so that at the time of writing the system outlined in the text was essentially still in operation.

[2] *Chłopska droga* (Peasants' Road), Warsaw, 23/5/1971, p. 7.

[3] Based on *Rocznik statystyczny 1970* (Statistical Yearbook for 1970), Warsaw, Central Statistical Office of Poland, 1970, pp. 551–2.

[4] *Kommunist*, Moscow, 12/1969, p. 66.

above-plan profit is allowed for housing construction. On the whole in 1969, 13 per cent of the gross profit of state enterprises in the USSR was placed in the two incentive funds. Taking the industrial enterprises which were operating under the new system, 43 per cent of their net profits went into the individual Incentives Fund and 19 per cent into the Socio-Cultural and Housing Construction Funds.[1]

The methods of forming incentive funds in other Socialist countries, except Yugoslavia, are similar to those described above but, naturally, with considerable national peculiarities. In Yugoslavia there are practically no state-imposed norms, and instead the Workers' Council of each enterprise determines the quota or the proportion of residual profits to be shared as 'dividends'. In the German DR the size of the incentive funds is dependent on the planned profit, the above-plan profit and the profit rate, and the scales of the amounts allowed are so devised as to induce enterprises to undertake progressively higher and higher planned targets. In Bulgaria, Czechoslovakia, the German DR and Yugoslavia, in addition to the individual incentives funds, there are social welfare and housing funds. Of the eight Socialist countries, Romania attaches least importance to material incentives. According to the system introduced since 1969, the Incentive Fund in industrial enterprises is formed from above-plan profits, but the maximum allocation must not exceed 2·5 per cent of the enterprise's planned Wage Fund.[2]

The practice of linking the size of incentive funds to wage funds has an inherent weakness in that it predisposes enterprises to the maximization of their employment or average base wage. To counteract this tendency, incentive funds have been linked in several Socialist countries to *planned* wage funds, or increases in average wages (compared with a base year) are taxable. More recently some positive measures have been introduced, designed to spur enterprises to minimize their employment – thereby raising efficiency and relieving labour shortages. Enterprises are encouraged to increase their output with reduced employment, and

[1] Based on *Narodnoe khoziaistvo SSSR v 1969 g.* (National Economy of the USSR in 1969), Moscow, Statistika, 1970, pp. 742, 765, 766.

[2] *Ekonomicheskie nauki* (Economic Studies), Moscow, 8/1969, p. 64.

the economies so achieved are then partly shared by the remaining personnel. The most publicized experiment in this direction was that at the Shchekino Chemical Combine in the USSR, initiated in 1967, where by 1970 employment was reduced by 3,300 persons, total output was expanded by 87 per cent, labour productivity rose by 108 per cent, the incentives of the retained personnel reached one-third of their base pay and average personal earnings increased by 32 per cent; in 1970 over 100 other enterprises adopted this scheme and the practice has spread further since that time.[1] In Bulgaria, the incentive fund (called the Additional Incentives Fund) is formed from a portion of the increase in the net profit mass above the preceding year, but in addition a portion of the savings achieved by reducing the wage bill below the planned level is allocated to the Fund.

C. THE DISTRIBUTION OF INCENTIVES

As a rule, base wages and salaries are paid monthly and are essentially considered as advance payments. The disbursement of incentive funds is carried out quarterly and/or half-yearly, with the final profit-sharing taking place in most Socialist countries at the end of the financial year or of the production period. Incentives are mostly distributed as cash payments, but they may also assume the form of awards in kind (food, clothing, etc.), services or the availability of special amenities.

In the repartition of incentive funds, the problem naturally arises as to whether the distribution to the participants should be in accordance with the socialist principle 'according to work' or the communist principle 'according to needs'. The latter basis is, of course, ideologically more commendable, but the former is now of great importance as it is more conducive to greater effort and efficiency. In practice, a compromise approach is followed – about two-thirds of the funds set aside for incentives is disbursed to individual workers according to the quantity and quality of work,

[1] *Voprosy ekonomiki* (Problems of Economics), Moscow, 10/1969, pp. 27–40; *Ekonomika i organizacja pracy* (The Economics and Organization of Labour), Warsaw, 11/1970, p. 483; *Izvestiya*, Moscow, 9/12/1970, p. 3.

mostly as cash payments, and about one-third as collective or personal benefits where individual needs are taken into account. The state lays down general regulations or guidelines for the distribution but otherwise the details are determined by workers' councils, factory committees or by all workers at special meetings.

In Hungary, according to the Decree issued in 1970, the Sharing Fund can be used for the following purposes:

(i) To pay cash incentives to individual workers in the form of general bonuses, special prizes for some specific achievements, awards to rationalizers and inventors, non-taxable allowances and terminal profit shares.

(ii) To make cash grants for specific purposes, such as housing loans, rent subsidies, scholarships, benefits to workers losing wages due to stoppages beyond their control and emergency aid.

(iii) To finance the operation of collective services and amenities for the workers in the form of factory cafeterias, facilities for the children of working mothers, social, cultural and sporting activities and individual plots run by workers on state farms.[1]

The details of the actual distribution of incentives according to different purposes and branches of the economy is shown in Table 16 by reference to Poland. It will be observed that over 60 per cent of the Enterprise Incentive Fund, catering both for individual and collective rewards, was disbursed in cash and the rest in the form of various facilities, services and grants for more or less collective purposes. Where separate socio-cultural and housing funds are maintained (in Bulgaria, Czechoslovakia, the German DR,[2] the USSR), they are used for obvious purposes – collectively, as well as for the benefit of individual workers and their families, according to needs.

On the whole, incentives represent about one-quarter of the personal base (or standard) pay. The proportion is lowest in

[1] *Magyar közlöny*, op. cit.

[2] In the German DR the Socio-Cultural and Housing Fund is not formed out of profits, but fixed centrally by the state and the amount so allocated is treated as part of the enterprise's cost.

Romania and the German DR and highest in Hungary and Yugoslavia (about one-third in the latter two countries). But the actual proportions, naturally, differ within each country according to the different branches of the economy and in different enter-

TABLE 16 PERCENTAGE DISTRIBUTION OF THE ENTERPRISE INCENTIVE FUND IN STATE ENTERPRISES IN POLAND IN 1969

Purpose \ Branch of the Economy	Industry	Construction	Agriculture	Transport and Communications	Trade	Municipal Undertakings	*Average for All Branches*
1. Cash incentives	61	63	53	64	69	73	*62*
2. Construction of dwellings	26	25	20	24	20	18	*25*
3. House repairs	1	n.	4	0	0	0	*1*
4. Various services *	11	11	16	11	10	9	*11*
5. Other purposes	2	1	7	1	1	1	*2*
All purposes †	100	100	100	100	100	100	*100*

n. = negligible, less than 0·5%.

* Provision of free excursions, grants for the maintenance of reading and common rooms and assistance to kindergartens and sporting clubs associated with the enterprises concerned.

† Figures in columns may not add up to 100 owing to rounding.

Source. Based on *Rocznik statystyczny 1970* (Statistical Yearbook for 1970), Warsaw, Central Statistical Office of Poland, 1970, p. 552.

prises within a particular branch. According to some Polish economists, to be effective under Socialist conditions, incentive payments should represent 25–50 per cent of the personal wage or salary.[1]

The part played by incentives in the total earnings of labour in different branches can be illustrated by reference to Czechoslovakia, the Socialist country which appears to be 'average' in this respect. As is evident from Table 17, incentives in the form of bonuses and

[1] See, e.g., B. Fick, ('Directions in the Perfection of the Incentive System'), *Finanse*, 8/1968, p. 25; J. G. Zieliński, ('Conditions of the Effectiveness of Incentives'), *Życie gosp.*, 10/10/1966, p. 2.

TABLE 17 THE ROLE OF INCENTIVES PAID IN DIFFERENT BRANCHES OF MATERIAL PRODUCTION IN CZECHOSLOVAKIA

Monthly Average in Korunas per Person Employed in the First Quarter of 1970

Branch	Base Pay	Bonuses	Profit-Sharing	Total Earnings	*Incentives as a % of Base Pay*
Designing offices	1,838	423	229	2,490	*35·5*
State forests	1,650	337	170	2,157	*30·7*
State farms	1,421	68	336	1,825	*28·4*
Fuels extraction	2,101	440	143	2,684	*27·7*
Wood working	1,403	300	83	1,786	*27·3*
Food processing	1,423	233	149	1,805	*26·8*
Building materials	1,611	318	103	2,032	*26·1*
Chemicals and rubber	1,515	336	51	1,902	*25·5*
Textiles	1,248	247	71	1,566	*25·5*
Ferrous metallurgy	1,744	342	84	2,170	*24·4*
Communications	1,369	304	24	1,697	*24·0*
Machine building	1,552	306	43	1,901	*22·5*
Clothing	1,272	230	43	1,545	*21·5*
Glass and ceramics	1,427	214	48	1,689	*18·4*
Construction	1,792	228	86	2,106	*17·6*
Railway transport	1,864	304	4	2,172	*16·5*
Leather, footwear	1,589	137	36	1,762	*10·9*
Public catering	1,415	*	143	1,558	*10·1*
Retail trade	1,425	*	124	1,549	*8·7*
Motor transport	1,900	113	45	2,058	*8·3*

* In these branches bonuses are built into basic pay rates and there is a faster promotion from lower to higher classifications.

Source. Based on *Prace a mzda* (Work and Wages), Prague, 6/1970, pp. 268–9.

end-of-the quarter profit-sharing in early 1970 constituted as little as 8 per cent of the base pay in motor transport but as much as 36 per cent in designing offices. There were, of course, differences amongst the enterprises within a particular branch, and these are bound to vary from one period to another. In Poland the share of incentives in the *total earnings* of the tradesman classified as 'locksmith technician' was reported in 1970 to have been 44 per cent in mining, 27 per cent in the textile industry, 26 per cent in machine construction, 24 per cent in the chemical industry, 23 per cent in food processing, 21 per cent in metallurgy and 19 per cent in foundries.[1]

The size of incentives paid to different categories of workers in each enterprise usually differs widely. Thus in Hungary, persons in the top managerial division may on the average receive incentives of up to 80 per cent of their base pay, those in the middle-ranking category up to 50 per cent but those in the ordinary workers' class only up to 25 (15 per cent before 1970). In 1968, when the minimum wage was 9,600 forints, the average amount of the cash incentives distributed per person in each of the three categories was 13,000 5,500 and 1,300 forints respectively.[2] However, these figures understate the range of the differentiation; the state does not regulate the award of incentives to individual persons *within* each of the three categories – only the maximum *average* percentage. Enterprises are free to devise their own 'points system' whereby qualifications, responsibilities, tasks, the intensity of application, the quality of execution, the length of service, etc., of different persons are evaluated.

In Poland in non-agricultural enterprises, incentives for persons in the managerial classification may reach 80 per cent of their base pay and in the case of the engineering and technical personnel 50 per cent, whilst in other cases only 15 per cent or even less.[3] In Czechoslovakia, according to the decree issued in 1971, managerial profit-sharing in industry may reach 40 per cent, and in mining 50 per cent of the annual base salary.[4]

Profit-sharing may also widely differ in agriculture depending on farming conditions, so that in effect members of some farms may capture substantial portions of differential rent. A Soviet journal quoted a case of two collective farms where on one the average net income per man-day was 2·80 roubles but in another 4·70 roubles.[5]

[1] B. Fick, *Polityka zatrudnienia a płace i bodźce* (Employment Policy, Wages and Incentives), Warsaw, PWE, 1970, p. 304.

[2] *Figyelő* (Economic Observer), Budapest, 29/10/1969, p. 3; *Ekonomika i organizacja pracy*, 1/1970, p. 43.

[3] *Finanse*, 7/1968, pp. 24–5.

[4] *Hospodářské noviny* (Economic News), Prague, 8/3/1971, p. 4.

[5] *Dengi i kredit* (Money and Credit), Moscow, 9/1969, p. 17.

A Czechoslovak journal reported the case of a subsidiary enterprise of a collective farm in Slovakia where, even though it was operated by unskilled workers, the average monthly earnings in 1969 ranged from 4,000 to 5,000 korunas (when the average monthly earnings on state farms were 1,800 korunas).[1] As in other types of enterprises, the incentives paid to individual workers depend on the position occupied. According to a recent report describing a Soviet livestock-raising farm, the incentives received by the brigade leader amounted to 143·22 roubles a month, representing 72 per cent of his base pay, but a mechanic received only 18·07 roubles, constituting 14 per cent of his base pay.[2] The disparities are probably greater than the known case quoted above suggest.

Before we leave the question of the distribution of incentives, it may be of interest to mention two other factors further contributing to the differences in the incentives received by different persons. On the one hand, a workers' council, or factory committee or trade union in the enterprise concerned may reduce or cancel the payment of incentives to particular workers for inefficiency, the violation of work discipline and anti-social behaviour. On the other, extra incentives may be paid to rationalizers and inventors. These incentives may be quite large now, owing to the Socialist drive to accelerate technological progress. For example in Bulgaria, where the average monthly base pay is about 100 leva, an inventor is paid an initial reward ranging from 30 to 200 leva and additional awards amounting to 20,000 leva, and moreover he may be granted extra paid leave of up to 12 days annually for five years.[3]

D. RISK AND INCENTIVE PAYMENTS

Under the new economic system, incentive payments are inherently exposed to greater fluctuations than before. The size of the transfers to incentive funds is at least partly determined by the size of profits or some other profit indicator. Profit, or profitability, by its very nature of being the most 'synthetic' criterion, is dependent

[1] *Prace a mzda*, 6/1970, p. 252.
[2] *Życie gosp.*, 7/11/1971, p. 11.
[3] *Durzhaven vestnik* (Government Gazette), Sofia, 20/6/1969, pp. 1–7.

on a great variety of factors, both on the cost and demand sides of an enterprise's operations.

Profit is now calculated on the basis of the output sold, not merely produced, so that products are no longer automatically allocated by central planners to designated recipients but have to meet buyers' preferences. As sellers' markets are less acute than they were in the past, sales are less predictable. Large proportions of prices can now fluctuate in response to market conditions, and furthermore, the existence of fixed and free prices side by side affect individual enterprises to different degrees. The drive for more effective methods and patterns of production, especially those involving innovations, brings success or failure in its wake. The de-insulation of domestic from foreign markets, where it has taken place, has proved advantageous to some enterprises but disruptive to others. Of significance is also the fact that, as a result of the decentralization of planning and management, risk-bearing has been largely shifted from the state budget to individual enterprises (see Ch. 3C).

But there are also other conditions which now entail a good deal of uncertainty, associated with the formation of incentive funds and the award of incentives to individual workers. In most of these countries, transfers to incentive funds may be reduced or blocked altogether if planned tasks are under-fulfilled – even if an enterprise has substantial profits on hand. The size of the transfers depends on the profit indicator applied by the authorities – the profit mass, the rentability rate, the profit rate, and further whether planned or above-plan, or some other variant. This may be illustrated by the figures available for the Polish woodworking industry, where experiments on different bases for incentives were carried out for the period 1967–9:

	1967	*1968*	*1969*
The profit mass	122m. złotys	138m. złotys	151m. złotys
The profit rate	27·6%	23·8%	17·3%
The normative level of costs*	86·4%	88·7%	90·1%

* Percentage ratio of prime cost to total revenue from the output sold.

Source. Nowe drogi, 5/1970, p. 52.

If the basis for incentives had been the profit mass, the industry would have earned incentives in 1968 and 1969, but if any of the other two indicators had been applied no transfers of profits to incentive funds would have taken place. In Czechoslovakia, 8 per cent of the average pay planned for the preceding year may be forfeited and used for absorbing enterprise losses.[1]

But even if there are ample financial resources in the incentive funds, individual (or groups of) workers may be deprived of incentives for inefficiency or breaches of labour discipline. Workers now also face a greater risk of dismissal because the retained personnel stands to gain thereby. In some countries, as in the German DR according to a decree issued in 1970,[2] workers are personally liable for damage to socialized property, whether caused deliberately or by negligence, and even if such property is insured.

At one stage, the Socialist countries experimented with profit-sharing on the basis of equality, i.e. each member of the enterprise receiving an equal share. This basis had the merit of being less removed from the ideal of distribution 'according to needs', but it produced disastrous effects on enterprise performance. The higher the skill and position of the person, the lower was the proportion represented by incentives in their total earnings. Yet it is this type of worker who can contribute most to the growth of production and efficiency. Consequently that practice has nowhere been applied to any significant extent, and instead a considerable differentiation is now the rule.

Incentive differentials are either in proportion to base pay differentials, or applied on a progressive basis, i.e. the higher the base pay the higher the allowed *proportion* represented by incentives. Although in obvious conflict with the egalitarian principle, the latter approach is now increasingly commonly followed. This practice amounts to the implicit recognition of the fact that even under socialism different categories of workers have different capacities for contributing to an enterprise's profits. The managerial, professional and administrative personnel is in a better position than ordinary workers to search for the most effective methods and patterns of production. But this search involves extra

[1] *Ekonomicheskie nauki*, 8/1969, p. 64.

[2] ('Compensation of Deliberate Damage of Socialized Property'), *Gesetzblatt der DDR* (Official Gazette of the German DR), East Berlin, 29/4/1970, pp. 267–74.

effort and uncertainty, and it could produce higher profits or losses.

The progressive basis for incentive payments, according to the degree of responsibility and skill, is meant to induce arduous but creative decision-making involving risk. By the same token, losses incurred by enterprises must be attributed more to these categories of the personnel than to blue-collar workers. Therefore, in the case of unsuccessful operations, incentives to white-collar workers are reduced by more than to ordinary workers. In fact in some countries white-collar workers may be penalized by losing a portion of their base pay as well; although this may also apply in some cases to blue-collar workers, the proportion is smaller than in the case of persons holding more responsible positions.

TABLE 18 THE EXTENT OF PROFIT-SHARING AND RISK-BEARING BY DIFFERENT GROUPS OF ENTERPRISE PERSONNEL IN BULGARIA AND HUNGARY

Group of Personnel	Maximum Average Proportion of Base Pay Receivable in Incentives*		Maximum Proportion of Base Pay which Can be Lost	
	Bulgaria	*Hungary*	*Bulgaria*	*Hungary*
Managerial personnel	†	80%	20%	25%
Middle ranking personnel	†	50%	15%	15%
Blue-collar workers	†	25%	10%	0%

* These proportions are *average* for each group of the enterprise personnel. Within each group the proportions of incentives for individual persons are not restricted.

† Not clearly laid down for these groups, but the effect is similar to that in Hungary. Actual payment to individual persons is based on a points system.

Source. Based on *Ekonomicheskie nauki*, 8/1969, p. 64.

The extent of profit-sharing and risk-bearing by persons in different categories is illustrated by reference to Bulgaria and Hungary in Table 18. In Poland, there is a separate incentive fund for white-collar workers (the Economic Achievements Incentive Fund) and for blue-collar workers (the Enterprise Incentive Fund).

From the preceding discussion it should be evident that the economic reforms, and in particular the adoption of the profit criterion, have enhanced the instability of incomes of both blue-collar and white-collar workers. In this brave new world many a worker finds that he may be remunerated neither 'according to his needs' nor 'according to his work'. No doubt, many of them may be reminiscing with nostalgia on the well-ordered, good old days gone with the wind. L. Sirc, in his study of the economic reforms in Eastern Europe, expressed the sentiments of many workers thus: 'Some people preferred the stagnation of the old system under which they had secure jobs and steady pay whether they worked or not.'[1]

It may be noted here that under capitalism workers do not normally bear the risk of the firms in which they are employed. Persons who participate in profits are shareholders who are either rich people or are earning regular salaries or wages, and are moreover in a position to spread their risk by holding shares in different companies. But a worker in a Socialist country is not in a similar position to withstand a loss of incentives or spread his employment risk.

Some Socialist economists have expressed strong views against workers bearing enterprise risk, especially to the extent of losing a portion of their base pay. Some writers have insisted that a worker should not forfeit more than the amount of the incentives received in the preceding year.[2] Others believe that the base pay of the personnel should not be reduced, with the exception of an individual person whose fault in causing the enterprise's losses can be clearly proven; but this penalty should not be applied to a group of workers as it clearly affects their livelihood – rather disciplinary action should be taken against them if the case is serious enough.[3]

There has also been a good deal of concern among some trade union leaders. Indeed, there are some indications, especially in Czechoslovakia, Hungary, Poland and Yugoslavia, that trade unions – traditionally 'transmission belts' for state policies (as Lenin called them) – may develop into quasi-protective

[1] L. Sirc, *Economic Devolution in Eastern Europe*, London, Longmans, 1969, p. 128.

[2] e.g., J. Županov, ('The Producer and Risk'), *Ekonomist* (The Economist), Belgrade, 3/1967, esp. pp. 23–5.

[3] e.g., Z. Madej, *Zysk w gospodarce socjalistycznej* (Profit in a Socialist Economy), Warsaw, PWE, 1963, p. 294.

organizations, akin to those in capitalist countries, buttressing workers against the state bureaucracy, managers and technocrats.

The inherent risk to which workers' incomes are exposed has been well recognized by the authorities in the Socialist countries. But the prevalent official view now is that the responsibility for protecting workers against the possibility of a loss of incentives, and a part of their base pay where applicable, should primarily rest with the enterprises themselves. The schemes in use today have been developed partly by state direction, partly by the encouragement of different authorities and in some cases on the initiative of the enterprise personnel. Seven forms of protection can be distinguished.

First, in some countries, as in Hungary, Poland, Romania and the USSR, incentive funds may also be partly formed from other sources than enterprise profit, such as wage funds, income from subsidiary activities and regular allocations and special awards by the state. Second, in contrast to previous practice, the norms laid down by the state regulating the formation of incentive funds are now commonly announced well in advance and are applicable for longer periods (usually two to five years). Where the norms are changed, the purpose is often to adjust them to a realistic level of attainment so as to enable each enterprise to pay reasonable incentives. For example, in the Polish heavy industry in 1967, if the rentability norms had not been changed, 70 per cent of the enterprises would not have qualified for incentives. Instead, on the average two revisions for different enterprises were made during the year 'to avoid depressing the level of earnings which would be bound to lead to social tension associated with the directive indicator of rentability'.[1]

Third, in some countries more than one variant of the profit indicator is laid down to regulate the allocation of profits to incentive funds. Thus in the German DR, Romania and the USSR, both the above-plan profit mass and the profit rate are applied so that fluctuations in one may be reduced or offset by opposite changes in the other. Fourth, the size of the transfer of profits to incentive funds is often defined as a percentage of the base wage fund, not of

[1] T. Kierczyński, ('The Operation of the Rentability Indicator'), *Życie gosp.*, 20/10/1968, p. 1.

gross or net profit. Base wage funds are much more stable than profits, and in fact in the German DR, Poland, Romania and the USSR they are still centrally fixed.

Fifth, in practice incentive funds are not necessarily disbursed to the full even at the end of the financial year, so that usually substantial sums are left for later distribution, especially in lean periods. For example, in the USSR in the late 1960s, about one-quarter of the individual and collective incentive funds was left undistributed at the end of each financial year.[1] This carryover acts as a sort of reserve which can be drawn upon in adverse years.

But the most systematic and direct scheme for shielding workers against the vagaries in enterprise profits consists in the introduction of 'reserve' or 'guarantee' funds. These funds are either held by each enterprise (as is usually the case in Czechoslovakia, Hungary and Yugoslavia) or are attached to an association of enterprises or the sectoral ministry (Bulgaria, the German DR, Poland and Romania), or sometimes additionally to regional authorities (as in Yugoslavia). The method of the formation of the funds differs from one country to another, but in all of them they are maintained out of enterprise profits (in Czechoslovakia in most cases out of profits and wages combined).

Thus in Hungary the prescribed level of the Reserve Fund amounts to 1·5 per cent of the value of the enterprise's fixed and circulating assets *plus* 8·0 per cent of the wage bill. The Fund is created by placing in it 12·5 per cent of the Sharing Fund and of the Development Fund, and then it is similarly maintained as the need arises. The Reserve Fund is used to absorb risk affecting the Sharing as well as the Development Funds and it must be replenished within five years.[2]

Finally if all other ways and means fail, enterprises can turn to the state or some other authority designated by the state. In all the Socialist countries there are now minimum wage legislations,[3] and

[1] *Narodnoe khoziaistvo SSSR v 1969 g.*, p. 765.

[2] *Magyar közlöny*, 27/10/1970, pp. 910–16.

[3] In the early 1970s the minimum monthly wages were: in Bulgaria, 70 leva; Czechoslovakia, about 500 korunas; the German DR, 300 marks; Hungary, 800 forints; Poland, 1,000 złotys; Romania, 800 lei; the USSR, 60 roubles; and in Yugoslavia, about 400 dinars. These figures may not necessarily apply to agriculture (where minimum wages may be lower). Minimum wages represent 45–55% of the average wage level in the economy (without incentives).

moreover at least a portion of the base pay of all workers is guaranteed by the state. To honour these obligations, the state may assist the enterprises' reserve funds out of centralized funds or funds maintained by the ministries, usually in the form of repayable advances. In the case of enterprises incurring planned losses, subsidies are paid out of the state budget. In Yugoslavia, if an enterprise has not sufficient resources in its own reserve fund, it may turn for assistance to the reserve funds maintained by National Councils or Republican authorities, but these 'loans' have to be repaid later. In Bulgaria, if the reserve fund of a branch association is exhausted it is allowed to borrow from banks.

E. INCENTIVES AND CONSUMPTION

The payment of cash incentives may produce an immediate direct response from workers, but ultimately their effectiveness depends on the availability of suitable goods and services in the market. Although this problem also existed before the economic reforms, it has assumed greater significance under the new system because material incentives have been assigned a greater role. Contrary to the expectations of the idealist dreamers, the 'new communist man' has not yet evolved. Far from it, the average worker appears to have become impatient with the leaders' promises and pleadings for continued sacrifices, and instead is now more demanding than ever before. In a study of incentives under modern Socialist conditions, a Polish economist described the workers' attitudes in the following words:

> There is a strong desire to catch up and surpass workmates and neighbours, which produces a dynamizing effect on the worker to increase his income. The worker's craving to increase his income is conditioned by a variety of considerations, and it does not subside even if his income is steadily rising because his wants are also expanding . . . As income rises, so does the demand for luxuries, and since luxuries are usually expensive, the worker's desire for increases in his income also rises.[1]

[1] S. Góra, *Warunki produkcji a dzialanie bodźców* (Conditions of Production and the Operation of Incentives), Warsaw, PWN, 1967, pp. 45, 64.

In contrast to previous practice, the authorities have adopted a more liberal attitude. First of all, there is a growing inclination to give greater attention to consumers' preferences. In all these countries institutes for the study of consumer demand have been established or expanded. At the same time, more resources are being allowed for the production of consumer goods and services, including a greater variety and better quality. Admittedly, this new posture can be partly explained on two other grounds. On the one hand, the consumer is allowed to shape the structure of production to relieve central planners of routine details and to eliminate the waste of unsalable production. On the other, as the Socialist economies have reached more developed stages, it is now possible to give higher living standards to the masses. Nevertheless, there is sufficient evidence indicating that the authorities have also been anxious to reinforce the effectiveness of incentives, which is indispensable to the success of the new system.

One of the peculiarities of the Socialist road to economic development in the past was a drive to maximize the output of producer goods, which was being achieved largely at the expense of current consumption. Thus taking the member countries of the Council for Mutual Economic Assistance (CMEA or Comecon) as a whole, over the period 1950–65 the output of industrial producer goods (the so-called 'Group A' output) rose six times but that of industrial consumer goods ('Group B') by only four times.[1] But since the economic reforms this gap has been narrowed down and in fact in some of them the growth rates have been reversed. Thus in the USSR, over the period 1928–67 the average annual rate of growth of Group A output was 10·5 and of Group B output 4·5; but over the period 1968–70 the respective rates were 7·7 and 8·0, and this (slight) priority to consumer goods is planned to continue over the current five-year plan (7·4 and 7·8 respectively).[2]

In this development, considerable importance is attached by the authorities to the provision of consumer durables, including such items as washing machines, refrigerators, television sets and cars, which for a long time were regarded by the masses as unattainable

[1] *Rozwój gospodarczy krajów RWPG 1950–1968* (Economic Development of the CMEA Countries 1950–1968), Warsaw, Central Statistical Office of Poland, 1969, pp. 16–43.

[2] *Kommunist*, 11/1967, p. 9; *Vop. ekon.*, 4/1971, p. 58.

luxuries. The increase in the number of passenger cars and television sets in use in the Socialist countries between 1960 and 1968 is shown in Table 19. Although the Socialist countries are well behind the most affluent capitalist nations, the improvements recorded in the 1960s are remarkable and they are certain to

TABLE 19 THE NUMBER OF PASSENGER CARS AND TELEVISION SETS IN USE PER 1,000 OF POPULATION IN 1960 AND 1968

Country	Passenger Cars		Television Sets	
	1960	1968	1960	1968
Bulgaria	n.a.	7	n.	74
Czechoslovakia	n.a.	36	58	199
German DR	17	48*	60	244
Hungary	3	14	10	136
Poland	4	12	14	105
Romania	n.a.	3	3	57
USSR	3	5	22	112
Yugoslavia	3	22	2	64
Great Britain	106	204	212	279
Japan	5	52	74	208
United States	340	414	307	409

n. = negligible (0·3). n.a. = not available.
* For 1967.

Sources. Based on *Rocznik statystyczny 1970*, pp. 583, 648, 667; *Rozwój gospodarczy krajów RWPG 1950–1968*, pp. 110, 137.

continue in the future. Of particular interest is the Socialist determination to develop the mass production of passenger cars, which are now manufactured (or at least assembled) in all these countries except Hungary (the latter country concentrates on trucks under a CMEA specialization agreement). Rapid progress is being made where the leading Western firms (Daimler-Benz, Fiat, Renault, Volkswagen and Volvo) are playing an important role. For example, during the current 1971–5 plan, the sale of cars in the USSR is to increase nearly four times above the 1970 level.[1]

Other recent developments strengthening the effectiveness of

[1] L. Brezhnev, *Report of the CPSU Central Committee to the 24th Congress of the Communist Party of the Soviet Union*, Moscow, Novosti PAPH, 1971, p. 62.

material incentives include the growth of consumer credit, the official acceptance of fashions as psychologically, sociologically and economically justified under modern socialism, occasional reductions in the prices of consumer durables for incentive purposes[1] and some relaxation on the imports of consumer goods and on foreign travel (especially to other Socialist countries).

In its inclination to back up cash incentives with a more generous supply of consumer goods and services for sale in the market, the Socialist leadership is confronted with a painful dilemma, a Marxian contradiction *par excellence* – the traditional tug-of-war between efficiency and equity. One of the principal long-range goals to which the Communist Parties are committed is the progressive expansion of social (or 'collective') consumption, with the consequent (at least relative) decline in private (or 'individual') consumption. Private consumption consists of goods and services purchased in the market and paid for out of the consumer's own earnings, whilst social consumption is wholly or largely provided by society and is financed by the state, local authorities and enterprises in the form of cash social benefits (maternity allowances, child endowment, scholarships, old age pensions, etc.), handouts in kind (medicines, communal feeding, literature) and services (education, health, entertainment, transport, housing, a.s.o.).

Before the reforms, in most Socialist countries the latter type of consumption was growing at faster rates than the former, as illustrated by the average annual rates over the period 1950–65 (the rates apply to total, not *per capita* figures):

	Private Consumption	*Social Consumption*
Czechoslovakia	5·2	5·4
German DR	6·7	7·4
Poland	6·5	9·6

Source. United Nations *Yearbook of National Accounts Statistics 1969*, New York, Statistical Office of the United Nations, 1970, vol. II, pp. 149–51.

[1] e.g., in March 1971 the following price reductions were announced by the Ministry of Domestic Trade in the USSR: bicycles, by 14%; motor scooters and washing machines, by 16% each; motor cycles, by 19%; TV sets, by 19–30%; electric razors, by 20%; plastic haberdashery and accessories, by 38%; ball-point pens, by 50%. *Izvestiya*, 1/3/1971, p. 3.

It appears that also over the period 1965–9 social consumption in the CMEA region as a whole grew faster than private consumption.[1] A progressive expansion of social consumption is the main avenue for implementing the Marxian ideal of distribution according to needs. In the mid-1960s the proportion of social in total consumption ranged in the European Socialist countries from about 20 per cent in Poland and Yugoslavia to about 30 per cent in Czechoslovakia and the USSR, compared with 5–20 per cent in most capitalist countries.[2]

Although preferable on ideological grounds, experience has shown that social consumption is not conducive to the maximization of enterprise performance and the growth of productivity. Social consumption is more or less automatic irrespective of the recipients' quantity and quality of work, and 'in fact it may produce disintegrating effects in enterprises and on society'.[3] On the other hand private consumption, being based on the consumer's freedom of choice and his own effort, activates the operation of material incentives, whereby the growth of production and efficiency are intensified. Consequently, many economists have in recent years advocated limiting, or arresting the growth of, social consumption in favour of private consumption.

B. Csikós-Nagy, a leading personality in economic thought and administration in Hungary, has recently stated that under the new system the improvement in the standard of living should proceed not via the redistribution of national income but through the growth of personal earnings according to work and that personal incomes should be further differentiated while social consumption should be limited[4]. A Polish economist, S. Góra, has emphasized that, if social consumption continues to grow in the future, it is imperative that more luxuries be available for private purchase on the basis of free choice.[5]

[1] *Życie gosp.*, 31/10/1971, p. 11.

[2] R. Krzyżewski, *Konsumpcja społeczna w gospodarce socjalistycznej* (Social Consumption in a Socialist Economy), Warsaw, PWN, 1968, pp. 116–20.

[3] Ibid., p. 90.

[4] B. Csikós-Nagy, ('Problems Associated with the Perfection of the Economic Mechanism'), *Közgazdasági szemle* (Economic Review), Budapest, 4/1970, pp. 455–6.

[5] S. Góra, op. cit., p. 72.

The authorities have recognized these facts of modern economic life and there are some indications suggesting revisions of previous policies on this question. Yugoslavia has done this earliest, following her first economic reforms of 1952, so that over the period 1952–68 her average annual rate of growth of total private consumption (7·6) exceeded that of social consumption (5·5).[1] In the USSR at the 22nd Party Congress in 1962, it was announced that by 1980 social consumption would be expanded to 50 per cent of total consumption.[2] However, since the late 1960s the proportion has settled at a level of about 33 per cent, and according to the current five-year plan it will remain unchanged up to 1976.[3] Similar slowdowns in the growth of social consumption are evident in the five-year plans of most other Socialist countries.

F. THE CRITICISM OF MATERIAL INCENTIVES

It is generally agreed amongst Socialist writers, political leaders and practising economists that the strengthening of material incentives and linking them to enterprise profits have produced beneficial overall effects in the form of a more economical use of materials, a greater utilization of idle capacity, a better adaptation of production to demand, diminished alienation[4] and an improvement in enterprise performance in general. However, the operation of incentives has been subjected to criticism in several quarters, and the arguments raised can be classified into five major objections – the limited effectiveness, the doubtful link to efficiency, undesirable differences in incentive payments, instability and ideological retrogression.

The basis of the formation of incentive funds and the methods of their distribution are too complicated to be easily understood by the majority of workers, which tends to weaken their impact. The proportion of gross profits distributed in incentives is on the whole

[1] *Yearbook of National Accounts Statistics 1969*, p. 151.

[2] *The Road to Communism*, Documents of the 22nd Congress of the Communist Party of the Soviet Union, Moscow, FLPH, 1961, p. 545.

[3] L. Brezhnev, op. cit., pp. 43, 49.

[4] For the origin and meaning of this concept, see Ch. 3A, footnote 1, pp. 54–5.

only about one-tenth, and even less in the form of cash payments to individual workers. For most workers, cash incentives constitute less than a quarter of their base pay (less than a fifth of their total earnings). Sharing in the socio-cultural and housing fund is on the basis of needs rather than the quantity and quality of work, so that its incentive effect on the managerial and professional personnel is small. The final sharing in profit at the end of the financial year is too far removed, as far as ordinary workers are concerned, from the time of the actual exertion at work. In recent years at least some of these countries have lifted minimum wages,[1] which has tended to blunt the unskilled workers' inclination to maintain their effort and in fact it appears to be encouraging slack labour discipline and absenteeism.[2]

But even where incentives are effective, they may stimulate enterprise production not necessarily in society's best interest. The incentive system based on profit suffers from the original sin perpetuated in Socialist prices. Owing to the continued price distortions and the consequent malformation of profits and hence incentive funds, labour is rewarded for achievements of doubtful economic validity from the standpoint of efficiency. As long as price irrationalities persist, the present system of incentives merely perpetuates sub-optimal patterns of resource utilization.

As in several Socialist countries the size of the transfers of enterprise profits to incentive funds is defined as given percentages of the base wage funds, enterprises find it to their advantage to maximize their employment. For example, it has been revealed that in the Soviet machine-building industry in the late 1960s, 80 per cent of the increases in the incentive funds was contrived through expanded wage funds and only 20 per cent was due to an

[1] e.g., between the mid-1960s and the early 1970s the minimum monthly wages applicable to the branches of the economy outside agriculture were increased from 50 to 70 leva in Bulgaria, from 220 to 350 marks in the German DR, from 750 to 1,000 złotys in Poland, from 570 to 800 lei in Romania and from 50 to 60 roubles in the USSR. In agriculture, where the nominal level of income has always been lower, minimum and average earnings rose even more – by about one-third over the period.

[2] For evidence, see, e.g., *Pravda*, Moscow, 10/1/1970, p. 3; *Probleme economice* (Problems of Economics), Bucharest, 2/1970, pp. 80–81; M. Syrek, *Wpływ substytucyjnego i niezależnego postępu technicznego na wydajność pracy* (The Influence of Capital-Using and Pure Technical Progress on Labour Productivity), Katowice, Wyd. Śląsk, 1967, pp. 242–3.

increase in the profit indicators.[1] Thus incentives can increase in anti-social ways without a corresponding improvement in labour productivity. Hence, some economists are in favour of linking incentives to a growth in labour productivity instead. Experiments to this effect are carried on in several Socialist countries, especially in the USSR.[2]

There are considerable differences in the personal incentives received by different members of an enterprise and amongst different enterprises. Many lower-grade workers are dissatisfied with the fact that persons in managerial positions are paid higher incentives not only in absolute terms but also in relation to their base pay, and in addition receive favoured treatment in the case of profit setbacks. Thus it has been claimed in Poland that the managerial incentive usually reaches the upper permissible limit of 80 per cent of the base salary, but other white-collar workers, who on paper can earn incentives of 50 per cent of their salary, in practice reach 15–20 per cent or even less.[3]

There is a wide range in the ability of different enterprises to pay incentives, owing to conditions inherited from the past (natural factors, the quality of the site and equipment, idle capacity), a differing capacity for technological progress and the varying incidence of price changes in different industries under the complex price systems (see Ch. 4E, pp. 100–4). It is a well-known fact that these external advantages are not, and cannot be, fully neutralized by differential levies.[4] These differences contribute to the instability in the labour market by inducing a greater labour turnover than was the case in the past – now reaching 40 per cent and even more in a year, compared with 20 per cent or less before the reforms.[5] The size of incentive payments in different enterprises and in different periods cannot be accurately predicted, and

[1] V. Rzheshevskii, ('The Reform and Labour Productivity'), *Kommunist*, 12/1969, p. 66.

[2] See, e.g., *Planovoe khoziaistvo* (Planned Economy), Moscow, 11/1970, p. 45; *Pravda*, 24/6/1970, p. 2.

[3] *Finanse*, 7/1968, p. 24.

[4] For evidence, see, e.g., B. Sukharevsky, ('Material Stimulation in the Context of the Economic Reforms'), *Ekonomicheskaya gazeta* (Economic Gazette), Moscow, no. 29, July 1968, p. 9.

[5] For recent evidence, see, e.g., *Figyelő*, 19/5/1971, p. 5; *Finanţe şi credit*, 11/1970, pp. 8–9; *Partien zhivot* (Party Life), Sofia, 8/1971, pp. 42–8; *Pravda*, 20/1/1971, p. 3.

such incentives represent an element of uncertainty to central planners as well as to the enterprises producing consumer non-essentials, which are usually purchased out of incentive earnings. Many workers are critical of the fact that they have to share in business risk.

Finally, many communist idealists cannot help but see the strengthening of material motivation – linked to profit at that – as a retrograde step amounting to economic revisionism. Some of them are, pragmatically, prepared to tolerate this step as a means of accelerating the growth of efficiency, but they assume that as soon as a sufficient level of productivity is attained the march towards the Marxian ideal of distribution should be resumed. The leaders hope that with higher levels of material welfare, education and social consciousness and the shortening of the hours of work, moral incentives will become increasingly effective, particularly in the case of white-collar workers. As a transitional move, some thinkers are advocating a switch to a greater differentiation of base pay and a gradual elimination of the movable incentive element of earnings. According to some writers, the phasing out of material incentives should begin with the managerial and professional personnel, followed by skilled blue-collar workers and then unskilled labourers.[1] This scheme has in fact been put into practice in China.

It must be pointed out that although the Communist Parties in the eight European Socialist countries have sanctioned the revitalization of material incentives as an essential element of the economic reforms, they have not renounced the Marxian ideal of distribution 'according to needs' as the ultimate goal. They are still committed to egalitarianism, amounting to the elimination of the differences between peasants and urban workers, between physical and mental work and between labouring and managerial personnel, and to a steady expansion of social consumption.

[1] K. Piotrowski, ('The Incentive Element of Earnings as an Instrument of Economic Management'), *Ekonomista* (The Economist), Warsaw, no. 2, 1970, pp. 239–60, esp. pp. 251, 259–60.

7 Investment

A. FINANCIAL INSTRUMENTS AND PROFIT

THE Socialist countries under consideration have passed through three stages with regard to the method of determining investment projects. Up to about the mid-1950s (1952 in Yugoslavia), investment decisions in practically all their details were made at the central level and imposed on individual enterprises. The decisions were essentially based on overriding macrosocial considerations, with little attention given to efficiency. In fact, the planned economic development by stages left little scope for choice in respect of major investment schemes.

But it did not take long for the authorities to realize that as the economy reaches higher stages of development, the number of investment alternatives rapidly multiplies. Hence, since the mid-1950s, and even earlier in the USSR, various types of indices of investment efficiency have been devised for the selection of investment projects not predetermined at the political level. An example of a commonly used index for comparative evaluation is the 'synthetic index of investment efficiency' (the coefficients embodied in the index are either constants or can be worked out from special tables prepared by the authorities):[1]

$$sIe = \frac{\frac{I}{T}(1 - d \,.\, f) - Cn \,.\, vc}{Vn \,.\, vp};$$

sIe = the synthetic index of investment efficiency;
T = the time of recoupment of the investment outlay (in years);
I = investment outlay;

[1] Based on: the State Planning Commission of Poland, *Instrukcja ogólna w sprawie metodyki badań ekonomicznej efektywności inwestycji* (General Instruction Concerning the Methodology of the Evaluation of the Economic Efficiency of Investment), Warsaw, PWE, 1962, pp. 30–5, 60–107.

d = the coefficient of discount indicating annual losses caused to the economy during the period of construction of the investment undertaking; it is usually fixed for the whole economy (e.g. 0·20 in Hungary);

f = the freeze period, i.e. the number of years necessary to complete the investment project;

Cn = the total cost of exploitation of the project, including maintenance and repairs during the whole period n;

vc = the coefficient of cost variation during the period of exploitation;

Vn = the total value of production in the entire period n;

vp = the coefficient of production variation during the period of exploitation.

These indices, some of which are highly sophisticated and complex, are still in use, especially at the intermediate level of economic management (industrial branch associations, industrial trusts, economic associations, centrals, as they are called in different countries) and banks when considering the extension of investment credits.

The third stage has begun with the economic reforms. One of the characteristics of the new economic system is the important role assigned to financial instruments or, as they are now often described, 'financial levers'. In the sphere of investment they consist primarily of capital charges, interest rates and other terms on bank credits, depreciation charges and allowances and awards to enterprises for achieving specific tasks. They are essentially meant to influence enterprise profits and consequently incentives to the personnel. These levers have been found in many respects to be preferable to centrally determined directives, and in particular they are compatible with the independence of enterprises. The general assumption is that the authorities can achieve macroeconomic objectives by manipulating the financial incentives and disincentives, whilst the relatively independent enterprises operating within these ramifications are in a better position to optimize microeconomic decisions, including the implementation of the details of investment undertakings.

Before the reforms, investment capital was allocated by the state to enterprises free, i.e. no initial payment was made by the enterprises nor any payment for its use in subsequent years (except the usual depreciation charges on fixed capital, but these were quite low). Consequently, enterprises made extravagant demands for such allocations, irrespective of their capacity for full utilization. This led to a widespread hoarding of assets and tremendous waste and inefficiency. This inherent weakness was officially recognized as early as 1953 in Yugoslavia, when annual capital charges were introduced on the use of fixed assets and in 1957 on circulating assets. Other Socialist countries took this step much later – Bulgaria, the German DR and Hungary in 1964 and Czechoslovakia, Poland and the USSR in 1966, Romania being the only country under consideration which has not done so yet.

Capital charges are regular levies payable by enterprises on the value of fixed and circulating assets held (in Poland only fixed assets are subject to these charges). The charges mostly range from 3 per cent p.a. in Bulgaria to 6 per cent p.a. in the German DR and the USSR. They apply to industrial enterprises, but they have also been extended to some other branches of the economy, although mostly at concessional rates. It is now in the enterprises' interest to acquire only those assets which can be fully utilized and to dispose of surplus equipment to minimize their capital charge liability.

Capital charges represent a sort of social opportunity cost – the price of the forgone alternative application of capital in some other use. In fact from the standpoint of enterprises in most Socialist countries the opportunity cost is higher, viz. by the interest rate which can be earned from banks on time deposits. For example, in Hungary, where the capital charge is 5 per cent and the time deposit rate is 7 per cent, industrial enterprises do not find investment worth their while unless the expected gross profit rate exceeds 12 per cent. For further details of capital charges and bank deposit rates, see Table 20. It may be noted here that there is a tendency to also extend capital charges to the land occupied by industrial enterprises (especially in Bulgaria, Czechoslovakia and Hungary).

In contrast to the previous practice, interest rates have become an active weapon for shaping investment through bank credit. Their level has been raised (from about 3 to 5 per cent, taking the region as a whole) and there is a remarkable range of rates charged according to the purpose of the credit and the type of borrower. Thus, according to the new scale in Romania announced in late 1970, the average level of interest rates has been raised from 2·9 to 3·8 per cent p.a. Credits to collective farms carry 2 per cent, to

TABLE 20 CAPITAL CHARGES AND INTEREST RATES IN THE SOCIALIST COUNTRIES

Per Cent per Annum

Country	Capital Charge*	Maximum Deposit Rate Paid by Banks to Enterprises	Interest Rates on Bank Credits	
			Total Range†	Normal Rates on Investment Credit
Bulgaria	3	5	2–10	2
Czechoslovakia	5	3	6–12	6
German DR	6	5	2–12	2
Hungary	5	7	4–10	8‡
Poland	5	6	3–12	3
Romania	–	5	1–12	1
USSR	6	0·5	1–15	2‡
Yugoslavia	4	6	5–20	10‡

* These charges generally apply to fixed and (except in Poland) circulating assets held by industrial enterprises. In most countries other branches of the economy are either exempt or subject to concessional rates. In Yugoslavia the charges are scheduled to be discontinued in the early 1970s.

† Including penalty rate.

‡ Maximum rate.

Source. Daily and periodical literature of the countries concerned.

state farms 3 per cent, to trading enterprises 3 per cent, and to those in industry, construction, transport and certain other classes of borrowers, 5 per cent. Overdue credits carry 6–10 per cent for three months and 8–12 per cent exceeding this period.[1]

A striking feature of the new interest scales, in obvious conflict with the dogmatic ideas prevalent before, is the existence of very high penalty rates of up to 20 per cent (in Yugoslavia). A summary

[1] *Viata economica* (Economic Life), Bucharest, 9/10/1970, p. 4.

of interest rates together with capital charges in the eight Socialist countries is given in Table 20. The modern responsibility of the banks is to examine the investment projects proposed by enterprises and to select and finance those which appear to be most profitable.

An active role is also being assigned to depreciation rates and allowances. Higher depreciation rates have been introduced in selected industries to accelerate the replacement of working equipment with the most up-to-date models.[1] There has been a tendency to leave higher proportions of depreciation allowances at the disposal of the enterprises, so that the budgetary absorption has been considerably reduced and in fact in some countries (Bulgaria, Czechoslovakia and Yugoslavia) discontinued.

One of the prevalent forms of waste in the past was the extension of the freeze periods of investment projects, i.e. exceeding the planned periods of construction and delaying the full operation of the completed projects, during which time resources were tied up without a return to the economy. To minimize this source of inefficiency various incentives have been devised whereby either costs to enterprises are reduced or incentive funds are directly increased.

For example, in Poland, if the actual date of the completion and the cost of the project are as provided for in the plan, the interest charge on the bank credit is reduced by 0·6 per cent; if the date of completion is shortened and the planned cost is not exceeded, the interest remission is 0·3 per cent; if both the period and the cost of construction are reduced below the planned figures, the interest remission is 1·0 per cent.[2] Furthermore, the incentive funds of the managerial personnel are now directly affected. In the case of the

[1] e.g., in Hungary in 1968 the annual rates were increased as follows (as a percentage of the initial value of fixed assets): in light industry, from 2·7 to 4·2; in agriculture and forestry, from 3·0 to 4·1; in heavy industry, from 3·9 to 5·2; in construction, from 5·2 to 7·8; in the economy as a whole, from 4·3 to 5·0. Between 1960 and 1970 the value of depreciation allowed in the economy was doubled in Poland and trebled in the USSR. Sources: I. Friss (ed.), *Reform of the Economic Mechanism in Hungary*, Budapest, Akadémiai Kiadó, 1969, p. 142; *Rocznik statystyczny 1965* and *1970* (Statistical Yearbook for 1965, and for 1970), Warsaw, Central Statistical Office of Poland, 1965, and 1970, pp. 76 and 84 respectively; *Narodnoe khoziaistvo SSSR v 1969 g.* (National Economy of the USSR in 1969), Moscow, Statistika, 1970, p. 768.

[2] *Finanse* (Finance), Warsaw, 4/1970, p. 34.

enterprise supplying major investment items (materials and equipment), an amount equivalent to from 0·2 to 0·4 per cent of the value of deliveries can be placed in the Economic Achievements Incentive Fund (as it is called in Poland) if the agreed items are supplied on time or earlier. At the same time the enterprise carrying out the investment project is allowed to channel an amount equal to 1·8–2·0 per cent of its salary bill to the Fund, if the normative period of construction is not exceeded; if the period of completion is exceeded by 20 per cent or more, the transfer to the Fund is not allowed.[1]

In the USSR, if a designing office furnishes the required design ahead of schedule, the incentive fund for the personnel is now increased by 5 per cent (previously by 2·5 per cent). If the period of the construction and commissioning of the project is shortened by 10 per cent below the planned period, the incentive fund is increased by 10 per cent; if by 20, the fund is raised by 25 per cent; and if by 30 per cent, the fund goes up by 50 per cent (i.e. on a progressive basis).[2]

B. THE FINANCING OF INNOVATIONS, AND RISK

Under the old system, practically all investment was financed out of the state budget, whilst the role of the enterprises was mostly limited to the maintenance and repair of the existing assets. Consequently, under that set-up technological progress was primarily possible via the construction of new projects. But the situation began to be changed in the late 1950s in favour of a greater share of non-budgetary financing.

The financing of innovational investments out of the state budget still plays an important part in Hungary, Romania and the USSR, where about one-half of such investments rely on budgetary allocations. They are of lesser importance now – but still not insignificant – in Czechoslovakia and the German DR; in Yugoslavia they have been virtually discontinued since 1967. The budgetary funds are usually devoted to projects involving the

[1] *Finanse*, 7/1969, p. 52.

[2] *Ekonomicheskaya gazeta* (Economic Gazette), Moscow, no. 3, Jan. 1970, p. 9.

formation of new enterprises, the centrally specified schemes to be carried out by existing enterprises and theoretical and developmental work related to new technology. Such undertakings involve a high degree of risk owing to the uncertainty associated with research and development, the large size of the scheme or a long period of recoupment. As a rule, budgetary allocations are in the form of free grants, but in some countries, especially in Bulgaria, Czechoslovakia, Hungary and Yugoslavia, they may have to be repaid.

The budgetary basis of financing commands certain advantages. Many risky innovations of great potential macroeconomic value to society might not otherwise be undertaken. The state is in a better position to evaluate the long-run macrosocial cost–benefit and initiate technological developments in desirable directions and to disseminate the new know-how. On the other hand, as risk is wholly or mostly borne by the state budget, budgetary allocations may be wastefully applied, and moreover, the initiative and independence of enterprises become restricted.

The non-budgetary financing of innovations is now derived from a large number of sources – centralized funds, funds attached to the intermediate organs of economic management, bank credits, enterprises' own liquid funds and in some cases other minor sources. Centralized funds are held in each Socialist country by the State Commission (or Ministry) for Scientific and Technical Progress (the exact title may differ in each country). It obtains its financial resources partly from the state budget and partly from the relevant ministries (and the latter derive them from the state budget, the intermediate entities of economic management and enterprises). This finance is mostly distributed to the more important research institutes for basic theoretical research and experimentation.

An increasingly important part is now played by the funds held by branch associations, industrial trusts, centrals, as well as by the ministries. These financial resources are derived from the profits of the associated enterprises. To illustrate, in Bulgaria 40 per cent of the enterprise Production Development Fund is channelled to the industrial trust and placed in the New Production Fund; in turn, 35 per cent of the New Production Fund is transferred to the relevant ministry New Production Fund.[1] The branch and ministry funds are used for research and development which are of common interest to that group of enterprises, or which entail a high degree of uncertainty, so that in effect risk is spread over a number of enterprises.

Innovations which are undertaken on the enterprise's own initiative and which are of local interest are financed out of the enterprise's own liquid resources. Finance for these purposes is held in the enterprise Production Development Fund (which may also be known under some other similar name), but in larger enterprises a separate Technological Progress Fund may be maintained as well. The Production Development Fund is formed mainly from enterprise profits (see next section of this chapter for details). It is relatively large because it is also used for other types of investment on the enterprise's own initiative. The Technological Progress Fund is usually smaller in size and it is derived mostly from special innovational mark-ups on the enterprise's prime cost, and less commonly from retained profits (only in Czechoslovakia, and in Bulgaria at the combine level, is this Fund financed out of profits).

These mark-ups vary according to the branch of industry or the economy, reflecting innovational needs and the degree of risk. For example in Bulgaria, the mark-ups allowed range from 0·1 to 3·5 per cent of the total prime cost in the branches of manufacturing industry; in transport the mark-up is 0·2 per cent, in agriculture 0·4 per cent and in communications 0·5 per cent. In the USSR, the allowed mark-ups in industrial enterprises range from 0·3 to 3·0 per cent.[2] From the standpoint of the minimization of risk to enterprises, mark-ups on costs are preferable to allocations from profits. Mark-ups on costs are a more continuous and reliable source of finance than withholding part of the profits because the latter are likely to fluctuate and differ widely from one enterprise to another. The remarkable growth of the Technological Progress Funds, the beginnings of which go back to 1958, is a reflection of the official determination to spur enterprises to innovations. 'The

[1] M. Marlewicz, *Finansowanie postępu naukowo-technicznego w krajach socjalistycznych* (Financing Scientific and Technical Progress in the Socialist Countries), Warsaw, PWE, 1968, p. 84.

[2] Ibid.

main reason for their formation and extension is to overcome the enterprises' reluctance to engage their general funds for risky and long term undertakings involving technological improvements.'[1]

Finance can also be obtained from banks as (repayable) loans. Credits used for innovations are usually granted at concessional rates of interest. For example in Poland, for ordinary investment the credit charge is 3 per cent, whilst modernization credit carries a charge of only 1·5 per cent p.a.[2] Bank loans are extended on the security of the enterprise's Production Development Fund or the Technological Progress Fund. In cases where a high degree of risk is involved, banks are allowed to apply higher interest rates or demand additional security.

A notable feature of the Socialist financing of technological progress which has emerged in the last decade is what can be described as the 'commercialization of research and development'. It is a logical consequence of the trend away from budgetary financing, the acceptance of the profit criterion, the strengthening of incentives to labour and the authorities' determination to shift the bearing of unmeasurable risk to the microeconomic sphere where it occurs. In contrast to the previous practice, research establishments have been freed from detailed bureaucratic control from above, and instead have been granted considerable economic independence.

Research entities are now supposed to operate on the basis of commercial accounting and be largely or completely self-supporting, i.e. to cover their expenses from the income earned from assignments carried out for the government agencies and enterprises and from the projects initiated by themselves. Their work contracts may be for expert advice, testing, designs, documentation, a new process or a prototype. Budgetary grants are usually extended only to national research institutes. The emphasis is on applied research and development, more or less related to the needs of the branch of the economy to which they are attached. Some research establishments, especially in Hungary, even engage in production closely related to their research.[3]

[1] M. Marlewicz, op. cit., pp. 65–6. [2] *Finanse*, 7/1969, p. 48.

[3] For evidence, see, e.g., *Figyelö* (Economic Observer), Budapest, 4/6/1969, p. 3.

Each research entity normally has a General Research Fund, for financing research on its own initiative, and a Material Incentive Fund for its personnel. There are scales of fees laid down by the authorities and the work is carried out on a contract basis. In these fees generous profit mark-ups are included over and above costs. For example, according to the East German schedule effective since 1969, the mark-up on research work for modernization carried out on the institute's own initiative is 5–10 per cent, on the work commissioned by enterprises usually 10–25 per cent, on projects which lead to desirable structural changes in the economy 20–40 per cent and on some crucial assignments commissioned by the state the profit mark-up may be as high as 80 per cent.[1] The rule is that payment has to follow even if the results of the research are negative, i.e. the risk is borne by the commissioning organ or enterprise. To protect the interests of the commissioning entities, contracts often include clauses regarding incentive payments for the work satisfying certain conditions on the one hand, and penalties for breaches of the agreement on the other. To reduce the risk of non-solution, or of a solution which is likely to be unprofitable, multivariant research may be sponsored (especially in the German DR and the USSR), whereby parallel, competitive research projects are carried on. Participants are paid at least for the cost involved to them and the best solution is awarded a prize.[2]

C. THE SELF-FINANCING OF ENTERPRISES

The term 'self-financing' is used today in the Socialist countries to describe the enterprise's capacity for undertaking operations which are financed out of its own resources, over which it exerts a direct influence without undue interference from higher authorities. In particular, this applies to investment involving both fixed and circulating assets. The increased ability and scope for self-financing is one of the cornerstones of the new economic system. It has

[1] J. Schulze, ('Performance Mark-ups for Scientific and Technical Work'), *Die Wirtschaft* (The Economy), East Berlin, 23/10/1969, p. 14.

[2] J. Moszczyński, ('Prospects for the Perfection of the Principles Governing Economic Accounting in Research Entities Attached to Industry'), *Finanse*, 4/1969, pp. 37–8.

proved to be indispensable to decentralization and to the effective independence of enterprises. If they are to maximize their performance (profit), they must be able to finance their projects themselves, taking advantage of the local investment opportunities which they are in a better position to recognize and exploit than remote central planners.

This particularly applies to the improvement in the organization and methods of production, the adaptation of the assortment of output to demand, the replacement of depreciated equipment with more effective models and the modernization of the plant in general. These are the points on which Socialist enterprises were found wanting in the past, particularly when compared with firms in capitalist countries. Self-financing also enhances the sense of pride and responsibility of the enterprise personnel. At the same time, it relieves central planners of the burden of the details of decisions of a microeconomic nature, and instead they can now concentrate on wider issues of long-term importance to the economy as a whole.

As we have demonstrated in Ch. 5, since the economic reforms not only has the absolute amount of profits left in enterprises vastly increased but so also has the proportion retained by them. One of the important functions of profit contributing to the independence of enterprises under the new system is that it is the chief source for the maintenance of the Production Development Funds, where liquid resources for self-financing are mostly held. In most Socialist countries the proportion of gross profits channelled to the Fund ranges from 10 to 40 per cent and about 50 per cent in Yugoslavia. In Hungary, the proportion so transferred in the first instance is about four-fifths, and then the Fund is taxed at a uniform rate of 60 per cent, in contrast to the progressive rate of 40–70 per cent applied to the Sharing Fund. The reason for the uniform tax rate is to enable the more profitable enterprises to maintain larger Production Development Funds and thus promote structural developments along the most efficient lines.

In addition to the retained profits, the Production Development Fund is also maintained from retained depreciation allowances and the sale of surplus assets. These amounts are now quite large. There has been a tendency in recent years for the depreciation rates to be increased and for the proportions allowed to be retained by enterprises to be larger. In Hungary the retainable proportion of depreciation has recently been 60 per cent, but since 1972 all depreciation may be retained in cases where it is justified.[1] Enterprises also find it to their advantage to sell those assets which they do not fully utilize in order to minimize their capital charges.

TABLE 21 SOURCES OF INVESTMENT FINANCE IN THE SOCIALIST COUNTRIES IN 1963 AND 1969

In Percentages

Country	Budgetary Allocations		Enterprises' Own Liquid Funds		Bank Credits	
	1963	1969	1963	1969	1963	1969
Bulgaria	70	32	29	38	1	30
Czechoslovakia	68	n.a.	28	n.a.	4	n.a.
German DR	46	16	42	61	12	23
Hungary	75	51	24	37	1	12
Poland	48	28	44	36	8	36
Romania	61	44	38	41	1	15
USSR	60	50	40	49	—	1

n.a. = not available.

Sources. Finanse, 12/1967, p. 35; 7/1971, p. 60.

The capacity for self-financing is further strengthened by the increasing possibility for enterprises of obtaining bank credits on their own initiative. Formerly, enterprises were extended finance more or less automatically for investment prescribed in detail by central planners. There was little chance of securing extra-plan credits, and banks acted as the superior administrative agencies of the Ministry of Finance. However, under the new system credits have come to play an active role in encouraging the most effective application of finance according to local conditions. But in contrast to previous practice, enterprises' dealings with banks are now based on voluntary contracts recognizing the equality of both parties.

[1] *Pénzügyi szemle* (Financial Review), Budapest, 9/1970, p. 712.

The part played by enterprises' own liquid funds and by bank credits in financing investment in the Socialist countries is brought out in Table 21. The trend away from budgetary financing is evident if we compare the situation in 1969 with that in 1963. On present indications, this tendency is likely to continue in the future.

D. LIMITS TO THE ROLE OF PROFITS AND INCENTIVES

By now, the reader may be inclined to believe that the Socialist adoption of the profit criterion and the development of different forms of incentives have created a satisfactory basis for the maximum efficiency of investment. Such a conclusion would be unwarranted yet, at this stage. Investment is still more dominated by non-commercial considerations than any other field of economic decisions.

Total investment is still determined at the political level and it is enforced by direct controls (mostly in the case of the so-called 'centralized investment') and centrally regulated financial levers. And so are what are known as 'major proportions' – the division of investment between the productive (material) and the non-material ('non-productive' services) spheres, the distribution of investment amongst different branches of the economy (heavy industry, the technologically most dynamic industries, light industry producing consumer goods, a.s.o.) and the regional distribution of investment. Investment in the so-called 'non-productive' services, such as banking and finance, housing, social amenities, entertainment, is a sensitive question in the Socialist countries. These services are not reflected in the rates of growth of national income, because they do not directly contribute to material production. Most investment decisions in this sphere are determined by the central and local authorities, usually with little reference to profitability.

Experience has also shown that although the intermediate organs of economic management (industrial branch associations centrals, etc.) were originally meant to be essentially part of the decentralization process, in reality in some countries (especially in

Bulgaria, the German DR, Poland and Romania) they have become more administrative instruments of the government than voluntary associations representing the interests of independent enterprises. Their influence and power are greatest in the field of investment. They hold considerable proportions of the enterprise funds, and in their investment policies they often in effect redistribute them from the more profitable to the less profitable enterprises.

The way in which capital charges are administered is open to criticism. In addition to the basic rate normally applicable to industry (as shown in Table 20, p. 160), there are other, mostly concessional, rates, and specified enterprises and branches of the economy are exempt from the charges altogether. For example in Bulgaria, where the basic rate is 3 per cent (it was 5 per cent before 1969), the rate applied to enterprises in construction is 2 per cent and to those in the local handicraft industry only 1 per cent; no capital charges are levied from the rest of the economy (agriculture, transport, trade, the 'non-productive' sphere), which means that the enterprises receive free allocations of capital and they pay nothing to the state for its subsequent use. In the German DR the basic charge in industry is 6 per cent, but in trade it ranges from 1 per cent (in catering) to 8 per cent (in the case of some enterprises in food distribution) and no charges apply to other branches of the economy. The concessional rate may be as low as 2 per cent in Czechoslovakia (compared with the basic rate of 6 per cent), 2·5 per cent in Poland (the basic rate is 5 per cent, and capital charges apply to fixed assets only), 2 per cent in the USSR (the basic rate being 6 per cent) and also 2 per cent in Yugoslavia (compared with the ordinary rate of 4 per cent).[1]

Furthermore, there may be temporary exemptions. With the exception of Hungary since July 1967, the fixed assets (and circulating assets in Bulgaria) purchased by enterprises on credit are free of capital charge until the credits are repaid. In the USSR, assets purchased out of the enterprise's own funds are exempt for two years and in Czechoslovakia for five years. Investment projects are not generally subject to capital charges until completed, even if the normative period laid down in the plan is exceeded. The

[1] *Ekonomista* (The Economist), Warsaw, no. 6, 1969, pp. 1385–8; *Planovoe khoziaistvo* (Planned Economy), Moscow, 3/1970, pp. 70–4.

differentiation of the rates and exemptions distort the profits of different enterprises and – where profit or profitability determines investment decisions – the distribution of investment. In no Socialist country are capital charges treated as part of the enterprise's prime cost, and the ideological loyalty to the labour theory of value will continue inhibiting a departure from this practice. In Hungary and Yugoslavia they are deducted from the enterprise's total receipts and are treated as part of the enterprise's total outlay for the purposes of calculating the balance-sheet profit; in Bulgaria, Czechoslovakia, the German DR, Poland and the USSR they are deductible from gross profits.

Romania has not introduced capital charges, and in fact in the countries where they have been introduced there is a good deal of disillusion and opposition. Some economists believe that the rates of the charges are too low to have any significant effect on enterprises, the evidence of which can be found in the continued existence of unutilized surplus capacity, hoarding and the excessive time taken for the completion of investment projects.[1] Other writers argue that capital charges are not only ideologically objectionable but in fact they impede capital-intensive economic development, mechanization and automation, and make labour (the only scarce factor of production under socialism) unjustifiably cheap.[2] It is generally assumed that in the long run capital charges will be abolished (and in fact Yugoslavia has already taken steps in this direction), and that enterprises will endeavour to utilize their assets fully if they are really interested in profit maximization or if they rise to the expected level of social responsibility.[3]

The differentiation of interest rates on investment credits is much

[1] e.g., see V. Gribov, ('Important Reserves for Increasing the Effectiveness of the Utilization of Circulating Assets'), *Dengi i kredit* (Money and Credit), Moscow, 6/1968, p. 22; W. Sztyber ('Theoretical Foundations of the Price Reforms in the Socialist Countries'), *Ekonomista*, no. 6, 1969, p. 1385; V. Zitek ('Machines–People–Effectiveness'), *Hospodářské noviny* (Economic News), Prague, no. 40, 1970, pp. 8–9.

[2] e.g., G. Anisimov, ('Determination of Economic Incentives, and Technological Progress'), *Voprosy ekonomiki* (Problems of Economics), Moscow, 11/1968, pp. 16–28.

[3] M. Breiev, ('Theoretical Problems of Perspective Planning'), *Planovoe khoziaistvo*, 3/1969, pp. 61–9; P. Kuligin, ('Budgetary Regulation of Economic Processes in CMEA Industry'), *Planovoe khoziaistvo*, 3/1970, p. 74.

wider than that of capital charges. For example, in Hungary the concessional interest rate for agriculture may be as low as 2 per cent p.a., whilst co-operative enterprises and tradesmen have to pay 5–10 per cent p.a. Experience has shown that this practice only distorts the profitability of different enterprises and in fact it has little effect on their investment policies. Some economists have emphasized that there is little point in differentiating interest rates because their influence on material incentives is too remote. That is why some writers advocate that interest charges should be deducted from the material incentive funds, especially that portion which is earmarked for the managerial personnel.[1]

Another distorting effect is produced by the disparity between the level of interest rates on investment credits and capital charges. As interest rates are, generally speaking, lower than capital charges, there is scope for manipulation by enterprises. As a Soviet writer pointed out, it is obviously economically wasteful if enterprises in the USSR pay 0·5–1·5 per cent in investment credit whilst the capital charge is 6 per cent.[2] This temptation is reinforced by the fact that, as a rule, assets are not subject to capital charges until bank credits are repaid. It is sometimes argued that the differentiation of capital charges and interest rates may compensate for the distortions in the Socialist price structures. Although this may be true in some cases, there is little evidence that this compensation is in fact carried out on a consistent and systematic basis; and where it is, it is obviously a roundabout and wasteful method.

A condition of the optimum distribution of investment is that its marginal product in different forms of application must be proportional to its opportunity cost or, as a Soviet economist expressed it, 'each rouble placed at the disposal of the enterprise should yield the same return, irrespective of the purpose to which it is applied.'[3] A well-known advocate of optimal planning, N. Fedorenko, put it more in Western than in Socialist terms – 'the condition of the

[1] e.g., S. Shvarts, ('Economic Reform and Some Problems of Credit Relations'), *Dengi i kredit*, 9/1968, p. 10.

[2] P. Yakovlev, ('Some Problems of the Organization of Financing Capital Investment'), *Finansy SSSR* (Soviet Finance), Moscow, 8/1968, p. 33.

[3] S. Shteinshleiger, ('Some Problems of the Influence of the State Bank on the Economy'), *Dengi i kredit*, 8/1968, p. 23.

optimal plan is the equality of the marginal efficiency of capital in all branches of the economy and enterprises'.[1]

Yet in reality the wide disparity in investment returns in different branches of the economy is still a feature of the Socialist economy. Thus in the USSR the incremental capital–output ratios (the cost of direct investment in roubles for each rouble's increase in annual production) recently reported were in selected branches of industry as follows:

Electrical engineering	0·46
Machine construction	0·86
Coal mining	1·51
Power generation	3·00
Oil extraction	4·52
Iron ore mining	5·46

Source. Berliner Zeitung (The Berlin Daily), East Berlin, 21/7/1971, p. 3.

The multiplicity of various *ad hoc* incentives and penalties and the continuation of directives indicate that Socialist profit alone has so far proved unequal to the task of ensuring the most rational size and distribution of investment.

[1] N. Fedorenko, ('Prices and Optimal Planning'), *Kommunist*, Moscow, 8/1966, p. 92.

8 Internal Trade

A. PROFITS, TRADE MARGINS, TURNOVER TAXES AND INCENTIVES

THE profit criterion and the material incentives to labour based on it have also been extended to domestic trade. Under the old system, distribution was highly centralized, it was tightly divorced from production by direct controls and turnover taxes – and, in general, trade played a passive role. Producer goods were distributed by central agencies on an allocational basis laid down in detail in directive plans. As a rule, only consumer goods were handled by trading enterprises. It was commonly accepted that under socialism trade should not be allowed to control production as this would interfere with planned development. Of the five major divisions of material production, trade was considered to be least important, the level of personal earnings in trade was well below the national average, there was a very high labour turnover and the public rating of employment in trade was near the bottom of the occupational ladder.[1]

There was no single criterion for the evaluation of the effectiveness of trading enterprises, instead a number of *ad hoc* indicators were in use singly or in combinations, with varying degrees of consistency. The most common indicators were the volume or value of trade turnover, the structure of goods handled, cost reduction, the number of hours during which the shop was open, the size and qualifications of the personnel, the number of customers serviced, the number of specific free services provided to customers and many others.

As part of the general move towards decentralization under the

[1] According to an investigation carried out in Poland in the early 1960s, on a scale embodying 30 occupations, trade ranked 20th according to remuneration, 26th according to social prestige and 27th in respect of the stability of work. J. Śliwa, *Rola zysku w funkcjonowaniu handlu socjalistycznego* (The Role of Profit in the Operation of Socialist Trade), Warsaw, PWN, 1969, p. 250.

new system, new trading enterprises have been set up replacing at least some allocational agencies in the sphere of producer goods. The number of goods subject to central allocation has been reduced and so has the number of directive indicators binding trading enterprises. The independence of these enterprises has been substantially extended and distribution is increasingly based on market relations. Trade is now viewed as a valuable link between production and distribution.

When profit was first adopted in industry, the authorities were sceptical about its suitability in trade. But many economists, such as A. Abaturov (in the USSR), V. Kobik (Czechoslovakia), W. Koepert (German DR), R. Nyers (Hungary) and J. Śliwa (Poland) took up the cause of trade and experiments with the profit criterion followed. The changeover to this basis was taking place gradually in the late 1960s and early 1970s, although in some countries (such as Czechoslovakia, Hungary and Poland) the beginnings could be traced back to ten, and in Yugoslavia to some fifteen, years earlier. What profit can do in Socialist trade can be judged from the following observation made by a Soviet writer:

> . . . profit, while not being the goal, provides a superior indicator of performance in the sphere of trade. It reflects all aspects of the enterprise operations – the volume of goods sold, their structure, the level of trade margins, trade expenses, the utilization of fixed and circulating assets, the efficiency and suitability of the personnel, the organization of commercial processes, the quality of service, financial discipline, etc.[1]

Profit maximization is particularly important for co-operative enterprises, which are well developed in trade and which have a greater degree of independence in the distribution of their profits. In contrast to state enterprises, they have little chance of survival if they suffer losses. The greater their profits, the larger their financial resources, which strengthens their independence from banks and their unwelcome investigations.

The income of trading enterprises is derived primarily from trade margins. The level of these margins has been substantially increased in the last decade, which provides further evidence of the importance now attached to profit in trade. To illustrate, in

[1] A. Prosandeiev, ('Indicators of the Effectiveness of Soviet Trade'), *Ekonomicheskie nauki* (Economic Studies), Moscow, 12/1969, p. 48.

Poland before 1961 the margins on textile goods (which usually carry average margins) were: retail, 4 per cent; wholesale, 3 per cent; and the commissions received by state disposal agencies 0·6 per cent. In the late 1960s the retail and wholesale margins were 10 and 4 per cent respectively.[1] Trade margins, naturally, differ according to the types of goods. The typical range of retail margins in the Socialist countries is now 5–15 per cent and of wholesale margins 1–8 per cent. They are still well below the levels in capitalist countries – 25–100 per cent in retail and 10–25 per cent in wholesale trade.

There is a trend for a greater differentiation of trade margins. They are becoming an active and flexible instrument for shaping the structure of supply and demand in accordance with consumers' preferences and social interest. The objective is to induce trading enterprises to provide better service to customers, so that they do not neglect low-priced items and those with a slow turnover. The flexibility and differentiation of trade margins are most advanced in Yugoslavia and to a lesser extent in Czechoslovakia and Hungary, where they are subject to negotiation between producing and wholesale enterprises and between wholesale and retail entities.

A financial instrument which is relevant to profits in trade is the turnover tax. This tax is normally raised on consumer goods when they are passed from the sphere of production to distribution.[2] It is the difference between the retail and producer prices (allowing for the retail and wholesale margins). Traditionally, turnover taxes have performed three functions in the Socialist countries: (*a*) a fiscal method of accumulation (savings); (*b*) regulating the profitability of the different forms of production; (*c*) ensuring an equilibrium in the market for consumer goods, whilst maintaining either producer or retail prices stable. These taxes were residual in nature, because they were largely a product of predetermined producer and retail prices, and consequently they were widely differentiated according to the type of product, the buyer, use, etc. In effect, turnover taxes were an instrument of insulating production from consumption, and each was regulated independently.

[1] J. Śliwa, op. cit., pp. 83, 153–4.

[2] But in Romania about 12% of the turnover tax revenue is collected from producer goods. *Planovoe khoziaistvo* (Planned Economy), Moscow, 3/1970, p. 72.

The problem of turnover taxes has been widely discussed by Socialist economists since the reforms. Two distinct views have emerged in the context of profit. Some writers, noted for their newly discovered fascination with financial instruments, have advocated an aggressive and flexible use of these taxes to induce enterprises to act in socially desirable directions. It has been argued that these taxes, including subsidies (which are a sort of negative turnover tax), should be highly differentiated to regulate the profitability of not only different branches of the economy but also individual enterprises. This in fact calls for embodying differential rent into turnover taxes. It has been further pointed out that their effectiveness in the past was clearly limited and it is only profit, the incentives based on it and the discontinuation of directive planning and management that have created full scope for the operation of these taxes. Some writers also believe that differentiated turnover taxes could be used as a compensatory device for the distorted price structure. These views have been put forward most forcefully in those countries where departures from the old system have been slow and reluctant, especially in the German DR, Poland, Romania and the USSR.[1]

The other school of thought is in favour of limiting the function of turnover taxes essentially to the fiscal sphere, or perhaps even abolishing them altogether. It is maintained that these taxes should be consistently expressed as *ad valorem* rates (and not as absolute amounts or residuals), the rates should be reasonably uniform at least for major groups of products, and furthermore the level of the rates ought to be reduced so that the gap separating producer and retail prices is narrowed down to sensible proportions. These taxes should then be treated as a price-forming element and not a consequence of the predetermined producer and retail prices. The main point of the argument is that in the interest of maximum consumer satisfaction and efficiency in general, there should be an automatic correspondence between producer and retail prices – producer prices should be influenced by demand, and similarly the conditions of supply should have a chance to exert an influence on demand via flexible prices. Consequently, turnover taxes should

[1] e.g., O. Niedziałkowski, ('A Residual or an *Ad Valorem* Form of Turnover Tax?'), *Finanse* (Finance), Warsaw, 10/1969, pp. 23–35.

only play a passive role and not interfere with the evolution of a flexible price structure reflecting scarcities. The support for this approach is strongest in Bulgaria, Czechoslovakia, Hungary and Yugoslavia, where several steps have been taken in this direction.[1] Some advocates of liberal economic reforms have been in favour of a complete elimination of turnover taxes, and consequently of the two-tier price system.[2]

It is evident that in each approach the importance of profit is clearly recognized as being of focal importance. But while the supporters of the 'flexible' policy seek to influence enterprise profits primarily via the manipulation of turnover taxes (and subsidies), the advocates of the 'passive' policy want to leave it essentially to the market mechanism, whereby profits are determined by prices. It is not difficult to see that the second approach is more conducive to economic rationality as understood in the market economies of the capitalist world. The actual developments in the Socialist countries have followed a pattern of compromise. In all of them the role of turnover taxes has been declining owing to the substantial increases in the level of producer prices and reductions in some retail prices, higher trade margins (largely at the expense of turnover taxes) and the emergence of profit as the main source of budgetary revenue (see Chs. 4B and 5C). On the other hand, even in the countries where the reforms have gone furthest (as in Hungary and Yugoslavia), turnover taxes are still an important feature of the economic scene.

The income of the trading enterprises, which comes mostly from trade margins and in a decreasing number of cases from state subsidies, is used for meeting material costs, wages, social insurance and payments to the state budget. Part of the remaining profits may then be devoted to material incentives and various awards to the personnel, and the residual profits are used for a variety of purposes, especially improvements of the facilities for customers and staff and the financing of stocks; a portion of the profits may

[1] e.g., B. Csikós-Nagy, ('Features and Tasks of the Price Policy'), *Pénzügyi szemle* (Financial Review), Budapest, 2/1970, pp. 89–102; K. Ivanov, ('Turnover Taxes under the New System of Economic Management'), *Planovo stopanstvo* (Planned Economy), Sofia, 10/1968, pp. 44–56.

[2] See, e.g., Ota Šik, *Plan and Market under Socialism*, New York, IASP, 1967, esp. p. 282.

be transferred to the intermediate organs of economic management or the local authorities for purposes of interest to a group of related enterprises. An example of the disposal of the total receipts of trading enterprises is shown in Table 22 on the example of Poland.

TABLE 22 PERCENTAGE DISTRIBUTION OF THE NET RECEIPTS OF STATE AND CO-OPERATIVE TRADING ENTERPRISES IN POLAND IN 1968

Apportionment of Net Receipts	State Trading Enterprises	Co-operative Trading Enterprises
Net Receipts	*100·0*	*100·0*
Material Costs	30·3	34·9
Wear and tear of non-durable assets	2·8	4·2
Depreciation of fixed assets	2·0	2·6
Transport	12·0	11·3
Deficiencies within permitted norms	1·8	1·7
Other material costs	11·7	15·1
Net Income	69·7	65·1
Wage and incentive funds	19·8	29·2
Other incentive awards	0·5	1·2
Social insurance	2·6	3·9
Other non-material costs	9·4	14·3
Net budgetary deductions, or subsidies (—)	3·8	—2·0
Taxes	9·1	0·6
Net balance-sheet profit	24·5	17·9

Source. Based on *Rocznik dochodu narodowego 1965–1968* (Yearbook of National Income Accounts), Warsaw, Central Statistical Office of Poland, 1969, p. 102.

The system of incentives to the trade personnel differs in detail in each country, but in general it is similar to that in industry. It may be observed that the effect of bonuses and other awards is greater in trade because of the continued lower level of base pay compared with other branches of the economy, normally 10–15 per cent below the national average. In Hungary in 1968 three-fifths of the trading enterprises' total profits was handed over in primary deductions to the state budget. Of the remainder (the 'balance-sheet profit'), 81 per cent was placed in the enterprises' Development Funds and 19 per cent in their Sharing Funds. The latter Funds were partly used for maintaining Reserve Funds, partly for increases in base wages and the remainder (after taxes on the above increases) was shared by the personnel. Profit sharing on the average represented 9·5 per cent of the base wage funds, but in individual state trading enterprises the actual proportions ranged from 1·6 to 34·0 per cent.[1]

In Poland the set-up is much more complex. According to the system introduced in 1967, incentives depend on the planned and on the above-plan fulfilment of tasks, and points are allotted for different indicators of achievement. If the profit plan is under-fulfilled by more than 2 per cent, no profits are transferred to the Material Incentive Fund. This fund usually represents 10–25 per cent of the Base Wage Fund. Individual incentives to the different categories of the personnel may reach the following proportions of the base pay: persons in the top managerial position, up to 60 per cent; supervisors and their deputies, up to 45 per cent; technicians, up to 30 per cent; and administrative clerks, up to 20 per cent. These scales are now much higher than they were before 1967 when, for example, managers could receive only up to 20 per cent of their base pay in incentives.[2]

In the USSR, according to the regulations introduced in 1971 and applicable to the trading enterprises which have changed over to the new system, two distinct funds are maintained (as in other branches of the economy): the Individual Incentives Fund and the Socio-Cultural and Housing Construction Fund. The size of these funds is governed by at least two standards: the profit mass achieved and the volume of the trade turnover, and in some cases by the *increase* in the volume of trade turnover. There are complicated scales of transfers of net profits to the two incentive funds according to the degree of fulfilment and over-fulfilment of the set targets. Up to 65 per cent of the above-plan profit after tax can be used for incentives; moreover, up to 60 per cent of the savings achieved from a reduction of losses in self-service stores below the

[1] *Pénzügyi szemle*, 10/1969, pp. 826–9. [2] J. Śliwa, op. cit., p. 148.

officially established norms and 5 per cent of the net fines received by wholesale trading enterprises from negligent suppliers may be added to the Individual Incentives Fund.[1]

B. THE PROBLEM OF STOCKS

Two phases can be distinguished in respect of the holding of stocks in the Socialist countries. In the earlier stages of economic development, roughly up to about 1960, both the stocks of material inputs (raw materials, components, equipment) held by enterprises for further production, and of final (not necessarily finished) products were generally small. Economic planning was noted for detailed 'tight balancing' whereby very small reserves were provided for, in order to reduce idle resources to a minimum and thereby maximize the rates of economic growth. At the same time, owing to the prevalence of shortages (acute 'sellers' markets') and the relatively unsophisticated requirements of these economies, there was little difficulty in disposing of the output produced.

However, in the last ten to fifteen years there has been an inexorable tendency for stocks to accumulate to alarming proportions. In a study of this problem, two Czechoslovak economists have demonstrated that the size of stocks in Czechoslovakia has tended to rise at a faster rate than the growth of production. On the other hand, in Western countries stocks grow at rates about 60 per cent *lower* than production, and in some capitalist economies the growth of production is in fact associated with falling stocks.[2] According to Polish estimates in 1970, 2·7 per cent of the total stocks held in industry was classed as 'abnormal' and a further 1·4 per cent as 'unnecessary'; in fact in some branches of industry (e.g. light industry) at least 7 per cent of total stocks was rated as excessive.[3] In the USSR between 1960 and 1969 stocks rose by over 100 per cent whilst the national income rose by less than 70

[1] *Ekonomicheskaya gazeta* (Economic Gazette), Moscow, 3/1971, p. 17; 10/1971, p. 13; 30/1971, p. 17.

[2] K. Knež and P. Piechaček, ('Problems of the Growth of Stocks'), *Plánované hospodářství* (Planned Economy), 3/1970, pp. 13–23.

[3] *Życie gospodarcze* (Economic Life), Warsaw, 2/5/1971, p. 5.

per cent.[1] Even in Yugoslavia stocks have been rising faster than production.[2]

The causes of the excessive stocks are complex, reflecting some serious faults in the functioning of the Socialist economies. Some of these causes are responsible for the large stocks of inputs whilst others lead to the piling-up of stocks of final products:

(i) a predisposition on the part of enterprises to acquire raw materials, components and equipment when it is possible, and not necessarily when needed, reflecting the uncertainty of supplies;
(ii) the poor quality or unsuitability of deliveries, so that large proportions of such goods are not utilized but are stored;
(iii) a greater independence of enterprises, the profit criterion for incentives to labour and a greater uncertainty associated with the strengthened market relations – larger stocks enable enterprises to seize profit-making opportunities when they arise;
(iv) the growing complexity of the Socialist economies, leading to a proliferation of the needs for products of exact specifications and quality, with precise conditions of delivery, etc., so that the declining substitutability of inputs necessitates a wider assortment of stocks;
(v) a greater role assigned to buyers' preferences consequent upon decentralization and economic liberalization in general;
(vi) difficulties in correct forecasting of the size and structure of demand owing to unexpected changes in plans on the initiative of higher authorities and poorly developed market research;
(vii) insufficient price flexibility, making it difficult to dispose of excess supplies at appropriately reduced prices;
(viii) improving market supplies of basic products, so that shortages are no longer as prevalent as they were in the past;

[1] *Narodnoe khoziaistvo SSSR v 1969 g.* (National Economy of the USSR in 1969), Moscow, Statistika, 1970, pp. 43, 747.
[2] *Privredni pregled* (Business Review), Belgrade, 25/5/1971, p. 2.

(ix) the priority assigned to production for export which is governed by irregular orders and usually involves higher quality and different specifications than for domestic use; as production for the internal market may have to be postponed at short notice, larger stocks may be necessary to cater for domestic customers.

Excessive stocks are obviously a form of social waste, and naturally they are viewed in the Socialist countries with great concern. They represent either idle resources or a type of output in defiance of the buyers' preferences. This adds extra pressure on the limited resources and – seemingly paradoxically – excessive stocks often lead to shortages and bottle-necks elsewhere in the economy. Therefore, to cope with the problem several measures have been adopted – a mixture of administrative controls, penalties and incentives.

First, directive norms may be laid down by higher authorities (especially in the German DR, Poland, Romania and the USSR) specifying the size of stocks of certain goods which can be held by enterprises under normal conditions. Infringements may be penalized by fines or direct action. This is essentially a continuation of the old administrative approach. Second, capital charges have also been extended in most Socialist countries to circulating assets.[1] These charges, which were first introduced in Yugoslavia in 1957 and in Bulgaria, Czechoslovakia, Hungary and the USSR during the period 1964–6, as a rule range from 3 per cent (in Bulgaria) to 6 per cent (in the German DR and the USSR) of the annual value of the circulating assets held by enterprises (see Table 20, p. 160). In Czechoslovakia the original concessional charge of 2 per cent has been raised (since 1970) to 5 per cent – the same rate as applicable to fixed assets.

Third, interest rates charged on credits for financing stocks are generally twice, or even more, as high as for financing investment (roughly 6 and 3 per cent, respectively). Fourth, an increasing use is made of consumer credit on a selective basis to facilitate the sale of consumer goods which are in excess supply in relation to demand. Fifth, trading enterprises have been granted more or less guarded

[1] In Poland only fixed assets are subject to capital charges, and Romania has so far not introduced them at all.

permission to apply price reductions to items which may otherwise be difficult to dispose of. Finally, in some countries (such as Poland) the allocation of enterprise profits to incentive funds may be conditional upon the goods produced not being obsolete.

These measures appear to be producing results with varying degrees of success in different countries. On the whole, it seems that incentive devices are more effective than controls and penalties. In Hungary, where in the early 1960s stocks represented 6 per cent of material production, the proportion fell to 4 per cent by 1969 and in 1970 to 3 per cent.[1] But elsewhere the problem of stocks is still serious. The measures applied reflect an *ad hoc* approach directed at removing symptoms rather than the fundamental cause deriving from the conditions created by faulty state policies.

C. TRADE RISK

The sources of trade risk under socialism can be classified into three categories: natural factors, socialist economic relations and economic reforms. There is hardly anything distinctive to socialism in the first category of risk (for a general discussion of natural risk, see Ch. 3A, pp. 52–3). Here we shall bring out the sources of trade risk which are peculiar to socialism, deriving from the social ownership of the means of production, central planning and the extension of market relations associated with the adoption of the profit criterion.

Contrary to what one would be inclined to think, trading enterprises in the Socialist countries are exposed to price risk. Retail or wholesale prices may be changed by higher authorities, and these prices are altered more frequently than the prices received by producing enterprises. Reduced prices may adversely affect profits, whilst too high prices may lead to the accumulation of excessive stocks. Where prices are allowed to be determined by the market (see Ch. 4E, pp. 100–4), profits or stocks may be similarly affected. Stocks may also increase as a result of the rigid bureaucratic links between trading and producing enterprises. By the time orders are completed, buyers' tastes might have changed. The holding of

[1] *Pénzügyi szemle*, 9/1970, p. 708.

stocks itself, especially if they are excessive, in addition to the cost involves the risk of damage, deterioration, theft, etc. (likely to be enhanced by inadequate storage facilities).

Trading enterprises are also exposed to the risk of losses caused by deficiencies both in merchandise and in money as a result of pilfering, fraud and the embezzlement of cash. Some well-organized abuses may be difficult to detect, and the losses may be skilfully shifted to the public. For example, as a result of collusion between some Polish trading and meat-processing enterprises, which was finally discovered in 1964, inferior meats and flour were substituted for pork in the production of sausage; the pork so 'economized' was being sold in black markets whereby over 10 million złotys ($2·5 million at the official basic exchange rate) was made in illegal profits.[1] The proportion of fraudulent deficiencies in Polish trade oscillates around 0·1 per cent of the value of trade turnover.[2] It appears that these deficiencies are largely due to a relatively low level of remuneration in trade, the depressed morale of the personnel and the small effectiveness of bureaucratic controls compared with private owners' vigilance.

The distribution agencies which previously handled producer goods have been partly or largely replaced by specialized trading enterprises (particularly in Czechoslovakia, Hungary and, of course, Yugoslavia). Such enterprises operate on a commercial basis and endeavour to maximize their profits. They order goods from producing enterprises or from foreign trade corporations at their own risk. In effect, risk-bearing in this field has been shifted from the state budget to such specialized enterprises. Occasionally, they may transact business for other entities on commission or act as agents, in which case they bear no risk unless agreed to in the contract.

Another source of risk is the increasing possibility of the accumulation of unsaleable goods. This is largely a consequence of the economic liberalization consisting in such developments as the allocation of larger supplies for the consumer goods market, a greater role allowed to be played by consumers' preferences and the

[1] J. Śliwa, op. cit., p. 52.

[2] Z. Abramowicz, *Ryzyko w działalności przedsiębiorstwa handlowego* (Risk in the Operation of the Trading Enterprise), Warsaw, PWE, 1968, p. 301; *Życie gosp.*, 18/10/1970, p. 10.

rising standards of living in general. It was easier to forecast demand for necessities, especially when they were few in number and in short supply. But there is an increasing amount and range of goods and services on the market, including luxuries which – in contrast to necessities – are highly substitutable, so that the demand for individual items is more elastic and unpredictable. According to studies carried out in Poland, from 5 to 10 per cent of the stocks held by the enterprises in retail trade in the late 1960s was classed as unsaleable (at the existing prices).[1]

The problem of unsaleable stocks, although exacerbated since the economic reforms, has existed in the Socialist countries for a long time. In an attempt to overcome this problem, risk funds have been established. Thus in Poland in 1958 the Ministry of Internal Trade established two funds in retail trading enterprises: the Fund for Price Reductions and Trade Risk (commonly described as 'Fund A') and the Trade Risk Fund ('Fund B'). In the following year, such funds were also created in wholesale trade.

The function of 'Fund A' is to absorb or minimize the losses that may arise from price reductions which may be necessary to facilitate the disposal of otherwise unsaleable goods. The implicit aim is to ensure that trade margins are not affected by price reductions. This fund may also be used for incentives to salesmen, to encourage them to apply a personal approach with customers to persuade the latter to buy such goods. The degree of price reductions as well as the type of goods to which they can be applied are still centrally regulated, but in recent years considerable freedom has been granted to trading enterprises regarding the details of these operations. But this freedom is bringing in train new forms of risk. There is evidence that price reductions are made in the articles which the personnel itself is primarily interested in buying, even if such articles are scarce and could be easily sold anyway; or prices may be reduced by one shop but not by others in the same locality, which creates unfair competition amongst socialized enterprises.[2] 'Fund B' is used for absorbing losses caused by the over-classification of goods, and such losses cannot be compensated for by the supplying enterprises. It is also used for paying incentives

[1] Z. Abramowicz, op. cit., p. 225; *Finanse*, 7/1970, p. 44.
[2] Z. Abramowicz, op. cit., pp. 212–13.

to the persons in the trading enterprises responsible for quality checking, and for covering the cost of expert examination and the re-marking of prices. The sources of finance for each fund are different. Fund A is maintained mainly out of deductions from profits – on the average 0·5 per cent of the trade turnover in retail trade enterprises and 0·1 per cent in wholesale trade enterprises. Fund B is replenished by fines received from suppliers breaking contracts.[1]

Other methods of reducing or spreading losses in trade may be briefly stated. To minimize the possibility of theft and to facilitate strict accounting, shops may be closed at the time of receiving supplies.[2] There are incentives to the personnel for the reduction of deficiencies below the allowed norms. The recovery of losses caused by negligent or fraudulent suppliers, trade personnel and customers is treated very seriously by the authorities, but it appears with little success. In Poland courts can normally pinpoint the guilty persons in 70 per cent of the cases dealt with, but only 1 per cent of the deficiencies is recovered.[3] The amount of property owned by private persons which can be seized is small. There is (now) no legal compulsion to work and an enterprise cannot recover its losses from persons out of work. There are also legal limitations on the amount and proportion of a person's income which can be seized for debt repayment. In the case of measurable risk there is the possibility of insurance, but its scope differs from one country to another (see Ch. 3E, pp. 72–5). The figures in the table overleaf summarize the cost of risk to a typical Polish trading enterprise (in percentages of total cost).

The question naturally arises of where the burden of risk should fall, especially in the case of faulty or new products – whether on the producing or trading enterprises. The traditional Socialist attitude has been that commercial functions should be divorced from production, and the risk of stocks and marketing must be shifted to the sphere of distribution, so that production is not subject to the fluctuations occurring in the market. This has been viewed as one of the most significant economic achievements of

[1] Z. Abramowicz, op. cit., pp. 186, 187, 196.

[2] For this and other reasons, shops in Poland are closed on the average for twenty-eight working days a year. *Życie gosp.*, 15/9/1969, p. 6.

[3] *Życie gosp.*, 18/10/1970, pp. 1, 10.

1. Insurable risk	*5·73*	*2. Other risk*	*12·12*
Social insurance	4·83	Doubtful receipts	0·66
Goods in transport	0·59	Deficiencies in stocks within norms	9·44
Fire	0·07		
Vehicles	0·03	Deficiencies in stocks above norms	0·57
Window glass	0·05		
Accidents to the personnel	0·05	Payments to white-collar workers for time not effectively worked	1·45
Robbery	0·07		
Civil suits	0·04	*3. Total cost of risk*	*17·85*

Source. Z. Abramowicz, op. cit., p. 83.

socialism. It may be observed that in capitalist countries producing enterprises not infrequently take back stocks unsold by trading firms and in fact may themselves engage in marketing in one form or another.

However, the traditional Socialist views on this question have been subjected to a thorough reappraisal in the last ten to fifteen years. It appears to be widely agreed now that it is in the social interest to make producing enterprises responsible for defective products (wrong specifications, poor quality), delays, etc., and that this is done by means of penalties. On the other hand, trading enterprises should primarily bear the risk of distribution. But there are cases where the area of responsibility cannot be clearly divided, particularly in respect of new products. In such cases, losses and rewards are usually shared in one form or another by the producing and trading enterprises and the public.

Thus in Poland, to encourage the production and handling of novelty products, temporary innovational mark-ups have been introduced which may reach up to 22 per cent of the basic producer price. The proceeds of the mark-up are divided as follows: 2 per cent is earmarked for the New Designs Fund, 58 per cent is transferred to the Ministry of Internal Trade out of which a centralized Price Reduction and Production Risk Fund is financed, and 20 per cent is paid into the state budget; in the second year, the budgetary deduction is increased to 50 per cent and then the mark-up is gradually reduced and removed in one to three years.[1] In an in-

[1] *Gospodarka planowa* (Planned Economy), Warsaw, 3/1970, p. 11.

creasing number of cases, producing enterprises now undertake some marketing activities themselves (see the next section of this chapter), so that the distribution risk is borne by them.

D. FROM SELLERS' TO BUYERS' MARKETS

Sellers' markets are noted for the dominant position of sellers over buyers, whilst under the conditions of buyers' markets the situation is rather the reverse. In the past, the former have usually been associated with the Socialist centrally planned economies whilst the latter with the market economies in the capitalist world.

Sellers' markets are a consequence of excess demand over supply at the existing level of prices. The reasons responsible for this excess in the Socialist countries in the past, on the demand side, have included the following conditions:

(i) the abnormal requirements for the factors of production to fulfil ambitious developmental plans, more via the outlay of resources than by increases in efficiency;
(ii) the rapid growth of the wage fund in the economy and incentive payments tending to outpace the growth of productivity;
(iii) the tendency for social consumption to exceed the levels provided for in economic plans;
(iv) the fairly even distribution of personal income;
(v) the relatively low level of prices maintained under official controls;
(vi) the priority given to export rather than the domestic market.

At the same time, several factors have contributed to the insufficiency of supply:

(i) the planned restriction of the production of consumer goods in order to maximize investment and the rates of economic growth;
(ii) the unduly low reserves, insufficient to prevent bottle-necks and shortages in the case of unforeseen developments;

(iii) the priority given to the fulfilment of targets for producer rather than consumer goods;
(iv) the low priority provided for in economic plans for the development of trade in respect of investment, the size and quality of the personnel, remuneration, etc.;
(v) strict controls over imports, especially of consumer goods.

The practical effects of sellers' markets are well known – queues, long waiting-lists, a small range of goods available, the poor quality of products and a demoralized and apathetic sales personnel. But at the same time trading enterprises find themselves in an inferior position when dealing with suppliers and they have little chance of influencing output, so that resources may be wasted in producing goods contrary to the social interest. Although sellers' markets were tolerated in the past, their disadvantages have become too obvious under the new economic system.

The adoption of profit is related to the development of buyers' markets in two ways. On the one hand, buyers' markets are highly desirable if the operation of profit is to bring full advantages to the economy, and on the other, profit itself is conducive to the evolution of buyers' markets. The existence of buyers' markets may enhance the effectiveness of the profit lever on two fronts. First, as producing enterprises can obtain their inputs when and where they wish they can minimize their costs, and thereby increase their profits, by pursuing the most economical patterns of substitution of their inputs; they can also reduce some costs otherwise associated with unsuitable deliveries, delays, etc. Second, the importance of profit in promoting the maximum enterprise performance derives largely from the fact that material incentives to labour are linked to it in one way or another. Workers, whether in producing or trading enterprises, will not sustain their effort for long if they are merely offered more money. Incentive payments must be backed up by the availability of goods and services in the market – in respect of quantity, variety and quality as desired by consumers. Socialist experience had clearly demonstrated that 'under the conditions of sellers' markets no system of incentives can work effectively'.[1]

At the same time, the efforts of enterprises to maximize their

[1] J. G. Zieliński, ('Conditions of the Effectiveness of a System of Incentives'), *Życie gosp.*, 9/10/1966, p. 2.

profits may serve the cause of buyers' markets in the following ways. First of all, the profit criterion is a better, or a more 'synthetic', basis for material incentives than any other indicator used before, as it takes account of both the cost and the demand sides. The distribution of profits – especially for incentives, production development and reserves – may be regulated in such ways as to provide sufficient inducement to enterprises to act in the best interest of the public. The enterprises' effort is then concentrated on the ability to sell, and not merely on obtaining supplies. Profit mark-ups for novelty and quality (see Ch. 4D, pp. 97–9) make it worthwhile for enterprises to produce and to distribute new products and of better quality, thus providing a wider range of goods on the market. It is in the interest of both producing and trading enterprises to speed up the circulation of goods, which in effect increases available supply.

There is evidence that profit is stimulating competition, particularly in the countries where economic reforms have been advanced furthest, especially in Czechoslovakia, Hungary and Yugoslavia. In these countries there is the possibility of retail trade enterprises dealing directly with producing entities, whereby they can by-pass wholesale trade (including wholesale margins). In Hungary 38 per cent of the goods retailed is now obtained directly from producers (57 per cent of food products, 23 per cent of clothing and 7 per cent of miscellaneous industrial articles).[1] In fact many producing enterprises compete with trading entities by establishing their own display rooms and retail outlets. Advertising, which in sellers' markets was largely pointless, is now becoming a feature of Socialist trade. Enterprises now find it to their advantage to advertise and at the same time the public is enabled to make a better choice. As a rule, only informative advertising is allowed, whilst persuasive and misleading publicity is banned.

Many trading enterprises, either individually or jointly, now carry on market research to minimize their risk of unsaleable stocks and to maximize their income by following, and indeed anticipating, buyers' preferences. As their position in dealing with producers is becoming stronger, the latter can be influenced to supply what the market wants.

[1] *Figyelö* (Economic Observer), Budapest, 9/12/1970, p. 3.

There are many indisputable advantages of well-developed buyers' markets, not only to consumers but also to the economy in general. There is better service to customers; there is no time wasted in queuing, which increases leisure time and promotes a better attitude to work; there is a more effective link between trade and production and resources are more likely to be utilized in accordance with social preferences. Buyers' markets also provide a sound mechanism for evolving efficiency (scarcity) prices.

Although considerable progress has been made in recent years, fully fledged buyers' markets are still far from reality in any Socialist country, and whether they are compatible with centrally planned economies remains yet to be demonstrated. Shortages of consumer goods and long waiting-lists for many consumer durables are still familiar features of the Socialist consumer goods markets. For example, as late as 1971 it was reported that in the USSR the extent of unsatisfied demand for consumer goods was typically 40–60 per cent (women's toilet articles, 40 per cent; table cloths, 60 per cent; leather gloves, 75 per cent; briefcases, 90 per cent).[1] It is well known that trading enterprises shy away from handling low-priced lines and new products, because either profit margins are too low or the risk is too high. A large proportion of enterprises is in a monopolistic position and they find that their profits can sometimes be increased more easily by restricting than by increasing their supply.

There are still compulsory channels of distribution in the case of some key products, even in the more liberal Socialist countries. The scope for demand creation is limited, considering that total consumption is centrally determined at the political level. Central planners, particularly in the economically more authoritarian countries (the German DR, Poland, Romania and the USSR), cannot be easily reconciled to the idea of trade interfering with the planned structure of production. Many political leaders, and even some economists, still believe that the excess of demand over supply is a healthy driving force conducive to full employment and dynamic development, and this is viewed as evidence of the superiority of socialism over capitalism.

[1] *Sovetskaya torgovlya* (Soviet Trade), Moscow, 24/4/1971, p. 3.

9 External Trade

A. PRICES AND EXTERNAL MARKETS

THE price basis which the Socialist countries employ in their foreign trade depends on the type of their partner country. In their trade with capitalist nations, normally current capitalist world market prices are adhered to. In actual transactions their export or import prices may naturally be lower or higher, reflecting their bargaining power and the terms of the trade contracts. The question of the prices used in trade amongst the Socialist countries, especially those belonging to the Council for Mutual Economic Assistance (CMEA or Comecon), is more complex.

Owing to the distortion of their domestic price structures, the Socialist countries have lacked a price system of their own which would be acceptable to all member countries. Before 1958, prices in their mutual trade were negotiated in individual agreements, which not only proved cumbersome but also entailed a good deal of uncertainty. In 1958 the CMEA countries signed the Bucharest Agreement, whereby they decided to use the average prices prevailing in world capitalist markets over a selected period as a starting base. These base prices are then corrected, in bilateral negotiations amongst the member countries by special mark-ups to take account of various national conditions, and remain fixed for several years. The corrected prices play a dominant role in the CMEA countries' foreign trade as their mutual exchanges constitute 65 per cent of their total foreign trade.

There are two significant features of the intra-CMEA foreign trade prices. Firstly, on the whole they are above world capitalist levels so that – ironically – the 'fraternal' CMEA countries charge higher prices to each other than to capitalist outsiders.[1] Secondly,

[1] To illustrate by reference to the commodities which are reasonably standardized. The average f.o.b. (or free to the Polish border) prices charged by Poland to different countries for black coal in 1968 in foreign exchange złotys

the 'correction' mark-ups are, relatively speaking, too generous for manufactures and insufficient for raw materials, reflecting more the marxist allegiance to the labour theory of value than the relative scarcities in the CMEA region.[1] However, it appears that these disparities in mark-ups are not as large now as they were in the 1960s.

The Socialist countries have traditionally been noted for the insulation of their domestic from foreign prices. This policy assumed the form of relatively stable domestic prices and various measures designed to neutralize price fluctuations originating from foreign countries. In practical terms it meant that exporting entities paid current domestic prices to producing enterprises, irrespective of the export prices received in foreign markets. Similarly, imported goods were sold domestically at the applicable internal prices, or at the prices of the closest substitutes, or at the prices set to equate the available supply with domestic demand. Foreign trade was carried on by relatively few and large foreign trade corporations, each with the right of exclusive dealings in specified lines of export and/or import, completely divorced from domestic production and trade. Their incidental 'profits' or 'losses' were fully absorbed by the state budget.

In all the Socialist countries under consideration, with the qualified exception of the USSR, general economic reforms have also been extended to foreign trade, and in particular links have been established between foreign and domestic prices. First, in the reforms of producer prices – carried out in Yugoslavia in 1965, in Czechoslovakia in 1967, in Hungary in 1968, in Bulgaria in 1968,

---

per ton were: Denmark, 21·05; Finland, 25·34; France, 32·92; the FR of Germany, 37·52; The German DR, 57·74; Czechoslovakia, 57·93; Hungary, 58·71; the USSR, 61·73. The average prices charged by the USSR for wheat exported in 1969 were in roubles per ton (f.o.b. or free to the Soviet border): Brazil, 49·51; the Netherlands, 55·38; Britain, 56·53; the FR of Germany, 58·74; Hungary, 59·11; the German DR, 67·37; Poland, 67·55; DPR of (North) Korea, 69·76; Czechoslovakia, 70·77. Based on *Rocznik statystyki handlu zagranicznego 1968* (Yearbook of Foreign Trade Statistics for 1968), Warsaw, Central Statistical Office of Poland, 1969; *Vneshnaya torgovlya SSSR za 1969 g.* (Foreign Trade of the USSR in 1969), Moscow, Ministry of Foreign Trade of the USSR, 1970.

[1] As reported in a Hungarian source, the mark-ups on raw materials ranged from 5 to 10%, whilst industrial products carried mark-ups of up to 60%. A Polish source, published in 1968, disclosed that the mark-ups on metal-working machinery ranged from 16 to 128 % above current world market prices. *Külkereskedelem* (Foreign Trade), Budapest, 9/1967, pp. 271–2; *Życie gospodarcze* (Economic Life), Warsaw, 2/6/1968, p. 11.

1971, in the German DR in 1969, 1971 and in Poland and Romania in 1970–71 – world market relations were taken into account; the Soviet price reform to be carried out in 1972–3 is expected to be in the same vein. Second, the prices received by domestic enterprises producing for export, as well as the prices paid by users for imports, are now largely or wholly in foreign-exchange equivalents. Consequently, prices in foreign trade can to some extent influence domestic prices – most in Yugoslavia, Hungary and Czechoslovakia and less so in Poland, Romania and the USSR.

The CMEA Permanent Commission for Economic Questions and the recently (in 1970) established International Institute for the Study of the Economic Problems of the World Socialist System have been working on the development of uniform principles and procedures in the member countries with regard to the treatment of such elements as wages, incentives, capital charges, depreciation rates, interest rates, transport costs, turnover taxes, trade margins and profit mark-ups. The objective is to evolve rational price structures so that prices in each country are comparable. Two other CMEA Commissions, for Currency and Finance and for Foreign Trade, have been co-ordinating work on the methods of evolving equilibrium exchange rates. So far only Yugoslavia has established exchange rates close to equilibrium, and she is the only Socialist country being a member of the International Monetary Fund.

As is well known, the official exchange rates of the CMEA currencies do not reflect their purchasing power. In their endeavour to gauge the relative effectiveness of their exports and imports and to facilitate a balance-of-payments equilibrium, these countries have been using special foreign-exchange coefficients correcting the official basic exchange rates. These coefficients have been based on the average or marginal cost of earning foreign exchange and they represent an important step forward. According to the time-table agreed upon in 1971, the CMEA countries will evolve single and realistic exchange rates in the late 1970s or the early 1980s. The Soviet rouble will at first become a reserve currency for the CMEA region, and later perhaps a convertible currency on the international scale.[1]

[1] For further details, see *Figyelö* (Economic Observer), Budapest, 11/8/1971, pp. 1, 5; *Finanse* (Finance), Warsaw, 10/1971, pp. 38–52.

The overall purpose of these efforts is to maximize gains from foreign trade, representing an important source of 'intensive' economic growth. Rational price structures, reliably reflecting scarcities in each country and responsive to foreign prices via equilibrium exchange rates, provide a basis for the comparability of outlays and gains. These considerations are of particular importance to the smallest Socialist countries (i.e. other than the USSR) which have limited resources and for which participation in the international division of labour in accordance with the greatest comparative advantage is now considered to be of the utmost national importance.

B. FOREIGN TRADE PROFITABILITY

In a free market economy profits from foreign trade transactions by and large indicate gains accruing to the economy. The profitability of the firms directly engaging in foreign trade, as well as of those producing for export and using imports, is affected by conditions in foreign markets and, taking risk into account, tends to be equal. This has hardly ever been the case in the Socialist countries. Where domestic markets are insulated from foreign markets, the financial balances of the enterprises directly or indirectly engaging in foreign trade in no way indicate the extent to which such trade is gainful. Their balances embody four major types of distortions.

First of all, domestic prices do not necessarily reflect factor cost. In general, the contribution of capital and land is inadequately reflected, owing to the low levels of capital charges, interest rates and rents, further accentuated by concessions and exemptions (see Chs. 4F and 7A). This makes labour appear relatively scarce; yet there is sufficient practical proof that the Socialist countries have a comparative advantage in many labour-intensive forms of production.[1] Second, the enterprises producing for export receive domestic prices from the foreign trade corporations and the enterprises using imports also pay the usual domestic prices, in

[1] As, for example, demonstrated by the nature of joint East–West ventures. For details, see J. Wilczynski, *Socialist Economic Development and Reforms*, London, Macmillan, 1971, pp. 303–13.

each case irrespective of the prices received or paid by the corporations in foreign markets.

Third, in the case of bilateral agreement trade, the negotiated prices may depart from world market (scarcity) prices. Even where both export and import prices are above world levels (as they often are), the maximized microeconomic profits (of each entity directly engaging in foreign trade) do not necessarily indicate maximum gains to the economy, because resources are not allocated in such patterns as to ensure the proportionality of marginal outlays to marginal effects. Fourth, the official rates of exchange of the Socialist currencies have traditionally been over-valued, especially in relation to the convertible Western currencies. Consequently, the Socialist entities directly engaging in foreign trade tend to incur book-keeping losses on exports and earn book-keeping profits on imports.

The Socialist countries have, of course, been aware of these distortions and they have endeavoured to overcome them in different ways. At first, beginning in the early 1950s, they devised various indices of the effectiveness of export in which, to generalize, costs in domestic currency were related to receipts in foreign exchange. By means of these indices, exportable items were arranged in descending order of 'effectiveness'. The marginal rate, below which goods were not to be exported, was fixed by the Ministry of Foreign Trade at such a level as to ensure a balance-of-payments equilibrium. As imports were more or less predetermined by the developmental needs embodied in the general economic plan, little attention was given to the study of their profitability. However, later indices were also devised to cover a portion of importables, mostly applied to the so-called 'comparative' imports, i.e. those needed for subsequent re-export in processed forms and which on balance were gainful in terms of foreign exchange. Another forward step was made when indices were prepared to show 'computational' profit, to guide the operations of the entities engaging in foreign trade within the planned framework.[1] These indices are still used in the countries where the insulation of domestic from foreign markets remains fairly tight, especially in Romania and the USSR.

[1] For details of the indices, see J. Wilczynski, *The Economics and Politics of East–West Trade*, London, Macmillan, 1969, pp. 311–30.

Since the economic reforms efforts have been directed in all these countries at gradually relaxing the insulation of domestic from foreign markets by reforming domestic prices, basing settlements between foreign trade and production on foreign-exchange equivalents, extending multilateralism in their trade and by some rationalization of exchange rates. The objective is to make actual profit, or profitability, the basic criterion of performance in foreign trade. Most progress has been made so far in this respect in Yugoslavia, and also in Hungary, and to a lesser extent in Bulgaria, Czechoslovakia, the German DR and Poland.

Is there any significant difference in the profitability of the Socialist countries' trade amongst themselves and that with the capitalist world? This question is most complex and it cannot be answered in precise terms. We shall examine it first from the macrosocial and then microeconomic standpoints. First of all it is important to realize that, as a consequence of the continued industrialization drive, there have been some far-reaching changes in the cost structure in the Socialist countries. Production costs in primary industries (especially in agriculture and mining) have been rising steadily in relation to those in manufacturing. This can be illustrated by the relatively high and rising capital–output ratio in agriculture as shown in Table 23 by reference to Bulgaria, Czecho-

TABLE 23 INCREMENTAL CAPITAL–OUTPUT RATIOS IN AGRICULTURE AND IN INDUSTRY IN SOME SOCIALIST COUNTRIES, 1951–1965

Average Annual Increase in Fixed Assets Necessary to Produce One Unit (1·00) of Increase in Output

COUNTRY	1951–5		1956–60		1961–5	
	Agriculture	Industry	Agriculture	Industry	Agriculture	Industry
Bulgaria	0·94	0·84	1·43	0·78	1·37	1·15
Czechoslovakia	0·96	0·78	1·40	0·83	1·40	1·08
Romania	0·68	0·76	1·09	0·88	1·06	0·85
USSR	1·15	0·91	1·13	1·03	1·26	1·15

Source. A Bodnar and M. Deniszczuk, *Wymiana międzynarodowa a rozwój gospodarczy Polski* (International Trade and the Economic Development of Poland), Warsaw, PWE, 1969, p. 146.

slovakia, Romania and the USSR over the period 1951–65. The need for raw materials – expecially cotton, flax, oil seeds, hides, certain foodstuffs, mineral fertilizers, metals, fuel and timber – has been expanding very rapidly, but at the same time these industries typically operate under increasing costs. By contrast, manufacturing industries have been benefiting from their greater experience, the economies of scale and externalities. These tendencies largely explain why in the CMEA region raw materials have become 'hard' items whilst manufactures are relatively abundant.

TABLE 24 PERCENTAGE COMPOSITION OF THE EUROPEAN SOCIALIST COUNTRIES' FOREIGN TRADE, 1957–59 AND 1967–69

The European Socialist Countries' Exports to and Imports from: *	1957–59 ¶		1967–69 ¶	
	P‖ %	M‖ %	P %	M %
Exports to:				
Other European Socialist Countries *	42	58	27	73
Developed Countries †	63	37	56	44
Developing Countries ‡	29	71	26	74
Imports from:				
Other European Socialist Countries	42	58	27	73
Developed Countries	36	64	20	80
Developing Countries	95	5	84	16
European Socialist Countries' Total Foreign Trade	45	55	31	69
World Trade as a Whole §	46	54	35	65

* The countries included in this table are Albania, Bulgaria, Czechoslovakia, the German DR, Hungary, Poland, Romania and the USSR. Both exports and imports are valued f.o.b.

† Europe (except Eastern Europe and the USSR), North America, Japan, Australia, New Zealand and South Africa.

‡ Latin America, Africa, except South Africa; Asia, except Japan and China, Mongolia, the DPR of (North) Korea and the DR of (North) Vietnam.

§ Excluding inter-trade among the four Asian Socialist countries (China, Mongolia, the DPR of Korea and DR of Vietnam.

¶ Three-year annual averages.

‖ P = Primary products, M = Manufactures, according to the Standard International Trade Classification. P – includes Classes 0–4, and M – Classes 5–9.

Source. Based on United Nations *Monthly Bulletin of Statistics*.

If we examine the structure of the Socialist countries' foreign trade represented in Table 24, the following conclusions emerge:

(i) The share of manufactures in the Socialist countries' foreign trade has been steadily rising, which to some extent indicates the growth of the industrial capacity and the sophisticated needs of these economies. The proportion of manufactures in their total foreign trade is now over two-thirds, slightly higher than the world's average.

(ii) About three-quarters of the Socialist countries' intra-foreign trade consists of manufactures, and only one-third is represented by food and raw materials. These proportions also apply to these countries' exports to the developing nations.

(iii) On the other hand, exports to developed capitalist countries consist largely of primary products. Even though this proportion has been declining, it still represents over one-half of the total.

(iv) The Socialist countries' imports from the developed capitalist world consist mostly of manufactures (about four-fifths), in which machinery and equipment play the most prominent part.

(v) The Socialist countries' imports from the developing nations are, as one would expect, dominated by food and raw materials (about four-fifths of the total).

At the existing levels of costs and prices, exporters of manufactures (especially Czechoslovakia and the German DR) to other CMEA countries reap larger gains, whilst those which export raw materials (particularly the USSR) gain relatively little.[1] The Socialist countries regard the overall structure of their trade with

[1] This complaint is now of long standing. For details, see O. Bogomolov, ('Current Problems of Economic Co-operation amongst the CMEA Countries'), *Mirovaya ekonomika i mezhdunarodnye otnosheniya* (World Economy and International Relations), Moscow, 5/1966, pp. 15–27; V. Diachenko, ('Desirable Directions of the Improvement of Prices in Intra-CMEA Foreign Trade'), *Voprosy ekonomiki* (Problems of Economics), 12/1967, pp. 64–74; Y. Kormnov, ('On the Mutual Benefits from International Specialization in Production'), *Vop. ekon.*, 10/1970, pp. 91–9. For a summary of arguments on the question of exploitation in Soviet–East European trade, see J. Wilczynski, *The Economics and Politics of East–West Trade*, pp. 336–41.

each other and with developing nations as natural and satisfactory, but they are highly critical of the composition of their exports to the West. In their view this composition does not reflect the high degree of Socialist industrialization attained but rather discrimination encountered in Western markets in the form of restrictive import quotas, the over-zealous application of anti-dumping measures and prohibitive tariffs.

Food and raw materials embody a low degree of value added, their production costs have been rising in the Socialist countries and at the same time their prices in capitalist markets have tended to decline in relation to manufactures (the so-called 'Prebisch effect'). The low degree of the macroeconomic gain has been further accentuated by the lower prices usually obtained by Socialist exporting enterprises, owing to competition from the well-entrenched local and other capitalist suppliers, the poor marketing techniques employed by Socialist exporters and the inadaptability of Socialist production to the highly demanding buyers' markets in the West. A Bulgarian economist complained:

> We offer those goods for export the production and marketing of which are easiest, and not those which promise the maximum gain and require flexible adjustments to foreign demand.[1]

With regard to Socialist imports, there is no doubt about the macroeconomic gains derived from Western machinery and equipment which contain advanced technology and speed up Socialist industrialization. Whether in actual deals Socialist importers pay higher or lower than the prevailing prices is difficult to generalize. On the one hand, as Socialist import deals usually involve large contracts, quantity discounts are often secured. On the other hand, this has sometimes worked with opposite effects. When large customers are known to be in the market, prices may actually rise to the disadvantage of Socialist buyers (as illustrated by Socialist purchases of Australian wool in the past).

Before we conclude this section, let us restate the extent to which profitability governs Socialist foreign trade. The official determination to maximize the gains from foreign trade as a source of

[1] D. Vasilev, ('The Role of the International Division of Labour in Increasing the Profitability of Foreign Trade'), *Vunshna turgoviya* (Foreign Trade), Sofia, 10/1968, p. 4.

economic growth, the progress being made in the de-insulation of domestic from foreign markets and the gradual extension of the profit criterion to the enterprises engaging in foreign trade and linking it to incentives (to be dealt with in Section D), are all enhancing the role of profit in shaping the flow of external trade. However, it must be realized that Socialist profit is still an imperfect indicator of the gains from foreign trade, particularly in those countries where the extension of economic reforms to foreign trade has been very cautious (in Poland, Romania and the USSR). With the partial exception of Yugoslavia, foreign trade is still subject to central planning and most of it is carried on on the basis of long-term trade agreements and annual trade protocols. This is particularly so in intra-CMEA trade (constituting two-thirds of the member countries' total foreign trade), where profitability is not necessarily an independent factor but rather an instrument which can be manipulated on a planned basis. In countries with their system of government so completely dominated by the Communist Parties, it is natural that in the totality of state policies non-commercial considerations are introduced in shaping the size, structure and direction of exports and imports, where political advantages may be considered as outweighing commercial losses.

C. RISK IN FOREIGN TRADE

On the whole, the extent of the foreign trade risk confronting a Socialist economy is smaller than is typically the case under capitalism. The participation of the Socialist countries in foreign trade is relatively low. Although the eight countries represent about one-quarter of the world's national income and one-third of the world's industrial output, their share in world trade is only one-tenth.

Their foreign trade is subject to planning and control, in greater detail in some countries than in others, and it is dovetailed into the general economic plan. A large proportion of these countries' foreign trade is with other Socialist planned economies. This is indicated by the percentage of the individual countries' exports absorbed by other Socialist countries (by the CMEA countries in brackets) in 1969:[1]

Bulgaria	79·0	(75·6)
German DR	73·0	(68·0)
Czechoslovakia	69·1	(62·7)
Hungary	68·0	(64·3)
USSR	65·9	(54·9)
Poland	65·7	(61·9)
Romania	59·4	(51·7)
Yugoslavia	31·1	(30·1)

Sources. Peace, Freedom and Socialism, Prague, 11/1970, p. 34; IMF and IBRD, *Direction of Trade*, 3/1970, pp. 90–1.

Trade with other Socialist countries is based on five-year trade agreements, and then annual trade protocols embodying firm commitments and terms as to quantities, prices, credits, etc. Risk is further reduced in intra-CMEA foreign trade by the co-ordination of the member countries' investment plans in accordance with the agreed fields of specialization.

The degree of risk is, of course, greater in trade with the capitalist world. Although the Socialist countries usually sign trade agreements and protocols with capitalist, especially developing, nations, they are too broad and not as committal (the so-called 'umbrella agreements'). This risk is further enhanced by the fact that on the capitalist side the trade partners are generally private firms not bound by inter-governmental trade agreements or protocols. A deterioration in East–West relations may disrupt trade either way by governmental intervention. Socialist exports may encounter boycotts (which were, for example, common in the USA in the past), indiscriminate anti-dumping measures (especially in Australia, the European Economic Community and the USA) and limitations on the transferability of the Socialist export earnings (especially in the EEC). On the Socialist import side, the

[1] The CMEA group includes Bulgaria, Czechoslovakia, the German DR, Hungary, Poland, Romania, the USSR and Mongolia. The remaining Socialist countries are Yugoslavia, China, the DPR of (North) Korea, the DR of (North) Vietnam and Cuba. Chile, although in several respects she can be considered a Socialist country (since 1970), is not included in these statistics.

administration of the strategic embargo by most Western countries represents the most obvious source of uncertainty.[1]

A peculiar type of risk to which Socialist trading enterprises are exposed is that of 'counter-sales'. The Socialist predilection for tying their import deals to export transactions with the same trade partner is well known; this is largely due to the Socialist difficulty of otherwise earning foreign exchange in Western countries. In such operations, one contract is conditional upon another, and it is most likely that the date of delivery in one case may differ from the other. Moreover, as the capitalist trader may not want the Socialist goods for his own use, he resells them (and perhaps re-exports them) at discount prices, thus prejudicing a subsequent Socialist export effort.

The risk of payment default by capitalist importers, in contrast to Socialist importers, is frequently stressed in Socialist literature.[2] Other factors contributing to the risk faced in capitalist countries include the highly competitive and demanding markets,[3] fluctuations affecting the volume and structure of trade, prices, the policies and practices pursued by exclusive economic groupings and the poor marketing and purchasing techniques for which Socialist trading enterprises are noted in the West. There is also a poor link in the Socialist countries between trade and industry, a reflection of the traditional divorce between production and distribution, which limits manoeuvrability when conditions change in foreign markets.

[1] The reader interested in further details is referred to this writer's *The Economics and Politics of East–West Trade*, pp. 138–307, and to G. Adler-Karlsson, *Western Economic Warfare 1947–1967*, Stockholm, Almqvist & Wicksell, 1968.

[2] S. Długosz and L. Osiatyński, *Problemy minimalizacji ryzyk w tranzakcjach handlowych z zagranicą* (Problems of the Minimization of Risk in Foreign Trade Transactions), Warsaw, PIHZ, 1967, pp. 61–83; C. Gavrilescu, ('Payment Guarantees in Trade with Capitalist Countries'), *Finanţe şi credit* (Finance and Credit), Bucharest, 10/1970, p. 54.

[3] e.g., in the Polish light industry producing for export a provision is made for extra output averaging 20% above the actual order in anticipation of rejections; but in some cases, rejects may represent 100%. Although rejects are usually marketed domestically, the degree of risk of disposal is high, because export production – especially for capitalist markets – is highly specific and there may be no local demand. See W. Samecki, *Ryzyko i niepewność w działalności przedsiębiorstwa przemysłowego* (Risk and Uncertainty in the Operation of the Industrial Enterprise), Warsaw, PWE, 1967, p. 115.

Compared with the past, the extent of the foreign trade risk confronting the Socialist economies is now greater and it is likely to continue increasing. Taking the CMEA group of countries as a whole, their foreign trade has been rising faster than their national income; this is illustrated by their average annual rates of growth:

	Foreign trade	*National income*
1951–60	12·0	9·5
1961–5	8·5	6·0
1966–70	8·8	7·0

Sources. Rozwój gospodarczy krajów RWPG 1950–1968 (Economic Development of the CMEA Countries 1950–1968), Warsaw, Central Statistical Office of Poland, 1969, p. 4; *Życie gospodarcze*, 15/8/1971, pp. 10–11.

In effect, the share of foreign trade in the Socialist countries' national income between 1950 and 1970 rose from about 20 to 50 per cent in Bulgaria, the German DR and Hungary, from about 20 to 35 per cent in Poland and Yugoslavia, from 15 to 25 per cent in Romania and from 7 to 9 per cent in the USSR (using the Western definition of national income). Their combined share in world trade rose during the period from less than 8 to more than 10 per cent. Economic reforms have further increased the extent of risk, consequent upon departures from the detailed planning and control of foreign trade, the gradual de-insulation of domestic from foreign markets and the tendency towards abandoning detailed trade agreements with capitalist countries. It is noteworthy that the capitalist world's share in the Socialist countries' total foreign trade rose from less than 18 per cent in the early 1950s, to 33 per cent by 1970.[1]

As in other spheres of economic activity, there has been a tendency for shifting the burden of risk in foreign trade away from the state budget. Before the reforms, the foreign trade corporations were passive executors of detailed export and import plans and they settled their accounts with domestic enterprises at the official domestic prices, irrespective of the prices received or paid by the corporations in foreign markets. The corporations' 'profits' or 'losses' were absorbed by the state budget. Under the new

[1] Based on United Nations *Yearbook of International Trade Statistics* and *Monthly Bulletin of Statistics.*

economic system, the automatic budgetary equalization settlements have been reduced or discontinued. Risk-bearing has been shifted partly (in Poland and the USSR) or largely (in Bulgaria, Czechoslovakia, the German DR, Hungary and Romania) or almost completely (in Yugoslavia) to the foreign trade corporations, branch associations and the enterprises dealing with foreign trade entities.

Except in the USSR, many domestic enterprises producing for export or (less commonly) those using imports have been granted the right of direct dealings in foreign markets. This process has gone furthest in Czechoslovakia, Hungary and, of course, in Yugoslavia.[1] At the same time, particularly in the remaining countries, the number of foreign trade corporations has been increased by a subdivision of the former large entities and the creation of new ones; their total number in the CMEA region has risen from 120 in the 1950s to 220 in the early 1970s. These developments have produced a measure of competition in foreign trade which was completely lacking before the reforms. Although this competition is conducive to greater efficiency, at the same time it has increased the degree of uncertainty facing individual enterprises engaging in foreign trade.

As has already been pointed out, risk-bearing in foreign trade has been largely shifted from the state budget to the microeconomic sphere. At this level, the burden of risk is shared between foreign trade entities and domestic enterprises. The precise shares of the incidence vary according to the basis of dealings, of which we can distinguish six:

(i) A foreign trade corporation may act on its own account, and it deals with domestic enterprises at fixed, negotiated or free-market prices. In such a case, it fully absorbs profits or losses from its operations. This basis of dealings is rather exceptional now.

[1] By 1970 the number of entities with the right of direct dealings in foreign markets was at least 36 (in addition to 25 foreign trade corporations) in Czechoslovakia, 70 (in addition to about 30 foreign trade corporations) in Hungary and 1,000 in Yugoslavia (compared with about two dozen exclusive foreign trade corporations in the early 1950s). *Zahranični obchod* (Foreign Trade), Prague, 10/1969, pp. 24–5; *Finanse* ,12/1969, pp. 66–7; *Yugoslav Survey*, Belgrade, Nov. 1969, p. 71.

(ii) A corporation may operate as a joint partner with a domestic enterprise so that profits and losses are equally shared.

(iii) A corporation may act as a commission agent for domestic entities, in which case it receives a commission proportional to the profit made on the foreign trade transaction.

(iv) A corporation may act only as an agent for a fixed fee, so that the principal fully bears the risk.

(v) If an enterprise producing for export, or one using imports, deals in foreign markets directly, it naturally bears the risk itself.

(vi) In those countries where the intermediate organs of economic management are actively engaged in promoting foreign trade, as is particularly the case in Bulgaria, the German DR, Poland and Romania, the risk may also be shared (or spread) by such associations.

In some Socialist countries, especially in Czechoslovakia, Hungary and Yugoslavia, there are companies with limited liability where capital is subscribed, and consequently risk is borne, jointly by the parent entities, which usually include a foreign trade corporation, a relevant industrial enterprise and a bank.

The main methods of protection against foreign trade risk consist of insurance and reserve funds. In all the Socialist countries under consideration, the transport, handling and storage of goods in foreign trade are now subject to compulsory insurance, and insurance contributions are treated as cost. In Bulgaria, Czechoslovakia, the German DR, Hungary, Poland and the USSR there are separate state entities which specialize in foreign insurance. It is also known that the Socialist insurance and even trading entities protect themselves against uncertainty in capitalist markets by hedging operations using capitalist forward markets.

As a logical development following the tendency towards shifting risk-bearing in foreign trade away from the state budget, various types of reserve funds have been established, some on an experimental and others on a permanent, comprehensive footing. The formation and administration of these funds are similar to those existing in industry and internal trade. For example, Hungary has developed two reserve funds: the 'Price Reserve

Fund' and the 'Import Price-Difference Reserve Fund', both designed to absorb fluctuations in the foreign prices of key commodities. These Funds are held by enterprises engaging in foreign trade and they are normally supposed to be self-supporting, without budgetary subsidization (but in reality state subsidies have been necessary). Poland introduced a 'Foreign Trade Risk Fund' in 1965 to compensate enterprises producing machinery and electrical goods for export. The Fund is held and maintained by foreign trade corporations. There is also a compensation scheme to protect enterprises dependent on imports.

A form of protection against the risk of excessive competition from imports is represented by tariffs. Import duties, which were practically non-existent and unnecessary under the old system of rigid quantitative controls on imports, have been reactivated in Bulgaria, Czechoslovakia, Hungary and Yugoslavia, where they are now flexibly used. It appears that Poland is also inclined to do likewise.

D. INCENTIVES IN FOREIGN TRADE

Socialist economies have always suffered from an acute pressure on their balance of payments. Ambitious development programmes, tight economic planning with very low reserves, the prevalence of poor quality, shortages and sellers' markets, the difficulties of marketing in foreign (especially capitalist) countries and the overvaluation of domestic currencies, have all created an in-built predisposition to excessive imports and an aversion to the pursuit of exports. Under the old centralized and directive system, to cope with this problem the authorities concentrated on a severe control of the size and structure of import and on import-replacement production. Although after the mid-1950s some efforts were made to expand exports, the measures relied upon were mostly of an administrative and directive nature.

The notable feature of the approach under the new economic system is the determination to expand exports and the reliance on incentives to enterprises engaging directly in export as well as those producing for export. On the import side, there has been a tendency to relax controls and to expose domestic producers to foreign competition, especially in Bulgaria, Czechoslovakia, the German DR, Hungary and Yugoslavia.[1] The objective of the new policies is to promote the optimum size, and the most efficient structure of export, and to some extent of import, in order to maximize gains from the international division of labour.

Although with greater hesitation than in domestic economic relations, profit has been accepted as the main criterion of enterprise performance and a basis for material incentives to the personnel, not only in the enterprises directly engaging in foreign trade but also those producing for export. Owing to the increasing practice of settlements between foreign trade and domestic entities at foreign-exchange equivalents, enterprise profits are now as a rule directly influenced by the prices received or paid in foreign markets. Consequently, it is in the interest of the enterprises and their personnel to adapt their activities to the market conditions prevailing in other countries.

The prices of many goods negotiated in intra-CMEA specialization agreements are set at such levels as to ensure sufficient profitability for the exporting member countries. There are concessional credit terms for export production and such credits may also be granted in foreign exchange. Incentives offered in export are usually higher in application to the earnings of hard Western currencies to compensate enterprises for a higher degree of risk faced in these markets. The different methods of protection against foreign trade risk, discussed in the preceding section, can also be considered as a form of incentive.

The independence of enterprises has been substantially increased to enable them, within socially desirable limits, to pursue their profit maximization. The state is now more inclined to rely on financial instruments influencing enterprise profits than on directives, especially in Bulgaria, Czechoslovakia, Hungary and Yugoslavia. In Hungary, enterprises producing for export are

[1] Béla Csikós-Nagy, President of the Hungarian Prices and Materials Commission, recently pointed out that under the influence of imports from Czechoslovakia, the German DR and the USSR, the domestic prices of trucks, refrigerators, vacuum cleaners and pumps were reduced in Hungary and the quality of many products was clearly improved. *Figyelö*, 9/12/1970, p. 3.

taxed only on their super-normal profits, i.e. those exceeding 15 per cent return on the assets employed.[1]

The incentive funds held by enterprises directly and indirectly participating in foreign trade are mostly designed to promote exports, and to some extent the effectiveness of imports. Although usually maintained out of profits, in most countries, the formation of these funds is regulated by one or more indicators, similar to those in industry and internal trade. In the German DR, according to the regulation laid down in 1966, 40 per cent of the above-plan profit is allowed to be retained by the enterprises concerned with export. Of this portion, normally three-quarters goes to the enterprise producing for export and one-quarter to the foreign trade corporation. Moreover, 40 per cent of the profit achieved by exceeding the planned profit rate can also be retained, but in this case as much as three-quarters goes to the foreign trade corporation because such an improvement is mostly due to its effort.[2]

In Poland, according to the revised system effective since the beginning of 1971, the allocation of profits to the incentive funds in the enterprises producing for export and the foreign trade corporations handling export is dependent on three indicators:

(i) The increase in the value of export above the planned level; different weights are assigned to the earnings of foreign exchange according to the 'hardness' of the foreign currency (this is done by the application of differentiated foreign exchange coefficients correcting the official basic rate).

(ii) The improvement in the profit rate above the planned level.

(iii) The degree of the plan fulfilment of foreign exchange earnings from convertible currency areas; penalties are applied for non-fulfilment.

To promote the provision of more and better-quality services, the foreign trade corporations are not allowed increases in personal incentives as a result of reduced employment.[3] In the enterprises

[1] *Rynki zagraniczne* (Foreign Markets), Warsaw, 1/5/1971, p. 5.

[2] *Vierteljahreshefte zur Wirtschaftsforschung* (Quarterly Research Papers in Economics), East Berlin, 4/1967, pp. 415–52.

[3] *Życie gosp.*, 31/5/1970, pp. 1, 4.

producing for export, 70–75 per cent of the incentive fund is reserved for blue-collar workers; incentives to individual persons must not exceed two to three times the average incentive paid, and the minimum to be paid per quarter is 300 złotys (the minimum monthly wage is 1,000 złotys).[1]

In some countries, such as the German DR, Poland and Romania, there are also centralized special incentive funds at the disposal of some ministries (mostly the Ministry of Foreign Trade) for promoting exports of particular national importance. In Yugoslavia there are virtually no planned indicators binding enterprises in respect of the size and distribution of incentive funds, and there is considerable freedom in this regard in Hungary.

In all the Socialist countries, enterprises participating in foreign trade, directly or indirectly, may be allowed a portion of their foreign exchange earnings for their own uses, such as obtaining imports outside the official channels, financing the improvement of their marketing activities in foreign countries and assisting the foreign travel of their personnel. On the whole, it appears that the level of incentives received by persons working in the enterprises directly or indirectly concerned with exports is about the same as in industry, and definitely higher than in internal trade.

There are also incentives operating on the import side of foreign trade. They are mostly based on the saving of foreign exchange and the fulfilment of planned targets. But the level of these incentives is relatively low, so that in effect persons associated with import only are worse off. However, this does not necessarily apply in Hungary and Yugoslavia. There are indications that this time-honoured discrimination is also being reappraised in the remaining Socialist countries because, as a Polish economist observed, 'a foreign exchange unit saved in import is equivalent to one earned in export'.[2]

[1] *Życie gosp.*, 21/8/1971, p. 8.

[2] B. Wojciechowski, ('Incentives for Economic Results in Import'), *Handel zagraniczny* (Foreign Trade), Warsaw, 1/1971, p. 10.

10 Conclusions and Appraisal

A. THE NEW SYSTEM AND ECONOMIC PROGRESS

THE adoption of profit as a criterion of enterprise performance and a basis for incentives to labour symbolizes the economic reforms on which the European Socialist countries (except Albania) have embarked since the early 1960s (since the early 1950s in the case of Yugoslavia). Although to varying degrees in different countries, industries and enterprises, on the whole profit is proving an effective economic instrument. Profit is the most synthetic of all the criteria ever used under socialism, as it reflects both the input and output aspects of an enterprise's operations, and thus it promotes a reduction of costs and a growth of production for which there is demand. It best combines the microeconomic interest of enterprises and their workers with the macrosocial benefit. It promotes the reallocation of resources according to changing supply and demand conditions, i.e. changing relative scarcities of factors and products. It stimulates competition amongst enterprises and individual members of their personnel. Profit is also the main source of the self-financing of enterprises and as such it strengthens their independence and freedom of initiative.

Enterprises are now more inclined to undertake risk, including innovational risk involving uncertainty. There is a stronger motivation than before because successful operations are reflected in enterprise profits and incentives to the personnel. At the same time several forms of protection against risk have been introduced or further developed, especially the legal exemption of managers from permissible risk, insurance against measurable and even unmeasurable risk, reserve funds and novelty and quality profit mark-ups.

Profit has also strengthened the effectiveness of material incentives. Not only are they now dependent on, and paid out of, enterprise profits, but their level has also been increased. Experience has shown that Socialist workers are more responsive to material than moral incentives, particularly where efficiency and a consistency of effort are required. The scope for the effectiveness of material incentives is enhanced by the fact that the level of personal income in the Socialist countries is low, particularly if compared with the affluent Western nations,[1] and that the supply of consumer goods (including luxuries) has been steadily improving.

The acceptance of the profit criterion has also prompted the Socialist countries to other complementary reforms conducive to a greater efficiency. These have included the decentralization of planning and management, moves to develop efficiency (scarcity) prices, the introduction of capital charges, some rationalization of interest rates, depreciation and exchange rates and some de-insulation of domestic from foreign markets. There has also been some relaxation of the restrictions on private enterprise, particularly in the fields directly catering for consumers' needs. The appointment of enterprise managers is now more related to business or professional competence than to political reliability.

The institutional set-up reinforced by the different incentives and disincentives, is more amenable to the minimization of costs and the maximization of output in accordance with market demand, so that waste is now less widespread than it was before the reforms. The new system is noted for greater economies in the use of resources, a reduction of idle capacity and the hoarding of circulating assets, an acceleration of technological progress, a larger variety of goods on the market and for improving commercial service to customers.

It is also noteworthy that economic progress is no longer so unequivocally identified with the maximization of the rates of growth of material production, irrespective of social cost. The authorities are now more reconciled to the pursuit of 'optimum' growth rates with due regard to the available resources and the social cost of economic development. Many Socialist economists now consider

[1] According to the writer's estimates for 1970 the *per capita* income (using the Western concept of national income) in the eight European Socialist countries ranged from $650 (in Yugoslavia) to $1,900 (in the German DR), compared with $3,900 in the USA and $2,200 in the developed capitalist countries as a whole. For details, see J. Wilczynski, *Socialist Economic Development and Reforms*, London, Macmillan, 1971, pp. 335–7.

that the maximization of the standard of living is a better indicator of economic progress than merely *per capita* income, because increases in material production per head may be incommensurate with extravagance in the use of resources and with consumers' privations.

However, it must be realized that in some respects the economic reforms have not gone far enough to create ideal conditions for the most effective operation of profit and incentives. The social ownership of the means of production is still the mainstay of the Socialist economies and, with the exception of Yugoslavia, at least some elements of directive central planning have been retained. In the late 1960s there was a good deal of enthusiasm amongst many economists and the public for further reforms in a liberal spirit, and official pronouncements sounded most encouraging until it came to the actual implementation of various reform proposals.

Many reforms have been diluted or sabotaged by Stalinist hardliners with a remarkable degree of success in Czechoslovakia, Poland, Romania and the USSR. Which bears witness to Marx's wise words written more than a century ago, 'The way to Hell is paved with good intentions.'[1] As the Communist Party still so completely dominates the national scene, non-economic considerations may prevail at the central level even if clearly in conflict with economic commonsense and efficiency. It may also be observed that the rapid economic progress in the German DR since the early 1960s has been due more to systematic planning and centrally coordinated management than to profit, incentives and liberalization.

The Socialist countries still have a long way to go before they evolve price structures reflecting scarcities, which means that Socialist profit does not necessarily indicate efficiency. The old reluctance to close down loss-incurring enterprises lingers on, and even in Yugoslavia and Hungary the subsidization of production is still continued on a substantial scale. Competition is still weak or even absent in some fields of production and distribution, so that many enterprises (especially in Czechoslovakia, Hungary and Yugoslavia) have found it easier to increase their profits by restricting supply. The aversion of risk-taking is much greater than in a capitalist economy. The level of material incentives appears to be

[1] K. Marx, *Capital*, London, George Allen & Unwin, 1946, p. 172.

too low in many cases, and their effectiveness is further blunted by the provision of generous social benefits, and by the obvious limits to private enrichment.

In fact, the adoption of the profit criterion has tended directly or indirectly to create new problems, which previously did not exist or could have been dealt with more effectively by the directive methods at the disposal of central planners. The new problems which may impair economic progress include fluctuations, inflation and unemployment; it is significant that they have appeared in their most striking forms in Yugoslavia – the country in which profit and the market mechanism play the largest part of all the Socialist countries.[1]

B. PECULIARITIES OF SOCIALIST ECONOMIC LEVERS

As has been emphasized throughout this study, the new economic system is noted for the importance being attached to economic levers. They have partly, largely or completely replaced centrally imposed directives, depending on how far the economic reforms have been advanced in different countries. These levers include interest rates, capital charges, rent, turnover taxes, prices, and of course the most important of them all – profit and incentives to labour. Although bearing familiar capitalist designations, their nature and functions differ in many ways under socialism.

On the whole, the level of interest rates on most credits in the Socialist countries is low, but their differentiation according to the purpose of credit or the type of borrower is very wide, ranging from total exemption to 20 per cent (and in some cases in Yugoslavia even more). With the exception of savings bank deposits, and debentures in Yugoslavia, interest cannot become a source of private income. Capital charges are not once-for-all levies but continuous taxes on fixed and circulating assets. There is also considerable differentiation of these charges – some branches of

[1] See Ch. 3E, footnote 3, p. 71, and Ch. 4F, p. 107. Further details can be found in, A. Bajt, 'Investment Cycles in European Socialist Economies: A Review Article', *Journal of Economic Literature*, March 1971, pp. 53–63; N. Čobeljić and R. Stojanović, *The Theory of Investment Cycles in a Socialist Economy*, New York, IASP, 1968; B. Horvat, 'Yugoslav Economic Policy in the Post-War Period: Problems, Ideas, Institutional Developments', *Amer. Econ. Rev.*, June 1971, Suppl., pp. 69–169.

the economy are exempt and the upper limits range from 3 per cent (in Bulgaria) to 6 per cent (in the German DR and the USSR).

Differential rent in practical terms is understood as surplus income produced under better-than-average (not better-than-marginal) conditions. As a rule, it is not allowed to be a source of income either to private persons or socialized enterprises. Turnover taxes are not the ordinary indirect taxes but still largely residual imposts consequent upon independently fixed producer and retail prices.

Prices are also used as active economic levers. Most Socialist countries have developed 'flexible' price systems, where some prices are free, some can move up to officially specified ceilings or down to specified floors or move within laid-down ranges. Where prices are officially regulated, and most prices still fall into this category, they may include special 'novelty' and 'quality' mark-ups or mark-downs. There is also considerable differentiation of the prices of identical products, depending on the nature of the materials embodied in them and the type of ultimate user. This approach to prices is known as 'target' (or 'goal') pricing.

But the greatest number of peculiarities can be discerned in the most sensational of all Socialist levers – profit. Contrary to what has often been said or implied in Western discussions on the subject, Socialist profit differs in many important ways from capitalist profit. First, whilst in a capitalist economy profit is a goal of economic activity, under socialism it is essentially regarded as a means, 'not an objective, but an instrument linking the interest of the enterprise with the macrosocial interest, i.e. the maximization of national income',[1] 'not a goal of communism, but a vehicle for building communism'.[2] The mainspring of economic activity is still central planning and the state's far-reaching involvement in the economy.

Second, under capitalism profit is an objective economic category. On the other hand, Socialist profit is a subordinate and flexible instrument wielded by the state. The authorities have the power to set directive profit indicators (planned profit norms,

[1] M. Krzak, ('Problems of the Soviet Reform'), *Życie gospodarcze* (Economic Life), Warsaw, 21/7/1968, p. 8.

[2] A. Birman, ('Profit Today'), *Kommunist*, Moscow, 10/1967, p. 101.

planned rentability or profit rates, planned increases in profitability). Furthermore, the state is in a unique position to radically change enterprise profits by manipulating financial levers, and the prices of the factors of production as well as of products.

Third, in a capitalist market economy, profits are usually indicative of not only enterprise performance but also efficiency. Prices normally reflect cost–preference relations and enterprises are in a position to respond to changing market conditions. But in the Socialist countries, even under the new system, price structures are still distorted. Hence, profits are a product of distorted price relations and although maximum enterprise profit reflects maximum microeconomic performance, it is not necessarily coextensive with macroeconomic efficiency.

Fourth, in a capitalist free-enterprise economy profit basically determines the allocation of resources. This is not necessarily the case under socialism. Although profit is allowed to govern the utilization of resources at the microeconomic level, their broad distribution is still largely shaped at the central level where current profitability is often disregarded. This is particularly so in the sphere of major investments. By the same token, differences in the profitability of different enterprises or even branches of the economy (i.e. those beyond the levels warranted by differences in risk) do not necessarily lead to shifts of resources from the less to the more profitable forms of production. In fact the state may reinforce the planned allocation of resources by appropriately changing enterprise profitability via financial instruments or directive profitability indicators, i.e. in a sense putting the cart before the horse.

Fifth, under capitalism in the case of imperfect competition (which is a typical situation), profits can be increased by actually reducing output to the level where marginal cost is equal to marginal revenue, and thereby forcing prices up. In the Socialist countries most prices are still fixed or regulated by the state, so that they cannot be freely manipulated by enterprises. Profits can be maximized mostly by increasing production to the level where the marginal cost is equal to the (given) price.

Sixth, in a capitalist society profit is the chief source of private capital and it is largely responsible for the large differences in the personal ownership of property, and as such the institution of profit perpetuates social stratification. Under socialism, with the exception of the insignificant private sector, profits are not reaped by private persons but by socialized (state and co-operative) enterprises. The portion of enterprise profit distributed to workers is small, they cannot acquire the means of production and consequently profit cannot produce social classes.

Finally, although in the capitalist world differences in profitability between different countries lead to international movements of investment capital, this is not so in application to the Socialist countries. The latter countries, on ideological grounds, are against foreign investments for the sake of profit. The Socialist export of capital, where it does take place, is motivated primarily by either political or humanitarian considerations, and mostly takes the form of repayable loans at low interest (usually ranging from 1 to 3 per cent p.a.) or of gifts.

There are also some distinctive features of the Socialist incentives paid to labour. Although material incentives usually represent distributed enterprise profit, they have little in common with dividends in capitalist countries. Only those who actually work in the Socialist enterprise concerned receive such handouts and they are treated as part of earnings from labour, not as remuneration for ownership or entrepreneurship. A good deal of importance is attached to collective incentives (recreation, amenities, housing, etc.) and (although less than in the past) to moral motivation.

C. SOCIALIST–CAPITALIST PARADOXES

If we examine recent developments in the European Socialist economies and in the capitalist world, we cannot help feeling like Alice *Through the Looking-Glass*, where everything was the reverse of what it should be, or like visitors to George Orwell's *Animal Farm*, where pigs were turning into capitalists and capitalists were becoming more like pigs. These developments are particularly striking in the sphere of profit, risk and incentives.

The very fact of the official acceptance of profit under modern socialism cannot be helped but seen – by observers in capitalist countries and by Stalinist diehards alike – as anomalous. The social system established in the USSR and Eastern Europe is based on

Marxian ideology. Yet to Marx and his orthodox followers profit was the hallmark of capitalism, to which all the evils of the capitalist social system could be traced. But whilst Communist leaders have embraced profit as an economic category, in the capitalist world profit is no longer such a dominant motive as it used to be. To many firms, including large 'monopolies', public relations between the management and workers, the goodwill of the public and patriotic sentiments are often more important than the maximization of profits.

The managerial personnel in large capitalist firms is not infrequently motivated by a variety of objectives, where personal interests, complex inter-personal rivalries and the quest for power and prestige may override profit considerations. The owners of large companies (shareholders) these days have little control over the management and over the size and distribution of profits. It is also common that the state directly or indirectly limits the size of enterprise profits, particularly dividends. Besides, there is increasing state participation in economic activities, which is usually not motivated by profit-making but by broader social goals.

The Socialist countries' recently developed enthusiasm for the workers' participation in enterprise profits contrasts with their view of similar schemes which have existed in the capitalist world. In a Soviet textbook of economics, addressed to readers in the English-speaking countries, in a discussion of the exploitation of workers under capitalism it is stated:

> The profit-sharing scheme can also be classed among the sweating systems of wages . . . The use of this scheme steps up the intensity of labour, retards the development of the workers' class consciousness, dulls their vigilance, disunites them and hampers their struggle against capitalists. The profit-sharing scheme creates the illusion that the workers have an interest in raising the profits of the capitalist enterprise.[1]

The irony of these tendencies is further underscored by the attitude of the Catholic Church, which historically has played an important role in Eastern Europe. It is paradoxical, as Ljubo Sirc recently observed,[2] that whilst Communist leaders are now in

[1] P. Nikitin, *Fundamentals of Political Economy*, Moscow, FLPH, 1962(?), p. 79.

[2] L. Sirc, *Economic Devolution in Eastern Europe*, London, Longmans, 1969, pp. 46–7.

favour of profit, competition and less central planning, and while they tolerate the private ownership of land,[1] Pope Paul VI should proclaim his Encyclical Letter (in 1967). It is strange that in this Letter he condemned profit as the key motive for economic progress, competition as the supreme law of economics and the private ownership of the means of production as the absolute right, and at the same time he advocated economic planning.[2]

In contrast to the prevailing official attitude, and contrary to what has been often implied in Western literature on the subject, many workers in the Socialist countries have not looked upon the economic liberalization with great enthusiasm. Some of them preferred the old paternalistic command economy which guaranteed stability and sheltered the common man, however apathetic and inefficient, from the uncertainty, competition and disruptive innovations associated with the new economic system. Some radical social reformers in the West also denounce profit and plead for a return to the idealism of Marx.

As a consequence of the decentralization of planning and management, the financing of research and innovations in the Socialist economies has been largely transferred from the state budget to enterprises and research and experimental entities. On the other hand, in capitalist countries an opposite tendency can be observed. Governments increasingly engage in, or subsidize, research and development;[3] it also appears that in their defence procurement programmes governments allow generous profit

[1] No European Socialist country, except the USSR, has socialized all land. In Poland and Yugoslavia, where in the early 1950s the proportion of agricultural land in the socialized sector was 22%, owing to subsequent de-collectivization the share was reduced to 15%, so that 85% of agricultural land is now privately owned.

[2] *Populorum Progressio* (*The Great Social Problem*), Encyclical Letter of Pope Paul VI, London, Catholic Truth Society, 1967, p. 15 (quoted from L. Sirc, op. cit., pp. 47, 62).

[3] The extent of state financing of R and D in the leading capitalist countries is surprising. According to a Soviet source (*International Affairs*, Moscow, 10/1969, pp. 33–4), quoting OECD and US sources, the percentage of total R & D financed by the state in the mid-1960s was as follows: in France, 66; the USA, 62; the United Kingdom, 56; the FR of Germany, 44; the Netherlands, 37; and in Belgium, 28. In the USA in 1967 the percentage of R & D financed by the government was 54 in industry, 61 in universities and colleges and 71 in other non-profit making institutions.

mark-ups to compensate suppliers for risk.[1] At the same time whilst the extent and degree of risk-bearing by Socialist enterprises have greatly increased, in capitalist countries the trend is rather in the opposite direction. There is a tendency for the risk faced by firms to diminish, owing to a reduction of competition consequent upon the growth of monopolies, oligopolies, cartels, state-supported marketing schemes and inter-governmental commodity agreements, and owing to the extension of planning and the perfection of forecasting, particularly in larger establishments.

The economic reforms in the Socialist countries have greatly enhanced the role of material incentives to labour. Incentive scales are so designed that persons in managerial and professional classifications receive higher bonuses than blue-collar workers – and not only in absolute terms but even as proportions of their base pay. This tends to increase the disparities in personal income. However in Western countries, owing to the rising levels of affluence, the appeal of incentives has on the whole been declining in recent years. Inequalities of income are being reduced by highly progressive taxation, the extension of educational opportunities and the expansion of social services. Most trade unions are against incentives in the form of payment by results, and they are increasingly pressing for more leisure rather than for more money. Some social scientists believe that the richest capitalist countries are on the threshold of a 'post-industrial society', to be noted for a decline of interest in advancement amongst the middle classes.[2]

D. PROFIT, INCENTIVES AND FULL COMMUNISM

There is little doubt that the official acceptance of the profit indicator, the strengthening of material incentives to labour and the activation of other related economic levers constitute a contradiction of Marxian thinking. They are essentially devices borrowed from the rival social system which Marx and his faithful followers have unflinchingly condemned. Marx's view of the communist society embodied the replacement of the market mechanism by

[1] e.g., see I. N. Fisher and G. R. Hall, *Defense Profit in the United States and the United Kingdom*, Santa Monica, Rand Corporation, Oct. 1968, pp. 12–16, 22–4.

[2] e.g., H. Kahn and A. J. Wiener, *The Year 2000*, New York, Macmillan, 1967, pp. 25, 57–60, 342–4.

planning, the abolition of property in land and other means of production, the repudiation of money and interest and the implementation of distribution according to needs, not according to work; furthermore, as labour was to become the sole source of value, the use of non-labour factors (capital and land) would not represent cost. The Socialist adoption of profit and the linking of material incentives to it, the increase in the level of interest rates and the application of capital charges and rent (however selective it is), obviously represent an ideological retreat in the march to ('full' or the 'second phase of') communism, and *as such* it can be described as a 'Great Leap Backward'.

The incorporation of these un-Marxian devices has bewildered many a communist idealist, brought up on Marxian teachings and further nourished by Party leaders with glowing promises of the communist paradise on this side of the grave. When the writer visited Eastern Europe at the height of the economic reforms a few years ago, he was told by a cynic that in one of these countries a group of enthusiasts proposed to celebrate the twentieth anniversary of the reconstituted circus after World War II by commemorative posters entitled '20 Years of the Socialist Circus'; but the authorities refused permission to display the posters.

However, a note of warning is in order here. Many eager Western commentators, guided more by wishful anticipation than by an accurate understanding of the issues involved, triumphantly acclaimed the Socialist adoption of profit as a return to capitalism. There is hardly any evidence suggesting developments in this direction. The social ownership of the means of production and central planning still prevail: even in Yugoslavia there is still a mono-party system of government controlled by the Communist Party and the ideological allegiance to Marxism is basically unshaken.

Many Western believers in the 'convergence thesis' have hailed the Socialist reforms as an unmistakable further evidence of the converging trend between socialism and capitalism, reciprocating 'creeping socialism' on the capitalist side. But most Socialist thinkers, not to mention the political leaders, categorically refute the possibility of the coalescence of the two social systems, as in their conviction the victory of communism is historically inevitable. What is rather happening, in their view, is that Marx's ideas are being reinterpreted in the light of new developments and partly adapted to the exigencies of new situations which Marx had never anticipated (and partly ignored where expedient). But the ultimate goal of full communism has nowhere been abandoned. At the 22nd Party Congress in the USSR in 1961, the main theme of which was the prospective transition from socialism to communism, it was pointed out that:

> It is necessary in communist construction to make full use of commodity–money relations in keeping with their new content in the socialist period. In this, such instruments of economic development as cost accounting, money, price, production cost, profit, trade, credit and finance play a big part. With the transition to the single communist form of people's property, and the communist system of distribution, commodity–money relations will become economically outdated and will wither away.[1]

At the same Congress, it was announced that the USSR (the most mature Socialist country) would begin entering the second phase of communism by 1980.[2] However, that vision was based on extravagantly optimistic assumptions. The USSR was to have overtaken the USA in total national income and in national income per head by the year 1970.[3] But the actual performance was far from that target. It was conceded in official Soviet statistical returns that in 1970 the Soviet national income (brought to a Western basis) was 65 per cent of the US total and the *per capita* income was only 55 per cent of the US figure.[4] At the East–West economic symposium held in Vienna in 1962 a Soviet economist, K. Plotnikov, told the International Economic Association that to enter full communism the USSR needed an increase in the volume of industrial output by six times and in agricultural output by three and a half times.[5] Between 1961 and 1971, according to official Soviet statistics, industrial output increased by two-thirds and

[1] *The Road to Communism*, Documents of the 22nd Congress of the Communist Party of the Soviet Union, Moscow, FLPH, 1961, p. 536.

[2] Ibid., p. 512. [3] Ibid.

[4] *Narodnoe khoziaistvo SSSR v 1970 g.* (National Economy of the USSR in 1970), Moscow, Statistika, 1971, pp. 82, 85.

[5] In E. A. G. Robinson (ed.), *Problems in Economic Development*, Proceedings of a Conference held by the International Economic Association, London, Macmillan, 1965, p. 68.

agricultural output by only a quarter.[1] By this writer's estimates, it appears that the USSR may reach the 1970 level of the US national income per head in the last decade of this century and catch up with the US current figure perhaps early next century.[2]

It is now widely agreed amongst Socialist leaders that the transitional phase ('socialism') to full communism will in fact be much longer than was commonly assumed a decade ago. In October 1970 a conference was held in Prague on 'The Place of Socialism in History and the Stages and Criteria of Its Development', which was attended by delegates from the European Socialist countries. The overall conclusion which emerged from the discussions was that:

> It [socialism] is a relatively independent phase of socio-economic development, its socio-economic nature differing fundamentally from mature communism. Socialism has its own system of objective laws and principles. This should not be taken to mean that some of these will not be valid in the higher, communist, phase.[3]

It was further pointed out at the same conference that:

> Disregard of the specifics of the socialist phase, reducing its function solely to removing the 'birthmarks' of capitalism and preparing the passage to communism, can lead to the wrong idea that what distinguishes socialism from communism (planned commodity production, distribution, categories such as value, money, profit, etc.) is an unavoidable 'evil' that should be removed with the least possible delay. That, in fact, is the erroneous foundation for extremist concepts and theories suggesting the abolition of commodity–money relations and material incentives in the process of building socialism, and denouncing these as 'birthmarks of capitalism', although, in fact, they are a very essential part of socialism.[4]

The prevailing attitude in the Socialist countries now is that profit, incentives and other quasi-capitalist levers are instrumental to the creation of the 'material and technical base' whereby progress to the communist cornucopia and consequently to the higher phase of communism can be accelerated. In fact, some of

[1] *Narodnoe khoziaistvo SSSR v 1970, g.*, p. 59.
[2] J. Wilczynski, op. cit., p. 338.
[3] *Peace, Freedom and Socialism*, Prague, 12/1970, p. 25.
[4] Ibid.

the developments associated with the economic reforms can be considered as steps towards full communism. Under communism, strictly speaking there will be no wages but simply a sharing of the output produced by enterprises owned by the workers. Receiving a portion of enterprise profit under the new system in a sense represents sharing in enterprise income on a similar basis. The earmarking of a portion of profits or incentive funds for collective benefits (mostly in the form of socio-cultural and housing funds) can be looked upon as a move towards distribution 'according to needs'. The departures from centralized and directive planning and management in favour of a greater independence of enterprises and workers' self-management can be viewed as heralding the 'withering away of the state'.

What are the prospects for profit and individual material incentives to workers under full communism? Socialist leaders are, on the whole, non-committal on these questions. But it appears that the following developments are likely. Profit will be retained as a yardstick of microeconomic efficiency and a device for ensuring the financial discipline of enterprises. The role of material incentives will be reduced, but it is unlikely that they will be eliminated altogether. They may mostly assume the form of collective incentives and penalty awards as a compensation for heavy, dangerous, unhealthy and otherwise unpopular work.

It is reasonable to expect that as economic progress continues the standards of general and vocational education will keep on improving. Work will be increasingly easier and more interesting, unskilled occupations will practically disappear, working conditions will gradually improve, workers will be more and more affluent and they will have more leisure time. Such developments, to which Marx attached great importance,[1] will probably moderate the workers' material inclinations and alienation, and will instead instil higher social responsibility. Consequently workers can be expected to be more responsive to moral incentives, such as the pride of achievement, professional standing, non-material awards (publicity, certificates, factory banners, medals, etc.) and what is known as 'social consciousness' in general.

[1] K. Marx, *Capital*, Chicago, C. H. Kerr, 1912, vol. I, p. 482; *The Poverty of Philosophy*, Moscow, FLPH, 1956, pp. 149–50, 155 et seq.

Index